ESTUARY

Land and water in the lower Thames basin

by

A. K. Astbury

THE CARNFORTH PRESS
9 LANCASHIRE COURT
NEW BOND STREET LONDON W.1

International standard
book number
0 9507246 0 2

Typesetting and artwork by
IMPADS of London
Printed in England by the
Anchor Press Limited
Tiptree, Essex

TO ROMMY

for the best of reasons

Contents

Appendixes

List of Plates

Plate

List of Figures

The air photographs which appear in Plates 4, 11, 18 and 25 were taken in May 1966 from a height of nearly three miles. The north is at the top of the photograph in each case. Plate 4 shows the Thames from the outfalls of the river Beam and Ingrebourne in the west to West Thurrock and South Stifford in the east. The outfall of the Darent is seen at the bottom in the centre, that of the Mardyke opposite. The industrial area of Purfleet, shown in Plate 28 under German air attack in 1940, can be seen on each side of the railway line south-east of the Mardyke outfall.

Plate 11. This air photograph, which overlaps the eastern edge of Plate 4, extends as far as Stanford le Hope in the east and Bulphan in the north. It shows the village of Orsett with its Roman field system (centre), the town of Grays (left centre) and part of the Lower Hope reach of the Thames (right). East Tilbury church is in the bend of the Thames where the wandering track from the west and the straight road from the north-west converge.

Plate 18. This air photograph, which overlaps Plate 11 to the north-west, shows Gravesend Reach, the southern part of the Lower Hope and, in the south-east corner, the bend in the Medway at Rochester. Gravesend is south of the Thames to the west, Tilbury and Tilbury docks north of it. Watling Street, its straightness showing clearly where it is by-passed south of Gravesend, is to the south. Higham Causeway can be seen running across the marshes and over the flood bank into Higham Saltings on the south-eastern bank of the Thames where the river turns north.

Plate 25 shows the built-up and industrialised area of Canvey Island to the north of the estuary and, to the south, the lonely and isolated area of north Hoo. Benfleet Creek runs east and west at the top of the photograph and there is a glimpse, in the north-east, of Westcliff and the beginnings of Southend.

Foreword

This book is about the Thames estuary and those parts of Essex and Kent which cradle it — Essex south and east of the London to Colchester road, Kent north of Watling Street. The choice of boundaries is not entirely arbitrary: the area so enclosed covers most of what geographers call the lower Thames basin.

The text was ready for publication in 1971, and during the nine years since then I approached all the publishers in this country who were likely to be interested in it, and doubtless some who were not.

Three said they would publish it, but after holding the typescript for over two years in total, decided against doing so.

I then thought I would apply for a grant towards publication, bearing in mind the offer by one publisher in July 1977 to issue the book provided he had a subsidy of at least £2,500. My application to a certain Trust for this sum, in return for royalties from publication in perpetuity, was gently and courteously refused. In the end I realised that unless I paid for publication myself the book would remain in typescript; and here is the result.

The matter of thanking those who have helped me calls for comment. In the foreword to his book *The Path to Rome* (which he heads *Praise of this Book*) Hilaire Belloc, who wrote so well about the lower Thames, has some caustic observations on this practice. But while it is to be admitted that readers are probably only mildly interested in acknowledgements, many unknown and kindly people often go out of their way to help writers of books for no return, and it is right that they should be thanked publicly.

Those who helped to fortify my flagging morale must have first mention. And for that reason (although the book contains only a glancing reference to his own subject) I am indebted to Sir Harry Godwin, FRS, Emeritus Professor of Botany in the University of Cambridge, for giving me more encouragement than he can ever realise.

I have also been strengthened over a number of years by the support given me — and not only in my topographical researches — by my friend Raymond Lister, Senior Research Fellow of Wolfson College, Cambridge.

On one specific occasion I was considerably cheered by Dr Struve, director of the Schleswig-Holsteinisches Landesmuseum in Germany, who while a stranger to me telephoned to say that a much wanted photograph was on its way.

In another specific matter my faltering steps were guided along the right classical path by Dr Hugh Plommer, the noted Cambridge savant and author of *The Ugciad*, who provided me with a detailed gloss of the word *gemitus*, used according to Gildas by the British in appealing for help to Aetius after the end of Roman rule in Britain; and traditionally translated, as I would like to believe, with some blurring of essential emotional meaning, by the word *groans*. I tried to persuade him that the Welsh (as in fact they were) would probably have had some greater feeling for words than the gloss might suggest, and that *heart cries* might be nearer the meaning of the word. He remained unconvinced.

Mr James Howson, archivist at the Valence House Museum, Dagenham, while yet a stranger to me, answered abstruse topographical and bibliographical inquiries over the telephone long after the eleventh hour; and Mr Randal Bingley, curator of the Thurrock Local History Museum at Grays, apart from valuable technical help over maps and photographs, for a time gave a secure home to the typescript in the museum safe.

Mr Desmond Collins, by recommending judicious excision, has I hope shielded me from gross error in dealing with the Ice Ages. Mrs M. U. Jones, director of excavation at the Saxon site at Mucking in Essex, gave painstaking attention to my attempts to present the technical aspects of the operation to a general readership; and if I have fallen into error in invading her field of knowledge in spite of her guidance the fault is mine alone. Finally, for over thirty years I have been encouraged in all my researches by present and former members of the Express Newspapers library staff in London. It is a pleasure to thank them here.

A note on the spelling adopted for certain proper names in the text is necessary. One of the three publishers who showed interest asked that I should write two chapters on the coming of the Saxons and the Danish wars. This I did; and have retained them after the possibility of publication in that quarter receded.

As a result one problem remained: that of how Saxon, Danish and Norse names should be spelt.

In this connection — indeed in any other — I believe the spelling of any name should be that which is likely to be most familiar. This avoids the not uncommon situation in which a reader is tripped up by coming across a previously familiar name (let us say Ethelred) spelt in an unfamiliar way (in this case Aethelred) and for him to ask, Does he mean Ethelred?

Where, therefore, Saxon, Danish and Norse names are concerned, I think the overriding argument must be that it is only by using the modern anglicised form that consistency and clarity can be guaranteed. Otherwise which, among the forms of Thurkill which appear in the *Anglo-Saxon Chronicle*, should be chosen? Thurcytel, Turketell, Thirkettle, Turkyll or Thurtell? There are also, in the *Chronicle*, at least four forms of the name Olaf, Olive among them, Anlaf preponderating, while for Canute we have also Nott, Knott and Knox, as well as the more familiar Cnut and Knut. Among these I conceive it better to use that which is most familiar in modern English — in the last case, Canute; and if that is used, then all other questions are superfluous.

While on the subject of nomenclature, I may add that I have purposely retained such old and familiar names as Westmorland and Huntingdonshire, not only because they are topographically more accurate, but also as a mild indication of the contempt I feel for those who wantonly destroyed counties the objects of men's love and loyalty for anything up to a thousand years.

CHAPTER I

The Thames Basin before the Ice Ages

Most men think of rivers, rightly enough, as living things. Even to the least imaginative they have some sense of purpose. Like men, they have their rising, their infancy, their youth, their maturity. They have seen many things both in time and space; and, like men, they are a part of all they have known.

Something of these aspects of rivers appears in Stevenson's story *Will o' the Mill.* It was doubtless this feeling that rivers have a personality which caused the Greeks to think of them as gods, and which caused John Burns to say (more or less) that while the Mississippi was plain mud, every drop of the Thames was liquid history.

All this is true. And yet, for the time being, I would present the Thames in different light, as a thing decided only by the nature of the land in the south-east of England and the rain which falls there.

One can be helped to see the Thames in this way by air photographs of its upper reaches, which show each slow fold of the land, and in the creases where those folds meet, the wandering watercourses which ultimately form the main river and its tributaries. Seen from this height, the infant Thames looks not unlike lost tidal water exploiting each slight depression in the sand as it drains back to the sea, something little more than the minor streams which make their own changing channels through the silt of Morecambe Bay, or the even smaller streams, which before motor traffic destroyed England, veined road dust in gutters after rain.

It is true that rivers, even when no more than collections of drainage water seeking their own level, their form, their direction, their very existence decided by rain and the fall of land, can still have a frightening power all their own. The Westmorland Kent, when massively swollen by rainwater from the hills, can roar past Grange over Sands like a lion, its tawny waters permanently banked towards the centre of the current as it cuts new canyons through the silt like a knife through butter. At Lynmouth, Devon, when in August 1952 some 300 million tons of water fell in the thirty-eight square miles drained by the two Lyns, the West Lyn moved over 50,000 tons of boulders in one day, some weighing more than ten tons, and a delta containing 200,000 cubic yards of rock debris formed at its mouth.

Slower moving Fenland rivers, when they set themselves, can in flood crumple houses as a man's hand crumples a paper bag. Even the Thames, in general a less fierce stream than these, pushed a steam locomotive on its side between Purfleet and Grays during the floods of 1953; and ten years later, on the muddy margins of the estuary, one could still see old reels of kraft lining paper washed out of the flooded Thames Board Mills by the river during those weeks of flood.

Yet even though rivers can have their own sudden and powerfully destructive life, even our usually peaceful Thames, I would still offer this river, at least for the moment, as drainage water finding its way to the sea. For while the Thames may reasonably be described as liquid history because it has followed its present course during historical times, it is geologically speaking little older than the newest channel which the Kent has forced through the silt between the coast at Grange and the sea. The Thames has not always been there. As far as the earth itself is concerned, it was not there yesterday. Further, in one sense it could be said that the Thames is making the best of a bad job. It did not, as other rivers have done, create its own basin. It has not, in one sense, even created its own bed.

For even if we look at the Thames, not against the whole of geological history, but only against that period during which the land mass of Britain as we know it today has been more or less complete, the river, at least in its present course, is still a product of recent history. Unlike many rivers, which are often older than the surface they drain and the hills they traverse, the Thames is not the oldest part of the landscape through which it passes. Its present course below London is only some hundreds of thousands of years old; even the course of the Mardyke, that minor tributary which joins the Thames at Purfleet, is millions of years older than the vaster stream into which it falls. Since, therefore, the Thames is a comparative newcomer, it would be as well to describe the country through which it passes, and its formation, before dealing with the river; and this means saying something about the earth itself.

The centre of the earth is a solid mass of nickel and iron, which were it not under pressure from the crust of the earth would be molten from heat today. This metallic core is covered, first with basalt, a stone which contains iron, and then a layer of granite, which is based on silicon. Then, above these, come the rocks we see on the surface of the earth today, or know of from borings.

These superficial rocks are of two kinds, igneous and sedimentary. Igneous rocks are older than sedimentary rocks, and their name, from the same root as ignite, shows they were made by fire. They took their present form at a time when they were not completely cooled, and while they do thrust themselves up to the surface in some parts of the British Isles, they are hidden over the whole of south-east England by later, sedimentary, formations. Sedimentary rocks, which include limestone, sandstone and chalk, were formed from igneous rocks by living organisms, or by the action of water or other influences.

In the London basin, basalt and granite are overlaid by a series of later rocks which are known as the palaeozoic, or ancient, platform. Above these are a series of surface rocks which were laid during the last 120 million years.

Deepest of the four main layers of these more recent rocks is a layer of sandstone known to geologists as greensand. Above that is a layer of gault clay, above that a layer of chalk, and above that a layer made up of varying amounts of clay, sand and pebbles. All four layers were laid in sea water, in the last of the seas which covered what is now the lower Thames basin.

The lowest of the four layers, the greensand, is the oldest; that on the surface, which is mostly clay, the most recent. All four rise to the surface north and south of the London basin, so that to the south of London the greensand, the oldest deposit, is farthest away, and in going north one passes across bands of gault and chalk before arriving at the central area of London clay and its associated deposits, each deposit being successively more recent. This succession is repeated, if less clearly, to the north of London, where clay gives way first to the chalk of the Chilterns, then to the gault between the Chilterns and Woburn, and finally to the greensand at Woburn itself, each deposit being older than that south of it.

The way in which three of the four deposits which cover the Thames basin come to the surface at the edge of the basin can be seen from the crest of the North Downs south of Caterham in Surrey, at a point slightly to the east of what is shown on the one-inch Ordnance Survey map as Gravelly Hill. Standing here, on what is the southern edge of the surfacing chalk, one can see the ground fall away abruptly at one's feet to the strip of gault, to rise after two miles in the long wooded greensand ridge of Tilberstow Hill.

This sandstone ridge runs south of the chalk and parallel with it in both directions. To the west it is the source of the dark sandstone one can see in St Martha's (formerly St Martyr's) chapel, on top of the ridge south of the chalk between Guildford and Newlands Corner in Surrey. Farther east, at Reigate, it produces a light-coloured sandstone which has limited uses in building. Farther east still the sandstone content of the stone falls and the limestone content increases, until towards Maidstone in Kent it is the source of that limestone known as Kentish rag.

I have referred to this sandstone ridge as greensand. The term is in common use for that type of sand containing glauconite or iron silicate and is thereby coloured green, although when the geological term Greensand with a capital G is used for this particular formation it includes sand coloured dark brown and gold, as well as that limestone called Kentish rag. At some points, for example near Leith Hill in Surrey, the greensand ridge divides into two parallel ridges; but in order to avoid loading the reader with unnecessary detail when so much that is necessary must be inflicted, I have purposely referred to one band of greensand only in the Thames basin. Except for one occasion earlier in this paragraph I have also avoided the convention of using capital letters to indicate particular geological formations. I also want, wherever possible, to avoid involvement with geological terminology.

The layer of gault above the greensand was laid when the sea in which the greensand formed had become deeper as a result of changes in relative land-sea levels, and had attained a depth of 600 feet or more. It is a stiff, blue mud clay of marbled appearance. One place where it can be seen in its original state, although well outside our district, is in the bank of the Old Bedford River under the bridge at Sutton Gault in the Isle of Ely.

Gault is softer than chalk or sandstone. For this reason where it surfaces south of the North Downs it forms a strip of almost sunken land which is known between Guildford castle in the west and Rochester castle in the east as the Vale of Holmesdale.

Chalk began forming above the gault, possibly some 100 million years ago, when the bed of the sea sank and the waters became deeper. It is made of the remains of microscopic unicellular creatures something like plankton which lived in the surface layers of the sea, and is therefore the product of sea plants rather than of sea animals. Chalk today contains deposits of flint and, in places, iron pyrites —

heavy, often kidney-shaped lumps of metal compounded of iron and sulphur, which when broken show a radial mass of shiny crystalline material. Broadly speaking, pyrites formed when the iron and sulphur in certain sea creatures' bodies settled out and combined to form small crystals, which by a process of accretion became the nodules we know today.

Flint will be familiar to readers in the south-east of England, if not farther afield. It is hard, compact, brittle, and easily formed by shattering into tools so hard that they can cut glass. It is to be found in many colours, although that used for making tools is commonly dark grey, honey coloured or (particularly in Sussex) white.

In their natural state flints have a skin which is lighter in colour than the flint itself, and is sometimes almost pure white. For this reason one might assume this skin to be of similar content to the chalk in which the flint is found. In fact it is simply flint whose structure has been broken down under outside influences into a sort of honeycomb formation, and it is the light reflected from the facets of this honeycomb which gives the appearance of lightness.

Flint is found in more or less level layers in the upper chalk, but not in the middle and lower layers. It is also clear that flint was in a fluid state when formed, because flints have been found which have "flowed" round fossils and other deposits. It is equally clear that flint, which was formed on the bed of the sea at the same time as the chalk, became hard in the absence of fire or extreme heat.

Flint is based on the element silicon, which is also the basis of such igneous rocks as granite. Chalk is based on the element calcium, as are all limestones. Very broadly, since chalk and other limestones are formed of the shells or bones of sea organisms which were also based on the element calcium, one might say that calcium-based rocks such as chalk were organically made, while rocks such as flint based on silicon were inorganically made.

To this generalisation, however, flint may be an exception. The way in which it was formed is uncertain. Some think it may have been made from the fossilised bodies of sponges whose structure was based on silicon, and not calcium. If so, then flint is of organic origin. Others believe flints were formed from the skeletons of minute creatures known as radiolaria, which are in some ways similar to the minute organisms from whose remains chalk is made — although radiolaria have skeletons based on silicon, not calcium. Others believe flint to have no connection with living organisms. Whatever its origin, it is not known how this silicon-based material, deposited on the sea bottom at the same time as the chalk, turned into the hard material we know today.

But to return to the chalk. In rising to the surface at the edge of the London "saucer", the chalk forms the Chilterns north of London, Salisbury Plain well to the west of London, and the North Downs south of London. Apart from the fact that there is, to the east, no chalk barrier which could be compared with those to south, north and west, the chalk could therefore be said to ring, and to be the only real boundary of, the Thames basin.

While the chalk forms no barrier to the east, it is represented there in the North Downs, which run east and west on the south side of river, estuary, and sea. It is also represented in a northern outcrop of those same Downs at Higham in north Kent (which causes the Thames to turn north at Higham Bight) and north of the river in an isolated chalk ridge running east from Purfleet in south Essex. There are also a number of chalk ridges in the bed of the lower Thames which connect with the chalk on each side of the river. The two main connecting ridges, which in times past have formed barriers to navigation, are an unnamed ridge at East Tilbury, and the shoal at Erith Rands.

Although chalk also underlies the whole of Essex and East Anglia, and a boring has shown it to be 890 feet thick at Harwich, few outside the area would associate chalk with south Essex. Where it surfaces by the river between Purfleet and Grays it peters out to the north under clay. But the chalk mines in Hangmans Wood near Grays, which are known as deneholes, dig deep into the chalk. Chalk is the basis of the cement industry, in south Essex as in north Kent; and on the high chalk ridges of North Stifford in Essex it is possible in summer, with the help of sunshine and the smell of thyme, to imagine without difficulty that one is on the Downs.

I have referred to the last of the four surface deposits in the Thames basin as London clay. This clay, which is up to 430 feet thick at Brentwood, and even deeper elsewhere in Essex, appears on the surface as a stiff brown clay which soaks up a good deal of water at the surface in wet weather, and shrinks and cracks in dry. With this clay are other deposits made up of varying amounts of sand and pebbles. Some of the most attractive heathland in Surrey — and in Essex too, at Brentwood and elsewhere — with its heather, birches and bracken, is found on some of these soils.

These sandy soils are also responsible for producing the only indigenous stone found in Essex north of the Thames, and in Kent north of the North Downs. These are the large sandstone boulders known in Berkshire and Wiltshire as sarsens or greywethers (wether being a kind of sheep), and the boulders made of that form of conglomerate known as puddingstone, which is sandstone containing rounded pebbles — the plums in the pudding. Sarsens are found north and south of the river, particularly in the Cliffe area of Kent; puddingstone, as far as I know, north of the river only.

Sarsens, whether of sandstone or puddingstone, come from the sand which was laid on top of the chalk. Water percolating through the sand left traces of iron and other chemicals which cemented the sand into hard shapeless masses. When weathering had removed the rest of the sand, these masses were left on the surface of the chalk in the form of boulders. The lumps of puddingstone found in Essex and Hertfordshire were formed in the same way as sarsens, but from layers of sand containing pebbles.

The London clay also produces stones of a kind called septaria, which are about the same size and shape as a half-pound pork pie. They are softer than sarsen stone or puddingstone, can be broken into small segments or layers with slight impact, and weather badly. They were formed by the segregation and concretion of the more limy parts of the clay, and now appear in the clay in strata in much the same way that flints appear in layers in the chalk. They are particularly common on the coast of Essex near Harwich.

I have said that the sandy soils of the estuary produce the only indigenous rocks found there. I used the word indigenous because during the Ice Ages the southern-moving ice cap carried other boulders into the area from hilly areas to the north. These boulders are called glacial erratics, and include limestone boulders from hundreds of miles away. Such glacial erratics are not found in Kent, because at the period of its greatest extent the ice cap came no farther south than a line drawn from north London, through Brentwood, to the coast of Essex at or about Maldon.

I have jumped ahead some millions of years in referring to the Ice Ages, for the London clay was laid some 60 million years ago while the Ice Ages ended some 10,000 years ago. They are therefore, comparatively speaking, a matter of recent history.

It is now necessary to return to a period some 30 million years ago, that is half way between the formation of the London clay and the Ice Ages, when there took place a vast upheaval in the earth's surface which at its central point so lifted the crust of the earth that it created the Alps. It also sent out waves of pressure which struck the chalk layer, lifted it and folded it to form the Chiltern Hills north of London, the shallow valley which now forms the Thames saucer, and the North Downs south of London. It also created, in the east of the Thames saucer, minor folds running at right angles to the main folding, which remain today in the chalk hill at Higham and the chalk ridges in the bed of the Thames. All these changes were caused, in the geologist's happy phrase, by "the outer ripples of the Alpine storm".

I have said the North Downs were caused by the Alpine storm. This is only partly true. What happened was that when the chalk and other deposits at the bottom of the sea were raised, they formed a great shallow dome above what is now Kent and Sussex, which in the centre reached a height of 3,000 feet above sea level. The chalk which formed the crown of this dome had under it a layer of gault, then a layer of greensand, and then layers of what are called Wealden deposits, which are mostly various kinds of sandstone and limestone. The Weald dome therefore not only contained extensions of some of the strata of the London basin, but in shape was like the London saucer turned upside down.

In time the chalk, gault and greensand layers were worn right away by frost, rain and rivers working from the centre of the dome. Frost, by turning into ice the water absorbed by surface chalk, and expanding the volume of that water by about a twelfth, broke down the chalk which had absorbed it. Rain, picking up carbon dioxide from the atmosphere, formed a weak solution of carbonic acid which attacked the chalk, and washed away in solution that which it had eaten away. Rivers wore away the softer surface rock, and began undercutting the ridges which remained. These processes, which continued for millions of years, stripped the top layers from the central area of the dome, exposed the deposits underneath, and left ridges of chalk and sandstone at the edges of the area of central erosion. These ridges moved progressively outwards from the centre, particularly to north and south, leaving in the North and South Downs, and parallel sandstone hills, truncated ridges where the main covering layers formerly arose. The result now is that if one travels across the Weald southwards from the North Downs one passes from chalk, across gault, and then across greensand — and then, after crossing the Wealden deposits in the centre of the area, which were laid in fresh water, and are not represented under London — the process is reversed, and one passes first over greensand, then gault, and then the chalk of the South Downs.

I have already referred to the valley of gault and the sandstone ridge which can be seen from the lip of the North Downs. Those who stand here may also see, on the other side of the Weald, the dim outline of the South Downs in the form of that recent addition to its profile, the wood on Chanctonbury Ring. It may be difficult for such observers to believe that they are standing on one side of a broken arch of chalk which once soared up for thousands of feet to connect with the other side of that broken arch, the South Downs, in the far distance. But it is so; and the sandstone ridge of Tilberstow also rose up beneath the higher chalk arch to connect with ridges of sandstone on this side of the South Downs which are now hidden in the distances of the Weald. Now only the stumps of chalk and sandstone remain, while the softer intervening layer of gault has been almost scooped out between them.

Here I must recall an earlier statement that rivers are often the oldest features of a landscape. This may have raised a passing question in the reader's mind. But the fact is that rivers can, and often do, survive great changes in the landscape across which they flow; and the existence of the rivers which flow into the Thames from the Weald proves it.

A glance at the map will show that at Tonbridge, in the centre of the Weald, the Medway in its upper reaches passes through country less than a hundred feet above sea level. Then, while the river is only a few feet above sea level itself, it passes through two parallel barriers, first the sandstone and limestone ridge between Sevenoaks and Maidstone, then the North Downs. The first barrier rises to a height of over 300 feet within a mile of the river, the second to a height of over 500 feet. This pattern is repeated by the Darent, which also has its rising south of the North Downs, and finds its way through the chalk barrier in a long narrow valley with the ground rising on each side to over 500 feet.

One might assume that these rivers were lucky in finding two such convenient valleys in the chalk through which to pass. The fact is that they carved out the valleys themselves; and it is now necessary to understand how they did so.

It may be assumed that when the chalk arch between North and South Downs was unbroken, the Darent, Medway and other rivers having their rising in the Weald took the same general courses across the Weald dome as they do today, although their upper reaches were then higher than the tops of the present chalk barriers which now exist to the north, and which were then only the lower slopes of the dome. But while flowing down the chalk slope from higher areas inland, the rivers began eroding their beds downwards. This process began at the outfall, and continued backwards up their beds — and it went on at a faster rate than the process of denudation which was lowering the level of the land surface in the central area through which the upper reaches of the rivers passed. This meant that the rivers always entered the remaining peripheral chalk areas from a higher level. This in turn meant that they still had enough erosive power to continue their process of downcutting, so that by the time the central area of the Weald had been almost completely destroyed, the rivers had already cut their channels through the chalk and sandstone ridges which remained at the outer edges.

It may now be helpful to bring together in one table all the main points in time which have been mentioned in this brief outline of the early history of the Thames basin.

	Million years ago
Greensand laid from	120
Chalk laid from	100
London clay laid from	60
Chalk lifted in Alpine storm	30

CHAPTER 2

The Ice Ages

SO far we have been concerned with the making of the Thames basin over a period of millions of years. We must now consider how that basin was changed as a result of the most recent series of Ice Ages — and therefore think, not according to a time scale of millions of years, but according to one of tens of thousands of years only. For the Ice Ages are in the history of the earth almost frighteningly close. If we assume that the earth's crust formed some 5,000 million years ago, and that the Ice Ages began some 600,000 years ago and ended some 10,000 years ago, then if the life of the earth is compared with that of a man celebrating his hundredth birthday, the Ice Ages began four or five days ago and ended an hour and three quarters ago. (I refer to the most recent series of Ice Ages. There were others at various times before, that is between 600,000 and two million years ago, but they left less mark on the area than those which followed, and for the sake of simplicity I must ignore them.)

Before considering the effects of the later Ice Ages on the Thames basin it is necessary to know what the area was like before they began. At that time, some 600,000 years ago, south-east England and the Thames saucer were with certain exceptions roughly as they are today, although the land, and the bed of the sea which now borders the whole area to east and south, were some hundreds of feet higher. That part of the sea bed known as the Continental Shelf (the North Sea south of a line from Yorkshire to the northern point of Denmark, and the English Channel east of about Dorset) was dry land, and England an extension of the Continent. The Thames did not follow its present course at the southern edge of the London saucer; it flowed farther to the north, possibly through what is now the estuary of the Blackwater below Maldon in central Essex, joining the northward-flowing Rhine off what is now the Essex coast. The combined river passed across east Suffolk and east Norfolk, whose north coast it crossed for the last time at Cromer. It then entered the north half of the North Sea through a wide estuary between the coast of Yorkshire and the Dogger Bank, which at this time formed the northern edge of the dry land which connected England and the Continent.

The sea may have already invaded parts of the Continental Shelf before the Ice Ages began, although east of Dorset and south of the Dogger was at this time still dry land. The ice cap, as at present, was limited to the Arctic and Antarctic, and to the higher parts of the Alps and other mountain ranges.

Then, as a result of variations in the amount of summer sunshine for which no cause has been established, the polar ice caps so increased in area that the one to the north came down at the two periods of its greatest extent to a line drawn roughly from the Bristol Channel to south Essex. At the same time it also covered almost the whole of that part of the Continental Shelf which now lies under the North Sea.

In the most recent series of Ice Ages the northern ice cap invaded northern Europe during four separate periods. The first period, during which the ice did not come as far south as England, began about 600,000 years ago. In the second and third Ice Ages the ice sheet came down as far as the south of England and almost reached what is now the present course of the Thames. In the fourth and last Ice Age it reached northern Norfolk, but elsewhere came no nearer the Thames than South Wales and the Midlands.

Attempts have been made, and continue to be made, to assess the duration of the individual Ice Ages, and of the warmer periods between them, but the only fairly reliable date is that for the end of the last Ice Age. Most authorities suggest that it ended some 10,000 years ago. Others regard it as ending as recently as 8,700 years ago, when the last ice sheet retreated to Ragunda in Sweden and split into two isolated caps. For our purposes, however, the accuracy of the figures, even were accuracy possible, is of minor importance. What is of importance is to get a rough idea of when the Ice Ages began, how many there were, and how recently the last one ended.

The first important effect of the ice on south-east England was to change the course of the Thames. During the second and third Ice Ages the river, which had previously taken a more northerly course, was forced to move south under pressure from the ice cap, from the debris dropped by the ice, and from the ice floes which broke off the face of the ice sheet.

Evidence for the pre-glacial courses of the Thames is provided by the existence, above London, of certain gravel deposits laid by the river in its earlier course. These bands of gravel are continuous along the Evenlode, a northern tributary of the Thames which flows from north Gloucestershire to join the main river above Oxford. They then follow the present course of the Thames, at intervals capping the high ground on both sides of the river, as far as Bourne End some twenty-seven miles west of central London, where they leave the present river and take a line towards Rickmansworth and Hertford. The existence of these gravel deposits suggests that the pre-glacial river followed its present course as far as Bourne End, and then a line through Beaconsfield, Rickmansworth, Watford, St Albans, and Hertford to Ware.

Ware is some twenty miles from central London at the northern end of the Lea valley, which runs almost due north and south to the east of London. It is difficult to suggest where the pre-glacial Thames flowed after that point. Two suggestions have been made, neither of which takes the Thames in an easterly direction at all. One is that the river flowed up the valley of the Stort to Bishops Stortford and then, by way of Granta, Cam and Ouse, to the Wash. The other is that it flowed from Ware to the Wash through a gap in the chalk at Stevenage. It is possible that a river did flow along one or other of these courses at some time; but if so it must have been at a time so remote that we could hardly regard it as the Thames.

What is of more importance is the course taken by the Thames immediately before the Ice Ages. My feeling is that after Ware it did not cross the chalk barrier to the north, but went across central or south Essex to some point on the east coast.

A number of courses have been suggested. One is taken from Ware directly to the Blackwater estuary. A second is taken down the Lea valley to Blackwall or some intermediate point, after which it is taken south of the high ground at Horndon, and so through the Crouch or Blackwater estuary. It is possible, if the river followed this second course, that it left the Lea valley somewhere near Tottenham, and then flowed east to Horndon through Romford — or that it went all the way down the Lea valley to the present course of the Thames, which it then left along the valley of the Mardyke.

One final suggestion is that there were two rivers flowing through what is now the lower Thames basin in pre-glacial times: one which took a course from Bourne End to Ware, and then across central Essex to the sea; and one which followed the present course of the Thames through and below London, but without the benefit of its headwaters. It is possible that the river followed all these courses in turn over a long period of time, or it may even have followed two or more courses at the same time — as the Fenland Ouse did until three centuries ago, and as the Lea and Rhine do today.

It is not surprising that there is so much variation in the courses suggested for the pre-glacial Thames east of the Lea, for the whole area is masked by glacial debris which has so far made impossible the identification of any possible course. But there are certain factors which may be considered in coming to a speculative conclusion.

The first is the depth and position of those sunk valleys on the coast of Essex along which the Thames might have passed in its passage to the extended Rhine — not only the estuaries of such rivers as Stour and Crouch, but also the sea channels which form their seaward extensions. If the depth of the main channel in the Blackwater and Crouch estuaries is anything to go on, then the Blackwater was the main outlet, and the Crouch estuary a temporary outlet during the Ice Ages.

The second factor to be considered is the height above sea level at which the pre-glacial Thames entered Essex on the west. A height of 300 feet above present sea level would have taken it above the highest pre-glacial barrier it was likely to face. It could then have chosen its course at will. Had it entered the area at a lower level, then the relief of the pre-glacial land surface underneath the later glacial deposits — and this is the third factor — would have been decisive. And of that relief we know nothing except that if the glacial drift were removed, much of Norfolk and Suffolk and parts of northern Essex would now be below sea level.

The fourth factor to be considered in speculating on the immediately pre-Ice-Age courses of the river is the existence in south Essex of a depression which may mark one possible course. When the Romford to Upminster railway line was built, the silted-up channel of an old river running for over one hundred yards east and west was found near the Victoria Road bridge in Romford. T.V. Holmes, who reported this in the *Geological Society Journal* for 1894, says the channel must have been wide, because more than eight yards from the bridge the bed still sloped towards the south, as though the centre of the channel had not yet been reached.

Holmes suggested that if the channel at Romford was that of an earlier Thames, then it flowed between the heights of Warley, Billericay and Danbury to the north, and those of Langdon Hills, Hadleigh, Rayleigh and Althorne to the south; then, after crossing the present valley of the Crouch, entered that of the Blackwater between Woodham Ferrers and Althorne, at a point where the watershed between the two basins is now little more than fifty feet above sea level. He suggested that it finally joined what is now the estuary of the Blackwater somewhere east of Maldon.

My own feeling is that while the Thames may at various times have followed one or more of the courses earlier described, immediately before the Ice Ages it flowed from Bourne End to Ware and then down the Lea valley, probably leaving it at Tottenham to flow past Romford and West Horndon. It then crossed the watershed between the Mardyke and Crouch between East Horndon and Dunton Wayletts at just over 100 feet, and then reached the Blackwater, either by way of the Wid, which flows northwards to the west of Billericay, or by a course passing Wickford and flowing down Lawling Creek. The former, which would involve crossing a fairly high ridge south of Billericay, is the less likely.

After flowing down what is now the Blackwater estuary the river then passed close to Mersea Island and the coast of Essex between Colne Point and Frinton. Deflected to the east by Gunfleet Sands, at that time a ridge of higher ground, it then joined the Rhine, which had flowed through what was until recently the Zuider Zee and then across the southern part of the North Sea.

Another possibility is that the river flowed all the way down the Lea valley to the Thames, and then cut across what are now the lower courses of the Roding, Beam, and Ingrebourne; or, first flowing for a period along the present channel of the Thames, flowed back up the Mardyke. I am inclined to think this course less likely than that through Romford, which is the only course for which there is any tangible evidence in the ground.

I have referred to a possible course up the Mardyke, and this is perhaps the best place to deal with this little stream. The Mardyke, now little more than a large ditch, has always puzzled me. It seemed curious that it should fall into the Thames opposite that nobler stream the Kentish Darent, and not only at exactly the same point, but in the opposite direction. It also seemed curious that its course through Stifford should be marked by a valley so deep that for Essex it has almost the appearance of a gorge — and that to pass through this chalk ridge at Stifford it should flow from a fen almost at sea level on the north, to river alluvium almost at sea level on the south.

The Mardyke has no very clear rising. It does take spring water from the southern slopes of the hills rising towards Brentwood and Ingrave, but much of its flow must now be such drainage water from Orsett and Bulphan Fens as is not pumped out by factories on the river. It is difficult to believe that this minor stream can have cut through the Stifford chalk ridge with what flow is now available to it.

It must have been the Kentish Darent which did this, and in the same way, and probably at the same time, as it gouged out its channel through the North Downs. For during the millions of years that the Thames took a more northerly course, the Darent must have continued right across what is now the bed of the Thames (at that time dry land) and then flowed up what is now the bed of the Mardyke to join the earliest pre-glacial Thames at a point somewhere south of the high ground at Horndon. Then, when the Thames was pushed south by the ice cap into its present course, its flow cut off the lower reaches of the Darent and turned it into the southward and westward flowing Mardyke we know today.

The idea that the flow of a stream or river should be reversed in the same bed is an acceptable one. In the Fens the water of the Old Nene has been known to flow through the town of March in one direction one day and in the opposite direction the next. As a result of human interference the waters of Well Creek, which in the Middle Ages flowed from west to east, now flow from east to west. The cause of this phenomenon is mainly lack of gradient, and it is liable to happen in any stream crossing an alluvial plain.

I have already said that the course of the Mardyke — its bed, if not direction of flow — is much older than the present course of the Thames, which is no older than the end of the second Ice Age. The Darent is at least as old as the period during which the chalk of the Weald was raised, which was getting on for 30 million years ago. This means that the course of the Mardyke is anything up to 30 million years old, while the course of the Thames into which it falls at Purfleet is some hundreds of thousands only. These figures are as approximate as figures could be, but they are correct enough to show how old is the Mardyke, and how young the Thames.

This diversion to deal with the age of the Mardyke has caused me to anticipate what was to have been a general comment on the way in which the pre-glacial Thames was forced to take a more southerly course because of the pressure of the ice cap. Present knowledge suggests that below London the ice cap came as far south as south-central Essex in both the second and the third Ice Ages — although in the second it came slightly farther south on what is now the coast of Essex as well as at two points above the site of London. Even with these three variations the way in which the ice seems to have been halted twice on much the same line seems to be something of a coincidence. But if we accept the fact that the line reached by the ice was the same on both occasions save for three southern extensions in the second Ice Age, then it follows that these earlier extensions of the ice must have been decisive for diverting the Thames into its present bed; and that at the end of the second Ice Age the Thames had already taken up its present course from London to the sea.

The ice did a number of things to the lower Thames basin apart from changing the course of the Thames. Through its physical action, weight and movement, it changed the surface soil of the area it covered. Through its temperature and the meltwater it produced it changed the surface soil to the south of the ice cap. It also changed relative land-sea levels, with far reaching results.

When the ice came down as far as south Essex, Britain was covered with ice sheets which moved slowly southward the whole time as fresh ice came down from the north to replace that which melted at the southern edge of the ice cap. The ice in its gradual movement southward picked up and carried rocks and other debris, often for hundreds of miles. Some of these rocks were carried on the surface, some inside the ice itself, and some in and beneath its lower surface. In the last case the ice became like a gigantic flexible file with embedded fragments of rock for teeth.

Sometimes the rocks picked up and carried by the ice were dropped singly when the ice sheet melted. These are the glacial erratics to which I have already referred. The boulder of mountain limestone by the churchyard wall at Manuden in Essex is an example.

Where an ice cap ends, stones are over the centuries dropped in much the same area, and often in line. The high ground known as Cromer Ridge, which runs westwards from Cromer in Norfolk to Holt, and reaches a height of 300 feet in places, is made of material brought to the edge of the ice cap during the last Ice Age. Such heaps of glacial material, which are called moraines, are more commonly found at the end of glaciers, because at such points material brought from a wider area is concentrated. There are, for example, moraines at the southern ends of Coniston Water and Windermere in the Lake District, brought down by the glaciers which formed in these valleys.

The ice sheet did not bring many boulders to its southern edge in Essex because the main stone areas of the country were some distance away. It did,however, pick up other material in its passage across the south-east midlands and East Anglia, and this it spread widely at its southern edge. In this material were flints picked up by the ice when it crossed the Chilterns and their extensions to south-west and north-east. These flints were ground down and rounded by the ice. Then, when they came towards the edge of the ice sheet, they were picked up, carried, and spread by streams of meltwater.

Some of these streams of meltwater ran under the ice itself, where the pressure of the ice above lowered the melting point of that below, and so produced water. Because of their confined course, and the head of water behind them, these streams moved at great speed. Their grinding power in spate was considerable, and in their onward rush continued that task of rounding flints which had already been begun by the ice. Sometimes they left heaps of pebbles in tunnels under the ice. When joined by water melted at the edge of the ice cap they heaped up pebbles there also. These pebbles — or gravels, to give them their common name — are one of the most important products of the invasion of the Thames basin by the ice cap.

The word gravel is applied here to a deposit which contains pebbles only, and not to that more familiar type which contains clay. Clay gravel, which is used for making garden paths, and was used by the Romans for surfacing many of their roads, is known to the trade as hoggin. It is of value because the clay often contains a good deal of iron, deposited by iron-charged water which over millennia filtered through the material. When used as road metalling the iron in the clay binds the gravel together and can make it as hard as stone —a somewhat similar process to that which takes place when iron-charged water filters through sand to form sandstone and, ultimately, iron-stone. For these reasons hoggin becomes hard and compacted with age and use, and provides a surface difficult to break.

When picking up the flints which formed glacial gravel, the ice also picked up the chalk in which these flints were bedded, as well as the surface soil and subsoil from other areas. This chalk, clay, sand and loam became frozen in the lower layers of the ice, or was dragged along beneath it. The material was then dropped, not only at the edge of the ice cap, but wherever the ice sheet melted in retreating at the end of the Ice Ages.

These deposits of chalk, clay, sand and loam were the basis of three other glacial deposits found near the southern edge of the ice cap: boulder clay, coombe rock, and loess. Boulder clay is so called because in other areas clay deposited by the ice contains boulders; but like many geological terms it can be confusing, because in Essex at least boulder clay contains no boulders. It is a stiff clay which contains chalk, and where this chalk content has been exhausted as a result of weathering, the result can be a plastic clay more unworkable even than London clay.

Glacial gravel and boulder clay formed under the ice sheet itself. The other two types of deposit, coombe rock and loess, although they resulted from the coming of the ice, were produced immediately south of the ice cap, where the average temperature was below freezing point for a large part of the year.

The fact that the climate here was one of alternate freezing and thawing meant that stones and rock alternately contracting and expanding tended to shatter, and so break down through weathering. This process was accelerated by the presence of meltwater from the ice cap, which when absorbed by the surface soil, or by porous rock such as chalk, shattered it as it expanded on freezing. In time these processes led to the formation of a great deal of rock debris from the chalk and other rocks in the area.

In winter the area south of the ice cap was covered with snow and ice, but when spring came this snow and ice melted, and the water so produced could not drain away to greater depths because the subsoil was permanently frozen. The surface soil became soaked with water as a result, and wherever there was sloping ground the debris resulting from weathering tended to slide down over the waterlogged surface and collect in great masses at the foot of hills and in valley bottoms. When these masses are made up largely of chalk, as they are in Essex and Kent, they are called coombe rock, which is found in Essex at West Thurrock and East Tilbury, and in the Ebbsfleet valley in Kent (which runs from Springhead to the Thames north of Northfleet station and is not to be confused with Ebbsfleet in Thanet).

Farther away from the face of the ice cap, and in areas less affected by floods of meltwater, the characteristic soil was formed by the fine wind-blown dust known as loess. Loess was produced in the absence of water by alternate expansion and contraction caused by freezing and thawing. This process caused particles of rock to shatter, and continued until the particles were so small that alternate expansion and contraction had no further effect.

Loess came mainly from heaps of glacial debris in dry areas south of the ice cap where the surface was not covered with vegetation. Finer material in these heaps, dried by the wind and reduced in size by the processes already described, was carried off by the wind as soon as it was formed, and deposited in nearby areas where grass, low lying vegetation and other obstacles halted the wind.

Loess is excellent agricultural soil. It is also used for making bricks, in particular the yellow bricks once used so widely in London. There are deposits in parts of Ockendon, along the edge of the West Thurrock marshes, in East Thurrock, and at South Stifford, all in Essex. Loess also filled a shallow depression which ran from South Stifford eastwards to the new cemetery at Little Thurrock. Much of this has since been taken for brick making. One worked-out brick-earth quarry was turned into Grays Park, while other sites have been built on. Arthur Street School, Grays, is built below the original ground level at the bottom of a worked-out brick-earth quarry.

It is now necessary to consider how the coming of the ice changed relative land-sea levels. One immediate result of the growth of the polar ice caps was that there was a drop in sea levels because seawater became "tied up" in the ice. The water resources of the world move in a cycle, evaporation from the sea forming clouds which turn to rain, which returns directly or indirectly to the seas again. However much water is caught up in this cycle, the bulk of the earth's water is stored in the sea, so that if some of it is taken out of circulation and locked away in ice sheets there must be a consequent drop in sea levels. It has been estimated by those who have worked out the extent and average depth of today's ice sheet, which at its deepest over Greenland is over 10,000 feet thick, that if all the existing ice masses of the world were melted, then the world's seas would all rise by 150 or 160 feet, and submerge many of the world's largest cities in the process.

There was a second and more prolonged result of the alternate formation and disappearance of the ice cap, and this was a change in land as well as sea levels. This affected two areas in particular: the Baltic area, where the land has been rising since the end of the last Ice Age; and lowland England, the Channel, the southern part of the North Sea, the Low Countries, and north Germany, where the land, and what is now the sea bed, have been sinking.

These changes in land level, which still continue, resulted from the removal by melting of a great weight of ice from the crust of the earth in Scandinavia and neighbouring areas. This had the same effect as pressure, imposed and removed, has on an incompletely inflated rubber ball, causing the surface to rise in one part, and to sink in another. In north-east Sweden, where the ice was at its thickest, there has been a rebound of some 1,500 feet in land levels, with a corresponding sinking, in south-east England, of over 200 feet since the end of the last Ice Age.

According to a map published with an article on land rising and sinking by Hartmut Valentin in the *Geographical Journal* in 1953, the Highlands of Scotland are rising at the rate of about four millimetres a year, and the land in the Thames estuary is sinking at the rate of about two millimetres a year, as a long-term result of the ice cap melting. What Valentin calls the hinge line runs roughly in a crescent with its two horns on St Davids in Pembrokeshire and Whitby in Yorkshire, and with its convex side to the south-east — a line which follows roughly the southern limit of the ice sheet in the last Ice Age.

So far we have observed changes in relative land-sea levels of two types: a rising of sea levels throughout the world which came with the end of the last Ice Age, and followed a period of some 600,000 years during which sea level varied according to the extent of the ice sheets; and a gradual and continuing sinking of land levels in south-east England and neighbouring areas.

These two factors, together with the need for the Rhine to find an outlet when it could no longer flow northwards because of the ice sheet, were responsible for the flooding of what is now the North Sea, the destruction of the land bridge between England and the Continent, and the creation of Britain as an island. Dudley Stamp, in *Britain's Structure and Scenery*, says there was marked and widespread lowering of land in about 6000 B.C., and that North Sea flooding linked North Sea and Channel by about 5000 B.C. after the rising waters had entered a shallow valley previously cut, or enlarged, by the Rhine or its ponded-back waters in what is now the English Channel. Archaeologists incline to believe that there was still a land bridge in 5000 B.C., when the immigration of certain Neolithic tribes took place. Others suggest the final linking of Channel and North Sea by flooding took place earlier, in about 7000 B.C., or gradually between 7000 and 6000 B.C.

The breaking of the Channel bridge is in a sense a diversion: what is important to remember is that both Channel and North Sea are parts of the European land mass flooded by rising seas; that both are extremely youthful and, since flooding is still continuing, that both are still growing.

One can gain an impression of the youth of the North Sea by realising that when the sea invaded its present bed it also flooded many of the valleys which led, and still lead, inland from what was then the newly formed east coast of England. These include the valley of the Stour below Manningtree and that of the Orwell below Ipswich. It is not difficult, when the tide is out, to look across one of these sunk valleys, all now invaded by each high tide, and see in the minor stream threading the central mud flats the freshwater stream which flowed along the valley before the sea broke in — and to see the whole area, not as the estuary of a great river, but as the bottom of a once dry valley whose grass and trees have been killed and washed away by the invading waves.

The youthfulness of the North Sea also becomes apparent if one walks along its shore at low water, for example on the Essex coast between Clacton and Walton. At high water mark at the southern limit of Walton the young and expanding sea which finally swallowed the old church in 1798 has eaten right into road and houses. It is not difficult to imagine that in time it will eat its way through Walton altogether. Yet beneath our feet, here and elsewhere on this stretch of coast, are tree stumps bearing witness to the forest which grew here in or since the Ice Ages; freshwater peat, which shows that at the time of its formation the land here was well above high water mark; and clay, which shows that the whole area was once under another and an older sea altogether.

Comparable observations may be made about the Thames estuary. It is natural to think of the estuary, either as the outlet of a great river, or as part of the sea which contains sandbanks exposed at low water. It is neither. As to the first, the Thames, whose real flow can be seen from Westminster Bridge at low water, could never have created this wide-ranging outlet. As to the second, the estuary is an extension of the North Sea at high water only; at low water, sea and river invest a series of valleys which run across the flooded land in a north-easterly direction. These valleys, which are flooded at all states of the tide, form the routes along which ships can reach London. Between these valleys are a great number of shoals, ridges and sandbanks which in sum cover an area roughly equal to that of the flooded valleys, and in some cases have their highest points as little as ten or eleven feet below the surface at high tide. In these conditions, which save in the figures I have exaggerated to make my point, the Thames estuary at low water is simply land seamed by tidal creeks.

These are perhaps subjective ways of appreciating how young and in a sense unestablished is that North Sea which Belloc referred to as "shallow, tumbling and yellow water" and Conrad as "that shallow and dangerous puddle". There is, however, one fact which proves that the North Sea was dry land after the last Ice Age: fishermen working the Dogger Bank often trawl up peat from depths of between 130 and 140 feet which is known to have formed some 9,000 years ago; and since peat can form in fresh water only, this means that in about 7000 B.C. there was no sea near the Dogger, and that since then there has been a rise of sea level relative to land level of at least the distances given. It is known that the peat on the Dogger formed about 9,000 years ago because it contains fossilised tree pollen which can be dated. These fossilised grains are immensely hard and practically indestructible. If they are isolated, examined microscopically, and then compared with current forms, it is possible to say what kind of trees were growing at the time the peat formed, and thus to date its formation to a certain botanical period. A three or four cubic centimetre sample of peat can contain over a thousand grains, so that there is no chance of statistical error; and since, when newly formed, pollen grains are light enough to be carried by the wind for a considerable distance, they can easily be taken from an area where trees are growing to a waterlogged or flooded area where peat is forming.

We must now return to the results, as far as the Thames is concerned, of that rising and falling of sea levels which resulted from the melting and freezing of the ice caps.

When sea level fell the water at the outlet of the Thames had a steeper fall. It flowed faster, and had greater power to erode its bed downward. Thus in cutting down to adjust to three separate low sea levels during the last Ice Age, the Thames cut three sunk channels in its lower reaches which have now all been filled with material deposited when sea levels rose and the eroding power of the river was reduced.

The second result of changes in relative land-sea level was the creation, each side of the river's main channel, of banks of gravel. These were deposited at times of high sea level when the river's slower flow could not carry away the glacial deposits washed into its bed by meltwater from the ice cap.

The gravel in these terraces is made of small rounded flint pebbles varying in size from that of a pea to a walnut. Sometimes the rush of meltwater from the ice cap was strong enough to move these pebbles right out to sea; when it was not, they were dropped on the edges of the streams formed by meltwater, and principally on the northern bank of the Thames. These gravel deposits, which are often several miles wide, are known as the Thames gravel terraces.

The highest and oldest of the three terraces, about one hundred feet above the present river, is known as the Boyn Hill terrace after an area near Maidenhead in Berkshire where such a terrace is found. The intermediate terrace both in height and age is the Taplow terrace, some fifty feet above the river, named after Taplow in Buckinghamshire; the lowest and most recent, which is usually some twenty-five feet above the river, is known as the flood plain terrace. The fifty and twenty-five foot terraces were formed in two separate warmer periods in the third interglacial, which came after the ice sheet had come as far south as Essex for the second and last time in the third Ice Age. (The heights as I have given them are those in the London area, which are slightly above those of the same terraces downstream. In the Grays area, according to Robert W. Ims writing in volume 3 of the Thurrock Historical Society Journal, they are ninety, forty-five and ten feet respectively, and I shall use these measurements in referring to terraces below London.)

It may help readers to identify these terrraces if I mention that Hyde Park in London is on what is there the fifty foot terrace, and that this terrace continues to Holborn Viaduct, where it drops to, and rises from, the valley of the Fleet river, and then continues under St Paul's and the City to the valley of the river Lea. The river edge of this terrace can be seen clearly by anyone standing at the top of St James's Street and looking south.

The ninety foot terrace is particularly clear in the lower Thames area. Those who walk southwards to the end of Bradleigh Avenue, Grays, and see the ground falling away at their feet towards the river, are on the edge of this terrace. It is the same terrace which can be seen rising from the flood plain of the river between Chadwell and West Tilbury, and which is breasted by the Tilbury to Chadwell road as it climbs up to the crossroads at Chadwell. It is the base of this terrace which is followed by the road from Little Thurrock until that point, south-east of Chadwell, where it turns north to breast Hob Hill. The base line of the ninety foot terrace can also be seen on the 2½-inch map of Tilbury, where the maze of blue lines which show water-bearing dykes in the marshes ends abruptly at its base.

North, north-west and north-east of the curve in the Thames between Woolwich and Erith the three terraces appear as in theory they should always do, with the youngest and lowest terrace near the river, and the oldest and highest farthest away. The oldest and highest, the ninety foot, runs farthest away from the present channel of the Thames from (say) Barkingside to Upminster. It is less continuous than the others, but it is there. Then to the south comes the forty-five foot in a broad band, then the ten foot, then the silt of the flood plain, then the river itself.

The gravel terraces are less extensive on the Kent side of the Thames because the ground rose fairly swiftly there, and the river had less play. The largest area of ninety foot terrace is that to the west of Dartford, which stretches almost as far as Bexley. There is another and a smaller patch east of Dartford, which is breasted by Watling Street as it rises up steeply from the low lying valley of the Darent.

With the end of the Ice Ages the increasing power of the sea to invade the Thames and Thames estuary led to the deposition of silt, and ultimately to the formation of the Thames and Medway marshes. Vast quantities of silt and other eroded material had of course been brought down by the Thames during and immediately after the Ice Ages, but as their effect died away so was the amount of silt brought down by the river reduced. Its place was taken by material brought in by the tide — millions of tons of fine grained clay, mud and silt torn from the surface of the land when the sea came down to form the North Sea and drove up from the Atlantic to form the Channel, as well as chalk torn from the hills whose remains we see in the white cliffs of Dover and France.

Nowadays erosion is less, but exposed areas such as the Yorkshire coast north of the Humber, and the coast of Suffolk and Essex where the ground is soft, are still being eaten away by the sea, which then drops its burden in sheltered inlets in nearby areas. This means that while the coast of Suffolk at Dunwich has been washed away, the sea inlets by the Broads have been filled, and that while the London clay cliffs on the north coast of Sheppey have been eroded, the channel between Thanet and the rest of Kent has been silted up — and that within historical times.

Silting works in this way. Anything which flows, whether air or water, can carry with it particles of a certain size and weight. In general the amount which can be carried, and the distance it can be carried, depend on the speed and density of the carrying medium and the density of the particles. The faster the flow of tide or river the greater the size and weight of particles which can be lifted, and the longer the distance they can be carried.

The flow of river and tide in the estuary is not now swift enough to lift and carry particles larger than those of silt, mud, or clay; and once the movement of the water is arrested — by a headland or other barrier in the bed of the sea, by the inertia of water already in occupation of a sheltered bay or inlet, by the opposition of fresh water coming down a river or estuary, or by the ebb itself — then the larger particles will begin to settle. If the period of arrested movement is short, then only the larger suspended particles will be dropped; if long, then the size range of dropped particles will be greater. In practice this means that silt is dropped first, then clay and mud; and since the arrest of tidal or river flow is gradual, and the incoming tide travels more slowly the farther it flows, the material deposited is actually sorted — the particles become smaller and smaller in size the farther away they are from the sea, and the slower the momentum of the carrying water.

This principle whereby moving water, when retarded, can drop material graduated by size may be illustrated by reference to the 9½-mile long shingle ridge of Chesil Bank, which connects the Isle of Portland with the mainland at Abbotsbury in Dorset. The stones in this bank are graduated from large at one end to small at the other, the tide having dropped the big stones first. The same principle (although here it is a matter of weight, not size) is used by prospectors to separate grains of alluvial gold from pebbles, sand and silt. If a spadeful of material thought to contain grains of gold is thrown into water running at a certain speed, then the large stones will be dropped first, smaller stones next, and pebbles,sand and silt thereafter in that order. And in this spectrum made of bands of gradually decreasing particles, the grains of gold will have their own predictable place — if gold is there.

It was the movement of the tide, and not of the river, which brought particles of silt, mud and clay in suspension up the estuary after the Ice Ages. And where that movement was arrested, there the sediment fell to form the marshes along both banks of Thames, Medway, and estuary. Now flood banks stop wholesale silting, but suspended solids still fall to form shoals and sandbanks in river and estuary, which depending on their position must be cleared by dredging for the sake of maintaining navigation channels.

CHAPTER 3

The Post-Glacial and Historic Thames

I have dealt with the short-term results of the Ice Ages. It is now necessary to consider the long-term results — the continued sinking of south-east England, the southern part of the North Sea, and certain areas in the Low Countries and northern Germany. This sinking continues today, and will continue for centuries to come.

The main effect of land sinking on the Thames, Thames estuary, and lower Thames basin has been to raise flood levels, to make high tides higher, and to create at our coasts a new, expanding, and more powerful sea which daily tries to increase its hold over parts of our south-eastern shores.

There is no need to labour the importance of flood levels in the lower Thames today, but it may be necessary to point out their importance historically. We cannot hope to know what the lower Thames and the Thames estuary were like at any period in history or pre-history unless we know what flood levels then were. What fords existed across the lower Thames at all periods since man settled there; what settlements there were in the area, prehistoric, pre-Roman and Roman; what roads may have led to fords, ferries, and settlements; what fortifications were built in the estuary, particularly in Roman times; to what extent areas of land in the estuary once populated have been lost to the sea — all these depend on flood levels and on the erosive power of a sea itself unleashed by higher flood levels.

We know what flood levels were in the lower Thames at the end of the last Ice Age from a study of terraces and other features already described; we know what flood levels were at various times in the last three or four thousand years because of the depths at which buried trees, peat, marine deposits and the evidence of human occupation have been found at certain points on sea and river margins; and we know what flood levels are today. What we know with less certainty is the state of flood levels in (say) Roman and Saxon times.

If buried trees are found on the shore of sea or tidal estuary at a certain depth below today's high tide or freshwater flood level, then sea or river must have been farther away, or flood levels must have been lower, when those trees were growing; how much farther away depends on local conditions.

I will give four examples. In the Thames at Grays three submerged forest layers have been recorded — an upper layer of yew and brushwood three feet thick, separated by three feet of mud from a lower layer, again three feet thick and mostly of yew, which was again separated by three feet of mud from the third and lowest layer, of yew, large elm trees and oaks so decayed that they could be dug out with the spade. The yew, when dry, was very hard, could be worked, and resembled rosewood.

The second example comes from slightly farther west — the stretch of the Thames from the Black Shelf at West Thurrock towards Stoneness which was in times past known as The Roots because of a submerged forest in the river bed hereabouts. When, farther west still, the railway was laid across the levels east of Barking, a ten feet layer of yews fourteen to sixteen inches in diameter, with willows more than two feet in girth, was found three to four feet beneath the surface of the soil; and as with so many of these reports, small brushwood was also found, including hazel nuts which appeared sound to the eye, but crumbled to the touch. Finally, an example from Kent. Murray's guide to the county says that in digging wells at Sheerness workmen came on a buried forest through which they had to "burn" their way. All these trees, whether in Essex or Kent, grew since the Ice Ages, and when in growth were all a certain minimum number of feet above flood levels.

The existence of peat is also an indication of flood levels at the time of its formation. Peat always forms in fresh water; it cannot form in salt. An underground layer of peat, when found near tidal waters, must therefore have been at a certain minimum distance from, and above, high water mark when it was formed. If we know when that peat formed, then we know that at that period the land was so many feet higher than it is now.

If alternate layers of peat and marine clay are found on a site, then alternate subsidence and rising of the land surface may be assumed — subsidence which resulted in the invasion of the sea which left clay, rising which caused the sea to retreat, freshwater flooding to take place, and peat to form. Such alternate layers of peat and clay are much in evidence in borings taken on the edge of the lower Thames and the Thames estuary; if they can be duplicated on other sites, then their evidence can be taken to prove alternate land rising and falling on an overall scale.

Sometimes, however, the evidence of flood levels from one site seems to conflict with that from others. For this reason it is always necessary to review any evidence concerning former flood levels in and near the estuary in the light of local conditions, which varied considerably. One way in which they varied was in the incidence of tidal breakthroughs, which could overwhelm one area while leaving another at the same level unaffected. Such tidal breakthroughs are known today: their existence in earlier times is proved by the fact that some submerged forest layers in and near the Thames contain trees and shrubs which were in full growth at the time they were overwhelmed by floodwater. There was clearly no gradual submergence here, but one or more sudden breakthroughs which overwhelmed trees normally above floodwater level.

Breakthroughs take place more often where there are artificial flood defences which are breached at one point. They take place least, or not at all, where the land rises away from the shore. Even in the London clay of the Isle of Sheppey, where erosion has gradually eaten away the cliffs to the north of the island and destroyed Warden church and churchyard, the course of marine aggression has been gradual and fairly predictable. It is in other areas of the estuary, where the land is not much higher than high tide level, and where there can be a sudden breakdown of resistance on the part of the land to tidal incursion, that breakthrough takes place.

Tidal breakthroughs such as these, which took place in prehistoric times at Grays, West Thurrock and Barking, and inundated trees in full growth, might be described as cumulative. The land sinks at a regular rate for some years; then, when an extra high tide is backed by an east wind, the tide bursts through and occupies square miles of country which it never leaves. It then not only invests the same area at each high tide, but it erodes soil and land at the inland edge of the flooded area. Features which before the breakthrough were an obstacle to every tide save that which ultimately overtopped them now become powerless against tides of lesser height and power. And the body of the tide, racing out through a channel which previously carried a lesser and slower stream, can erode that channel to greater depths. By attacking areas of soil not previously exposed to flood or tidal action it can so vary the shape of the river that the very mechanics of the movement of fresh and tidal water within the river are changed. The power of the tide, or perhaps of tide and river combined, will become greater in areas where previously it was weak, and weaker where previously it was strong. Nor will there be any return to the state of affairs which existed before the breakthrough. The tide which caused the breakthrough may be only inches higher than the previous tide which caused no breakthrough, but it may still carry away ridges feet high and miles long, and inundate square miles of low lying countryside — simply because of those extra inches. Nor, after the breach has been made, will lower tides ever again be limited to their previous boundaries. They will return to the areas already invaded by higher tides; and although, before the breach took place, those lower tides would have been unable to obtain entrance, now they will do so with ease, and create still further havoc.

Two and perhaps more of the effects I have described are illustrated by the tidal breakthrough which took place at Dagenham in Essex in 1707. This resulted in the flooding of a large area of low lying land behind the north bank of the Thames, much of it still flooded today, and caused a shelf to appear in the main stream of the river with only twelve to eighteen feet of water above it at low water spring tides, which threatened to bring shipping to a standstill. (Spring tides have maximum rise and fall because pull of sun and moon coincide; they come once a month, and are known as spring tides because they spring higher than others. Neap tides, which come a fortnight after springs, have minimum rise and fall because the pull of moon and sun is opposed.)

The processes I have described continue today. The flooding which drowned fifty-eight on Canvey Island alone in 1953 is the way in which gradual land subsidence shows itself. There is an "accidental" piling of the tide such as takes place every ten or twenty years, and the flood defences are overtopped. There can be no doubt that incidents like this have been taking place on the banks of the Thames and Thames estuary since man first settled there, and these apparently arbitrary developments must always be allowed for in examining the history of the Thames.

The most reliable evidence of flood levels in post-glacial and prehistoric times comes mainly from borings, of which a number have been made in the lower Thames basin. These borings, taken through layers of peat, silt and other alluvial deposits, all tell much the same story. One at St Mary's Island, Chatham, which is reported by John H. Evans in the 1953 volume of *Archaeologia Cantiana,* may be used for the purposes of illustration. At the point where the boring took place, the post-glacial land surface, which is of gravel, is thirty-five feet below ordnance datum, and the present ground level eleven feet above. Above the post-glacial surface are the following layers in rising order: six inches of peat, fourteen feet six inches of alluvial clay, two feet of peat, eighteen feet of alluvial clay, one foot of peat, and ten feet of alluvial clay. This last forms (or at the time of boring in or shortly before 1923 then formed) the surface soil.

As I understand it, these and other details of land sinking and rising suggest that in 4000 B.C. the land here was forty-six feet higher than it is now. Since then there have been three periods of land sinking (shown by the three layers of marine clay) separated by two periods of land rising (the two higher layers of peat). The lowest peat layer immediately above the original surface has been ignored in these calculations — it probably indicates some ponding back of river water resulting from slightly higher flood levels, resulting in turn from the beginning of subsidence.

The first period of subsidence ended shortly after 3000 B.C., when the land surface was thirty-one feet above its present level. This was followed by a short period of rising, when the land rose to thirty-six feet above its present level. The second period of subsidence then began shortly before 2000 B.C. and continued until shortly before the Roman Occupation, when the land was some eleven feet above present levels. There was then a second rising during the Occupation which took the land surface to some fifteen feet above its present level. The third subsidence began after the Occupation, and has continued until today.

These figures are partly confirmed by those of a Dutch geologist, J. H. F. Umbgrove, who estimates that since 2000 B.C. land level relative to sea level on the coast of Holland has sunk 11¾ inches a century as a result of combined land sinking and sea rising, while in recent times the figure has increased to thirteen inches a century.

If, as these figures suggest, the land surface in the estuary was fifteen feet higher in Roman times, one might assume it possible to draw a map of the then coastline, marking as islands such banks in the estuary as would then have been above high water mark. The difficulty is that fifteen feet is not enough to allow us to ignore the effect of tidal range in a low lying area. Tidal range in estuary and river was less in Roman times, but we do not know by how much; nor can we have any certainty about the extent to which — and sometimes at what points — arbitrary effects of tidal breakthrough should be taken into consideration.

This is where archaeological evidence — the existence of human remains at certain levels — becomes of importance in assessing tidal effects. There is a certain amount of generalised historical evidence concerning land subsidence since Roman times. Towards the end of the Roman Occupation of Britain, and after it, there was constant pressure on living space in European coastal areas from tribes making their way westward. Many of these tribes settled in what had been the Roman Empire, and their presence in northern France made it difficult for newly migrated tribes to move farther west by land. As a result,tribes which had settled on the southern boundaries of the North Sea and were already under pressure from the east but were unable to move farther west — and also found their areas of settlement becoming more and more restricted by rising sea and flood levels — decided to settle in the island across the sea.

This theory is supported by the results of excavation on the coasts of Holland and Germany which show that settlements built at the end of the Roman Occupation had to be set higher and higher to avoid rising flood levels, and were in time completely abandoned for this reason. In many cases the refugees settled in Essex and other parts of south-east England, and to this extent at least subsidence might be said to have been one of the causes of the Anglo-Saxon settlements. The fact that there was land subsidence in the Low Countries and on the south and south-western shores of the North Sea at the end of the Roman Occupation of Britain also suggests that corresponding land subsidence took place then in south-east England.

The height to which flood banks in the Fens have been raised since the end of the Occupation provides both direct and indirect evidence of Roman land-sea levels. It is known that the Fens were thickly colonised and intensively farmed during the Occupation, particularly south and south-west of Wisbech, and that during the whole of this time this densely populated area was completely without defence against the inroads of the sea. According to C. W. Phillips writing in *Antiquity* in 1932, the Roman Banks, tidal walls at the Wash now something like eleven or twelve feet high, are medieval — they were built section by section without the central direction they would have received had they been Roman.

The fact that these "Roman" Banks between Fens and Wash are Saxon or later means that the Romans did not find it necessary to protect this rich agricultural area from the inroads of the sea, although in later centuries a tide bank eleven or twelve feet high had to be raised by gradual, irregular and piecemeal additions. The only conclusion must be that the land sank by this amount between the Roman Occupation and the Norman Conquest, by which time the Roman Banks had been replaced by other banks nearer the sea.

Whatever is true of relative land-sea levels in the Wash will be true also of the Thames estuary. According to F. J. C. Spurrell writing in the *Archaeological Journal* for 1885, the Essex and Kent river and sea walls below Gravesend were built by the Saxons, while those above Gravesend,where banks were at first less necessary, were built in the thirteenth century. All have been added to ever since.

More specific evidence of higher land levels in Roman times comes from Lambeth, Southwark, Bermondsey, Rotherhithe and Deptford, the low lying areas immediately to the south of the Thames in London, where numerous discoveries of Roman pottery in areas now five to six feet below high water mark show this area to have been freely inhabited in Roman times. This suggested to the author of the volume on Roman London in the report of the Royal Commission on Historical Monuments that in Roman times the high tide must have been at least fifteen feet below its present level in relation to the land surface.

J.A. Steers, in his book *The Coastline of England and Wales*, records the fact that Romano-British hut sites at East Tilbury are thirteen feet below high water mark. These huts must have been built above high water, although how much is not known. If they were five feet above, then in Roman times the land here must have been at least eighteen feet higher. Steers also mentions that yew stumps on both banks of the Thames are at the same level as these huts, which suggests to me that the Thames in those days must have been much narrower and perhaps completely non-tidal at this point.

The most reliable evidence that the river was not tidal in London during the early years of the Occupation is that (according to F.W. Reader, writing in volume 16 of the *Essex Naturalist*) when the Roman wall was built at Moorfields across the Walbrook stream which fell into the Thames just west of where Cannon Street station now stands, the stream had a clear and swift current flowing over a

By courtesy of P. & O. Steam Navigation Company

Plate 1. The *Jervis Bay* at Tilbury landing stage by night.

Plate 2. Where it all begins. A photograph taken near the World's End inn at Tilbury.

Plate 3. Out in the estuary. *John Topham*

Plate 4. River Beam to South Stifford from the air. For further details see list of plates

By courtesy of Fairey Surveys Limited and the Greater London Council

John Topham

Plate 5. Coastal erosion on the Isle of Sheppey. Several hundred feet of this road at Warden Point had already been lost to the waves when the photograph was taken in 1975

By courtesy of Tony Withers

Plate 6. "The main effect of land sinking on the Thames. Thames estuary and lower Thames basin has been to raise flood levels, to make high tides higher, and to create at our coasts a new, expanding and more powerful sea which daily tries to increase its hold over parts of our south-eastern shores." This car, parked on the promenade, was smashed by the waves at Margate in January 1978.

Plate 7. The new tidal wall at Tilbury. In the background the World's End inn, Tilbury power station, and the entrance to Tilbury Fort.

gravel bed. This was proved by the uniform presence of Roman remains in the lowest layer of the deposits which subsequently filled the bed — and by the fact that the wall, where it crossed the depression along which the Walbrook flowed, was so accommodated to the fall of the ground as to prove that this original depression was still largely free from such deposits when the wall was built.

In later years, probably in the third century, the Walbrook became a sluggish quagmire, its bed filled with peaty mud. This suggested that the peat formed as a result of the ponding back of the stream behind tidal silt, perhaps at its outfall into the Thames; if so the stream, once unaffected by the tide, did later become so affected.

Direct evidence of occupation of areas now below sea level or lost to the sea is the only certain indication of what flood levels were in Roman times; but there is also value in evidence which suggests that flood levels rose in Saxon and medieval times, for this confirms that in Roman times the sea had not established such dominion over the land as it did in later centuries.

The evidence of post-Roman flood levels in the Thames is fragmentary and conflicting. Birch's *Cartularium Saxonicum*, a collection of Saxon charters, contains eleven concerning grants of land in the Higham and Hoo areas of Kent, the first dated 664, the last 961. Some of these refer to land which would be regularly under high spring tides today but for the existence of the main Thames flood bank. According to these charters the land was then regarded as valuable meadow land. One charter, that of Coenwulf in 801, refers to arable land near a fishery called Fishness — and no land in danger of the most infrequent flooding would be ploughed. Yet it is fairly certain that this land was in an area which is marsh today.

Since it is thought unlikely that the land referred to in these charters was then protected by the main river wall; since it may be questioned whether the Saxons had the resources to build river banks round the areas described; and since there is no mention, in these charters, either of marsh, or of river or flood banks, which would be the most obvious marks by which boundaries of land could be described in such low-lying areas — for all these reasons one may suppose that in the period from 664 to 961, land now under high spring tide level near Higham and in Hoo was in no danger of regular flooding.

These facts are given in the article by Evans quoted earlier. He suggests that the land in the Thames estuary, including the area of

Higham and Hoo, became subject to floods from the tenth century, at a time when the land surface, previously above high spring tides, became level with them. He further suggests that the first marsh innings, or reclamation, probably began at the end of the twelfth or the beginning of the thirteenth century, and that the period of intense inning was from about 1250 to 1450.

Evans' suggestions are confirmed by the *Belgian Chronicle*, which refers to two storms in 1014 and 1099 which were both followed by "appalling inundation and frightful loss of life". These storms and inundations are also mentioned in the *Anglo-Saxon Chronicle*, that of 1014 in the following words: "In this year, on St Michael's eve [September 28] the swollen incoming tide swept far and wide through many places in the land; and it ran farther inland than it had ever done before, and submerged many homesteads and drowned a countless number of human beings". The tide of 1099, according to the same record, sprang to such a height, and did so much damage "that no one remembered anything like it before".

Evans concludes that the Roman land surface at St Mary's Island, Chatham, stood some five to six feet above then high tide level, which was a maximum of ten feet below present high tide level, and that the Roman land surface therefore stood some fifteen or sixteen feet above the present land surface.

It is now necessary to consider (subject to the reservations already expressed as to tidal range) what the estuary may have been like in Roman times if the land was fifteen feet higher than now. There are a number of banks in the estuary which are dry at low water by up to the number of feet I now give: Margate Sand (western section) eight feet; North Shingles, six feet; Shingles Patch, five feet; West Barrow, seven feet. Greatest tidal range today in the South Edinburgh Channel, which is in the centre of the estuary between the North Shingles and the Shingles Patch, is 14½ feet. If there has been no change in tidal range since Roman times, then the banks listed were at that time as much above high water as they are today above low water. In a word they were islands.

The case for these banks being islands in Roman times has been expressed conservatively. The Thames itself was less tidal then, so there may have been less tidal play in the estuary also. Whether this was so or not, sea and tide had not then the dominion over our south-east coast that they have today. They were still in process of breaking down the barriers; and the very existence of those barriers in the estuary, and farther out to sea, would reduce effective tidal play. If anything, therefore, I have understated the case for suggesting that banks now dry at low water were islands during the Occupation.

If they were islands it follows that the Maplin and Foulness Sands were an extension, at all states of the tide, of the land between Thames and Crouch, while Dengie Flat and Buxey to the east of it were an extension of that between Crouch and Blackwater. (If the ending -ey in Buxey means island, as in Whittlesey and Thorney in the Fens, then Buxey had become an island in Saxon times.) It also follows that the western part of Margate Sand, the North Shingles, Shingles Patch and West Barrow, and parts of the Sunk and Long Sand, as well as the whole of the Gunfleet, were islands in Roman times.

I must now refer to certain islands which Ptolemy marks in the Thames estuary in his map of Britain. Ptolemy was a Greek geographer, and his map is shown in the Ordnance Survey map of Roman Britain. It is compiled from the co-ordinates given in the second book of his *Geography*, which was published in the second century A.D., although much of the material used relates to the first century and was collected by Marinus of Tyre. The map is not a brilliant one, but it is far better than anything which followed it for centuries; and two islands are plainly marked in or off the Thames estuary, and named Toliatis and Covnvs, which I shall transcribe as Covnus. The estuary is also marked Tamesae Aest, although its angle is so oblique as to make it little more than an almost straight stretch of coast with a nick in it for the Thames. Toliatis is placed about as far east of the North Foreland as London is west of it, and Covnus as far east of Toliatis as Toliatis is east of the North Foreland.

In the Rome edition of 1478 the two islands are named Toliapis and Covennos; and while in the 1482 edition the spelling is given as Toliatis, the difference between Covnus and Covennos remains. The Ravenna Cosmography written in Ravenna in the seventh century, gives Toliatis as Taniatide.

Camden suggests that Covnus, which he calls Convennos, is Canvey, and Toliatis, Sheppey, although this puts Covnus west instead of east of Toliatis. Later commentators have taken the islands to be Thanet (Toliatis) and, with less consistency, Canvey (Covnus).

Thanet was separated from the rest of Kent by a waterway in Roman times. Roman ships, making from Richborough to London, used to pass up what is now the valley of the Stour and down that of the Wantsum by this waterway, and then along the north Kent coast to the Swale, the creek which separates Sheppey from Kent. They then crossed the mouth of the Medway estuary to the Yantlet creek which formerly separated Grain from the rest of Hoo, and so made the south bank of the Thames estuary opposite what is now Leigh on Sea. Thereafter they followed the south shore of the estuary until they were in the Thames itself. This was the main waterway approach route to London until the fourteenth century.

Since Thanet could be regarded as an island in Roman times it is a reasonable candidate for Ptolemy's Toliatis. The name Toliatis is usually regarded as an error for Tanatus, which according to Solinus (who lived about 280), Isidore of Seville (560-636) and Bede was, with Tanatis, the Latin form of Thanet. It is thought to be connected with the Welsh, and earlier Celtic, word for fire, *tan*, presumably with the idea of a beacon in mind.

There may, however, be dangers in offering an explanation which seems to fit present day ideas by assuming a mistake in earlier times which cannot in itself be seen to be a mistake; and it is curious that the name Ruim — according to Asser in his life of Alfred the Celtic name of Thanet— should have been replaced by another Celtic name in this way.

But while Toliatis may have been Thanet, it is difficult to believe that Covnus (which Defoe calls Candy Island, and which the official guide *Captivating Canvey*, in a happy error, says was referred to by Ptolemy as Cnossos) can ever have been Canvey, mainly because Ptolemy has Covnus as much east of Toliatis as Canvey is now west of Thanet.

The similarity of names is deceptive. Covnus, which is also recorded as the name of a Gaulish silver coin from Pannonia, might also be a mistake for, or a variant of, Caunus, which is recorded as the name of a hill in Spain. It has no connection with the Saxon name of Canvey, which means the island of Cana's people.

If the creeks which separate Canvey from the rest of Essex are held to have made Canvey an island in Roman times (which is a large assumption) then this very fact could also be held to break the assumption down. For before the island was reclaimed by the Dutch in the seventeenth century it was crossed by two north-south creeks of comparable size to Benfleet Creek, the creek which is held to make

Canvey an island today — and these two pre-reclamation creeks could be held to have made Canvey three islands, not one. Certainly Norden marks three Canvey islands on his map of Essex, and describes them in the following words: "Nere the Thames mowth below Beamflete, are certain ilandes called Canuey Ilandes, low merishe grounds". (It may be mentioned here that according to a note in the 1976 Transactions of the Essex Archaeological Society the recent discovery of three fifth-century Anglo-Saxon sherds on Canvey establishes for the first time the presence there of early Anglo-Saxon settlers — and proves that the island was not then liable to be submerged by high tides.)

It is difficult to see Canvey an island so far from the coast as that shown by Ptolemy. Benfleet Creek, narrow though it is, can never have been wider, for the high ground at South Benfleet rises to over 200 feet a matter of yards away; and if the large square stepping stones leading down to the central channel between Canvey and South Benfleet and now hidden by mud are Roman (as has been suggested) then Covnus was not Canvey.

But what must surely be decisive is that Ptolemy marks Covnus as many miles east of Toliatis as it should be west — and west of Canvey there is no island of any kind, let alone one which could be related to Ptolemy's map.

I am inclined to think that such banks in the estuary as the Pan Sand, North Shingles and Margate Sand are as likely to be Covnus and Toliatis as are Canvey and Thanet.

I do not know whether the remains of buildings can be seen at low water on the dried-out banks in the estuary, or whether aerial photographs would show up anything on them. There is evidence of buildings at one, and possibly three, places out there — but these are all at points not dry at low water. They are on the Kentish Flats, the shallows which form the northern extension of the Kent coast north of Whitstable and Herne Bay. The best known is Pudding Pan north of Herne Bay. The others are Studhill, half way between Pudding Pan and the shore at Studhill Bay, and Clite Hole Bank north of Tankerton Bay. All are marked on the Admiralty chart as having "cement boulders" on the bed of the sea. In the case of Pudding Pan it is known that there is, or has been, Roman brickwork there held together by mortar. If the boulders at Studhill and Clite Hole Bank are not natural formations (for example sarsens) it is possible that these also are the remains of Roman buildings.

Pudding Pan, or Pudding Pan Rock as it is also called, was given its name because fishermen out of Whitstable, dredging for oysters after stormy weather, used to bring up Samian dishes from this bank which were put to domestic use. Gough's *Camden* says that in his time the rock was half a mile long from east to west, and thirty perches wide. It was then covered with "various loose stones" which were also frequently dredged up. Thomas Pownall, writing in *Archaeologia* in 1779, described how in 1773 his brother went out with a fisherman to the bank, and by sounding with a boat's yard thought the bank to be not much larger than the hulk of a moderate size ship. It then had nine feet of water above it at low tide, and sounding suggested it was of a rocky substance. At the first haul with the net a half hundredweight fragment of brickwork "cemented" together was brought up, together with small pieces of pottery; a second haul produced more fragments of pottery, and a third haul three complete "pans".

Spurrell says in the paper already quoted that pots are, or in his day were, dredged up from an area several miles in extent over the Kentish Flats, of which Pudding Pan was the shallowest point; and that large masses of brick, stone masonry, and roofing tiles were brought up as well as pottery. He does not say where these came from, but I would first wish to find out whether they were in the neighbourhood of Studhill or Clite Hole Bank. Spurrell adds that thirty red roofing tiles measuring 17½ by 13½ inches, with turned up edges, were dredged from one spot which he does not identify, "not two years ago". I think he assumes his readers will regard these as Roman. Spurrell thinks that too much pottery has been dredged up at Pudding Pan for it to have come from the wreck of one ship bringing in Samian ware, as others have suggested. He adds, "I would rather suppose it the wreck of a town or village of potters from the abundance of bricks, mortar, stones and tiles which accompany the pots". And so would I.

In speculating on the islands shown by Ptolemy I have assumed that the map based on his co-ordinates is a reasonably accurate record. However much one questions historical evidence one must at first assume it is reliable — it may be a bridge to truth, even if the bridge collapses when one has got to the other side. But I should point out, that apart from obvious errors in cartography, the accuracy of the spelling of names on the map is not high. Camudolanum is an error for Camulodunum, Gariennus for Gariannus, Darvernum for Durovernum, and Bullaeum for Burrium. A number of Ptolemy's names, including Urolanium somewhere near Lincoln, Brannogenium somewhere in North Wales, Iscalis on the south bank of the Bristol Channel, and Voliba somewhere in Cornwall, do not appear in the index of Roman names in the Ordnance Survey Roman map list in any form I can recognise. The chances of there being errors in the spelling as well as in the positioning of Toliatis and Covnus must therefore be accepted.

CHAPTER 4

All river crossings save Roman

I have no doubt that in prehistoric times there was a ford across the Thames which exploited the chalk ridge connecting the Essex bank at East Tilbury with Kent. I suggest that it was in regular use until (say) 2000 B.C., when the land at Chatham, and therefore in the Lower Hope, was thirty-six feet above present levels, and the river was non-tidal and, at this point, shallow. The track which can be traced leading from just west of Hangmans Wood, Grays, to the church at East Tilbury presumably led to this crossing.

While the Thames below London was probably never forded with regularity in historical times, it was in regular use for the movement of men and goods up and down. For where the only roads available were tracks kept open by the passage of men and animals, unmetalled and undrained, liable to flood and morass, then rivers were a better means of travelling, and more used. Belloc put the point well, if partially, in one sentence in *The River of London*, "In the decline of civilisation, or in its absence, water carriage — suited to heavy burdens, requiring no repair of ways, and providing a means of traction ready made — is, wherever available, the chief economic factor of commerce".

There can be no question, however, that in historical times cross river traffic was discouraged by the presence of marsh in the lower Thames. In general it is not easy to operate a regular ferry unless there is hard ground for embarking and disembarking men and animals; and while it may be possible by building a wooden landing stage to overcome this difficulty where the water level remains the same, the difficulty can be vastly increased by wide tidal range, particularly that between neap and spring tides. Where this is considerable, high tides may overflow or at least saturate the marsh, while low tide will leave yards of mud to cross.

Belloc outlined the difficulty in the following words in *The River of London* "...if there is any very considerable difference in the state of the tides throughout each fortnight, then the opportunities for using the crossing are very much reduced unless one has a steep shore to deal with. Under such conditions one might find a spot where crossing was easy enough at the springs, and yet impossible at the neaps; and instead of a ferry regularly in use twice in 24 hours, you would have one which could be depended on only a few times in a month. Since the

Thames is a river in which this difference is considerable, this has greatly strengthened the power of the waterway to act as an obstacle to travel north and south."

The difficulties so far outlined might be ignored if the hard ground came down to the river on opposite sides; but there is no point between London and the sea with hard ground on both sides of the channel at once. Every hard has marsh on the opposite bank. Places where hard ground comes down to the river — or, to be more accurate, places where the river has eaten into the hard ground — are at East Tilbury on the north bank, Gravesend on the south, Grays (north), Greenhithe (south), Purfleet (north), and Erith, Woolwich, Greenwich and Deptford (all south). These places, which are mostly on the outer edges of a curve in the river where the stream is eroding chalk brought to the surface by Alpine folding, are listed upstream from the estuary; all have marsh on the opposite bank.

The first place upstream from the estuary where a bluff of hard ground faced at least a spur of dry land near to the main stream was in the City of London, and the greatness of London is based on the fact that it was the lowest place at which the river could in historical times be forded, and then bridged.

The difficulties of operating ferries across the Thames as Belloc describes them are real, but even in the Middle Ages some half dozen were in regular operation.

We will now consider the matter historically. The *Anglo-Saxon Chronicle* records that councils of the English church were held in 742 and 822 at a place called Clovesho, which Ingram, mentioning the chronicles of Gervase, gives as Cliffe at Hoo, which is next door to Higham in Kent and opposite East Tilbury. Later translators have not followed Ingram, and have left the place unidentified. But Gervase was a native of Tilbury, and is indeed called Gervase of Tilbury (which could have meant only East or West Tilbury). He is known for his compendious *Otia Imperialia* written in Latin between 1211 and 1214 to interest the Emperor Otto IV. I have not read it, but I assume Ingram did so; and the possibility must be allowed that somewhere in it Gervase, a native of the area, identifies Clovesho as Cliffe at Hoo. For other reasons which I need not give here I believe the identification to be correct.

Evans, to whose paper in *Archaeologia Cantiana* two separate references have already been made, also accepted the identification, and took the matter further by stating that between 716 and 825 ten councils of the English church were held at Cliffe attended by delegates from East Anglia, Mercia and other areas north of the Thames. This suggested to him that there was a ferry at East Tilbury in the eighth century, because a place for meeting which required delegates to cross the Thames would not have been chosen unless facilities for crossing were available nearby. If those facilities were there, then the ferry known to exist between East Tilbury and Higham in the thirteenth century was already in existence in the eighth.

The Domesday Book says nothing about ferries across the lower Thames, but it does say that Higham in Kent had pasture for a hundred sheep across the river in Essex, and its entries for Chalk and Woolwich, both in Kent, also extend across the river into Essex. This suggests some regular cross river traffic at these points in the eleventh century.

In later centuries there were ferries between Rainham and Jenningtree Point; Coldharbour Point and Erith; Purfleet and the site of the Long Reach Tavern on Dartford Salt Marshes; West Thurrock and a point east of Greenhithe; Grays and a point below Swanscombe; Tilbury Fort and Gravesend; and East Tilbury and Higham. I have not listed ferries above Erith, of which there were many, and in all cases I have given the Essex name first.

The ferry from Rainham went from near the mouth of Rainham Creek, as the Ingrebourne is known in its lower reaches. There was a documentary reference to this ferry in 1580, and to Bounsinge Bess of the ferry house in 1591. I would like to have met her. The original ferry house, as one might expect, was also an inn, known then or later as The Three Crowns, although the most recent inn on the site is now in use as factory offices. The road which runs from Rainham station down to the river at this point is still called Ferry Lane, and is marked, though not named, on Chapman and André's map of Essex in 1777. A lone building on the river bank at the southern end of this road is shown on this map as Rainham Ferry.

The ferry from Coldharbour Point to Erith is marked on the first edition of the one-inch Ordnance Survey map, which suggests that it may still have been in use in the 1840's. Most of the area at Coldharbour Point is now twenty or thirty feet under refuse tips, but in 1777 a building known as Great Coldharbour stood on the point, while another riverside building, half way between Great Coldharbour and the ferry house at Rainham, was called Little Coldharbour. According to Wallenberg (whose two books on Kentish place names were published in Uppsala in the 1930's) the name Erith appears as early as the seventh century and means an earth or muddy-soil harbour or landing place.

The ferry from Purfleet to the Kent bank (in later years to the Long Reach Tavern) is said to have been used by pilgrims travelling from the eastern counties to the shrine of St Thomas at Canterbury, although I believe the bulk of pilgrims to have used the ferry at West Thurrock. In later times it had more secular use — to take bare fist fighters and their followers to contests on the lonely Kent marshes. The ferry was referred to in 1589, while a Chancery case of 1664 mentions a ferry, and a ferryman's house, at Purfleet.

When I worked at the Thames Board Mills at Purfleet between 1934 and 1936 I used to sit on the river bank at lunch time and look across the river to the Long Reach Tavern standing utterly isolated among the marshes on the river wall. The ferry was then closed, and the tavern impossible of access from the Essex side of the river. Many years later, some time in the 1950's, I went there from London, walking across the marshes from Dartford station. It was a lonely place, and although a Saturday evening in summer, I was the only customer. As twilight fell a liner passed upstream with lights blazing. It formed a curious contrast to the loneliness of the inn. I had no mind to walk back all the way to Dartford, and the licensee's wife suggested I should hail the tug at one of the oil depots opposite. It would then come over and drop me on the northern bank at a convenient distance from Purfleet station. I found such neighbourliness and freedom from authorised ideas of transport refreshing; but it seemed a liberty, and I went back to Dartford by taxi summoned by telephone. I thought, being driven back, that Dracula, who crossed the river at this point at low tide on his way to Bermondsey after being flushed out of Purfleet, must have had a good walk from the Long Reach causeway to the station at Dartford, a matter to which Stoker makes no reference. The Long Reach Tavern is now no more.

The ferry from West Thurrock to the Kent bank just above Broadness salt marsh is with reason credited with taking the great mass of Canterbury Pilgrims from the eastern counties. Pilgrims are said to have heard mass in the church on the river bank at West Thurrock, and in an earlier church which preceded it on the site, before making the crossing. The track on the Kent side is known as Pilgrims Road today.

J.R. Hayston, writing in volume 4 of the Thurrock Local History Society Journal, points out that the first reference he has come across to the West Thurrock ferry was in the fifteenth century and while he accepts that it must have been a main crossing point for pilgrims, adds that no documentary evidence has come to his notice which proves this.

A second ferry at West Thurrock ran from Stoneness about a mile south-west of West Thurrock church to Greenhithe. It was still in operation in the 1860's. Volume III of *The Beauties of England and Wales* edited by E. W. Brayley and published in 1808 records in its Kent section that there was then a ferry from Greenhithe into Essex for horses and cattle.

There are references to a ferry at Grays in 1228, and a further reference in 1600 which suggests that by this time it was a by request ferry only. Broadness, on the opposite side of the river, was in the 1950's veined with deep muddy creeks. It must have been possible to cross it on foot in earlier days: it was impassable then.

The ferry from Tilbury to Gravesend, which is shown in Glover's map of Kent of about 1571, is the only one of those described still functioning at the time of writing. The magnificent steam boats which used to cross from Tilbury to the landing stage at the bottom of Gravesend High Street have now been replaced by smaller diesel vessels which call at a point higher upstream formerly used by vehicle ferries. The old landing stage was the main departure point in England for the Continent in the last century and has (or had) a brass plate commemorating the fact that the Swedish playwright Strindberg (of all the famous men who in the nineteenth century passed this way) once landed here. It is now used as a restaurant, but the character of this attractive corner at the bottom of the Old High Street has not been improved by the pulling down of some of the riverside property and the driving of a one way motor road between it and the river.

In the early part of the sixteenth century the ferry house on the north bank was actually inside Tilbury Fort. Following the Dutch attack on the Thames in 1667 the fort was extended, the ferry house demolished and the ferry cut off. A new ferry house was built outside, which I take to be either the World's End inn, or a house previously on its site.

The ferry no longer runs from the World's End, and the causeway which ran down into the river here, and was once used for loading cattle fattened on the marshes, was removed after the Second World War. The "new" landing stage for the Tilbury-Gravesend ferry is now farther west and more than 600 yards from Tilbury Fort — as is required in the London, Tilbury and Southend Extension Railway Act of 1852 under which the ferry was established.

Early documentary evidence of the lowest ferry of all, that at East Tilbury, is fuller than for any other. There was a reference to it in Fine 24 of Henry III in 1258, while in the Placitae Coronae 21 of Edward I, 1292-1293 — pleas of the Crown in the 21st year of Edward I — the boatmen of the prioress of Higham were indicted for overcharging horsemen and foot passengers passing over the river between Kent and Essex. The prioress was also found liable to maintain a bridge and causeway which led from Higham to the river to give better and easier passage to such as would cross to Essex.

Volume II of the Victoria County History of Kent says that the prioress was found liable to maintain a causeway running to the Thames "and a bridge over the river" —implying, as I suppose, a bridge over the Thames, which is of course nonsense. Spurrell suggests in the paper already quoted that the bridge was an inclined way leading from high to below low water mark in the Thames. It would be made of blocks of stone retained by side walls of timber; and was what used to be referred to in London as "stairs". I think this must be the right way of it.

Earlier references in 1219 and 1240 which were "probably" to the ferry at East Tilbury are quoted by Hayston in his article, who adds that in 1449 and 1450 the ferry was said to be an excellent source of profit.

All the ferries I have mentioned, including that at Tilbury which is still in operation, continued until at least the seventeenth or eighteenth century. That at West Thurrock was working in the nineteenth century, those at Rainham and Purfleet within living memory.

One other crossing on the lower Thames may be mentioned, although it is not on the Thames itself. The ford across the creek between South Benfleet and Canvey Island, and the stepping stones which ran beside it on the bed of the creek, are still remembered, although the ford has been replaced by a bridge, and the four central stepping stones have been moved from the bed of the creek to the garden by the Council Offices in Canvey. The stones which led down to these four central stones still remain a few inches below the surface of the mud, as yachtsmen dropping anchors there sometimes discover. They were some three feet square and fairly close together, and when in use duckboards led down to them on each side.

The four stones formerly in the centre of the ford are conical, and have been set in the ground outside the Council Offices in the same way that they were set in the creek, that is with their pointed ends buried, and the flat base of the cone, which is almost two feet in diameter, forming the stepping stone. The bases have been hollowed by much use, and because the ridges so formed on the two opposed sides of the saucers are higher than the ridges at the other two quarters, the direction in which the stones were originally set is clear.

The material used is a dense limestone, more consistent and more compacted than Kentish rag. There are suggestions of saw or chisel marks running from point to base. The stones are all the same size, and substantial well-made pieces of masonry. I would say they were staddle stones put to unusual use. With their base on the ground, and with a flat piece of stone on the top of the cone to prevent rats and mice climbing in, such stones were commonly used to form the four corner supports on which the wooden floor of a farm building was based. There is a good example of such stones in use on the other side of the river on the Lower Higham road at Chalk in Kent, where a wooden farm building on the north side of the road opposite Filborough Farm stands on four, or possibly six, of these stone supports.

CHAPTER 5

Roman sites in Essex

Military sites

Roman fortifications are known according to size and function as camps, forts, or fortresses. Soldiers on the march or campaigning defended their camp, even if they pitched their tents for one night only, with a ditch and earth rampart. These, the commonest kind of temporary camp, were known as marching camps. The usual shape was a round-cornered rectangle — the shape of a playing card — and without exception the sides were straight. They varied greatly in size from (say) 500 to 2,000 feet across. Forts and fortresses were permanent strongholds, and save for the Forts of the Saxon Shore, which are dealt with later, do not appear in our area.

There are however in the Grays and Tilbury area a number of rectangular enclosures which can be dated to the first century A.D. It has been assumed that they are Roman marching camps built at the time of the invasion, although this assumption has been questioned.

The fact that the function of these enclosures, or earthworks, has not been confirmed by excavation is in itself interesting. What is more interesting is their possible connection, if they are in fact Roman marching camps, with the route taken by the invading armies from the Medway to Colchester.

The earthworks are listed and described by Adrian Babbidge in volume 16 of the Thurrock Local History Society Journal. They are at the Orsett Cock; Gun Hill, West Tilbury; Mucking; East Tilbury; and Orsett Hall. I give his descriptions here.

The earthwork near the Orsett Cock, about an acre in area, is a double-ditched sub-rectangular enclosure destroyed in part by road building. It is assumed to have had a single entrance on the east side. Within the enclosure is a ring ditch, possibly a house gully. Finds from the site are mainly first century A.D.

The earthwork at Gun Hill is a single-ditched enclosure of about two acres now destroyed by gravel working. It had an entrance gap on the east side.

The rectangular double-ditched enclosure of about 1½ acres at Mucking had a V-sectioned ditch with square corners and a simple entrance to the north. There was first century pottery in the primary fill.

The earthwork at East Tilbury is a fragment of a sub-rectangular enclosure partly destroyed by gravel digging, but probably about an acre in area. The ditch was about five feet wide and some 2½ feet deep.

There are also two sub-rectangular earthworks near Orsett Hall, the first a single-ditched enclosure of about 1½ acres with no obvious entrance, but with what looks like a hut circle about forty feet in diameter inside. The second, about an acre in area, has a possible entrance on the south side. Neither has been excavated.

Turning now to the descriptions and interpretations of other observers, I should first mention that the Orsett Cock earthwork has been referred to elsewhere as "probably Claudian" — that is built during, or shortly after, the invasion.

In the 1971 Transactions of the Essex Archaeological Society the earthwork is described as a first-century Roman marching camp about 300 feet square, both its ditches V-shaped, the outer one fourteen feet wide by four feet deep, the inner about ten feet wide by five feet deep, the two separated by a berm twenty-two feet wide.

In the 1974 Transactions, Warwick Rodwell describes it as a first century A.D. regularly laid-out double-ditched rhomboidal enclosure; and adds, "A precise functional interpretation of this earthwork is difficult, and since the evidence is quite incompatible with a domestic or agricultural origin, but strongly indicative of a small, short-lived defence, the latter interpretation must, for the time being, prevail..."

A particularly detailed account by P.J. Drury and W.J. Rodwell of the excavation of the Gun Hill site (which is Iron Age and Saxon as well as Roman) appears in the 1973 Transactions of the Essex Archaeological Society. The Roman enclosure, described as "massive", and measuring 203 feet east-west by 164 feet north-south on the east side, and 197 feet north-south on the west, and with all corners rounded, had a breastwork some seven feet high and a ditch some nine feet deep. But while according to the authors it belongs to the first century A.D. and there can be no doubt about its defensive function, "who built the Gun Hill enclosure, for what purpose and precisely when, are unfortunately unanswerable questions at the moment" they comment.

Mucking probably means something like "muddy creek". Its importance as an early Saxon site to some extent overshadows its interest as a Roman site. Both aspects are dealt with in a later chapter. It should, however, be said here that the Roman enclosure is exactly rectangular; and that there was discovered, within the enclosure, a bronze pendant such as was used to weigh down the leather straps which formed part of a first century legionary's armour.

A final reference, this time to the East Tilbury site, is by Randal Bingley in a later issue of the Thurrock Local History Society Journal. He says that there is "no military usage" of the site.

Mr Babbidge comments on the sites earlier listed in the following words. "...it is very hard to see a Roman military inception for any of the sites; none has produced finds of Roman military equipment that one would expect as a consequence; nor do the sites have either the form or the size of military installations of the Claudian period; even if one interprets them as temporary camps then the defended entrances so typical of that type are missing." He adds, "it is perhaps not unlikely that these sites reflect nothing more grand than the farmsteads of single families".

It may be that these comments were made before the discovery of the legionary's pendant at Mucking. The argument might also be strengthened if we knew how many comparable rectangular earth-works of the first century A.D. in other parts of the country have been proved by excavation to be farmsteads, and under what arrangements the labour to dig the ditches and raise such banks as existed was provided — I would have thought the work beyond the resources of a single family. I incline to think that the enclosures at Orsett Cock, Gun Hill and Mucking are Roman military works whose precise function will become clear in time.

Two other sites, possibly military, have been identified from the air. The first is at Mill House, formerly Tilbury Mills, at West Tilbury, where there are rectangular enclosures and parallel ditches. The second is north of Low Street, where aerial photographs show a rectangular crop mark suggesting the existence of a ditched enclosure of unknown date and purpose.

A site at Stifford Clays near Grays, described later in this chapter as a settlement, shows evidence of a square, or possibly a rectangular enclosure, with a double ditch to the south and a single ditch to north and west. The site is at William Edwards School, and is contained in a right angle bend of the road from Stifford to Orsett. The general course of this road is east and west, but it turns due north at one point before running east again, and the site is to the east of the north-south section of road.(Clays has nothing to do with the soil. Like Greygoose, of neighbouring Greygoose Farm, it was a man's name.)

There is a hint, no more, that there may have been some form of Roman defence work on an otherwise civilian site at Palmer's Girls' School, Grays (now, I believe, called a Sixth Form College). The report of the excavation there, in its only military reference, mentions "a single ditch with a profile of particular interest as it is reminiscent of Roman military earthworks".

Villas

One of the Roman villas in Essex nearest to the Thames was that at Mucking Hall, Barling, three and a half miles east-south-east of Rochford. Another villa has also been sited at Grays on the strength of a "fine tessellated pavement" said to have been found on the site of the stationmaster's house in 1857, and then re-laid in the vestry of the nearby parish church.

The Rev. William Palin, between 1833 and 1872 "curate, priest and rector" of Stifford, and author of *Stifford and its Neighbourhood* (1871) and *More about Stifford and its Neighbourhood* (1872) is one authority here. He says in the first book that a "tessellated pavement" was found with pieces of masonry when the foundations of the stationmaster's house were dug; and that this was re-laid, as found, to form the present floor of the vestry. He does not refer to it specifically as Roman. Worley, describing Grays parish church in his book on Essex churches, refers to "tesserae (discovered on the spot with other Roman remains) with which the new vestry has been paved". He has a note at the end of the entry *See Palin, History of Stifford;* but if he has relied only on Palin, then he has added something.

A Colchester Museum report quoted in the Thurrock Local History Society Journal says, "A tessellated pavement, reputed to be Romano-British, was found in 1857 during the building of the railway station. It is now in the vestry of Grays parish church". Volume III of the Victoria County History of Essex, published as late as 1963, reports "A fine tessellated pavement, discovered with Roman foundations in building this [stationmaster's] house, was removed complete to the vestry of Grays Thurrock church". It gives the *Home Counties Magazine* as its authority for this statement.

It seemed to me that the existence in the vestry of a Christian church of a Roman pavement, both fine and complete, was a matter of some interest, and I called at the church more than once without managing to see it. Then, deciding it was time to be certain, I waited for the end of evensong one Sunday, and with the help of Mr D. J. Agnew the then churchwarden, lifted up the edge of the carpet which covered the tiled floor. It was not possible to see the whole of it, for a heavy table covered the centre at which church officials were sorting out the collection; but what I did see of the floor was not made up of the small and partly glazed squares called tesserae with which the Romans made mosaic floors, but of unglazed flooring tiles of triangular and rectangular shape up to three inches at their greatest length. Nor was there any design save such as resulted from the arrangement, in mechanical fashion, of tiles of two indeterminate colours. I was told that the centre of the floor was even less patterned than the surround which I saw. Mr Agnew thought the tiles might be medieval, possibly from an old school whose site was taken over when the church was enlarged in 1846. It was clear that they were not Roman, nor was there any masonry in the church which might have come from a Roman site.

Later Mr Agnew wrote, "I am bound to say that the story seems to be a myth. All I have been able to find out for certain is that traces of a pavement, thought to be medieval (1300-1400) were found in the vicinity of the stationmaster's house during the 1920's. The find consisted of yellow glazed tiles, and I understand that some samples are in the Thurrock Local History Museum".

I suppose it is possible that the tiles found during the 1920's were similar to those found in the nineteenth century, and formed part of the same floor. But for the suggestion that the tiles were fourteenth century I would say the chances are they came from a schoolhouse which was built in 1710 in West Field "opposite Grays churchyard" by William Palmer. Palmer was a London merchant with waterside property in Grays, who in 1706 settled estates in Lombard Street and Cripple-gate, London, to provide, among other benefactions, a school he had given to Grays. The present Palmer's Schools are named after him. It is known that the schoolhouse was being built at the time of his death in June 1710; it was pulled down, and a second Palmer's School built, in 1848 . But whether the tiles in the vestry of Grays church came from Palmer's schoolhouse or not, they are not Roman; and if the Roman villa at Grays shown in figure 4 of the same volume of the Victoria County History is based on this "fine tessellated pavement found on the site of the stationmaster's house" then the entry is erroneous.

(A happier error appears on the first page of the second volume of the Victoria County History, where Norden is quoted as describing Essex as "the englishe Goschen". This is the mechanism whereby cafe proprietors in the late 1940's advertised "beveridges" on their blackboards, and London telephone operators, in accepting calls for Marple near Stockport in later years, repeated the exchange as Marples, the name of the then Postmaster General. The volume of the County History appeared in 1907; Goschen, one time Chancellor of the Exchequer, died in that year. The first of a number of references to the land of Goshen, the land Pharaoh gave Joseph, appears in Genesis, chapter 45 verse 10.)

The matter of the tessellated pavement is correctly reported in the fourth volume of the report on Essex of the Royal Commission on Historical Monuments,, in which the entry for Grays church reads "Tiles. In vestry, black and yellow glazed tiles laid in patterned bands, found on site of cottage north of church, and relaid here".

A map of the Romano-British site at Chadwell which appears in volume 19 of the Transactions of the Essex Archaeological Society shows a tessellated floor in the south-western angle of the crossroads near the church. No reference was given for this discovery, but it was said to have been found during building work some time before archaeological excavation took place.

It has also been suggested that there may be a villa about three quarters of a mile west of the crossroads at Chadwell, and on the same gravel terrace overlooking the river. It is a likely site. No direct evidence of the existence of a villa has been found at the time of writing, but excavations in the summer of 1970 produced evidence of a field system such as might be found attached to a villa, as well as a pottery kiln and much broken pottery.

The discovery of tesserae near East Tilbury church during gravel digging in the eighteenth century, reported in volume 2 of the Thurrock Local History Society Journal, suggests that a villa or other substantial Roman building may have been built on or near this site.

Two further discoveries which might have some bearing on a villa on or near the river bank at Purfleet are reported in volume III of the Victoria County History for Kent. They were of box tiles dredged from the river opposite Purfleet, and of box tiles and an earthen pipe dredged from the river off Dartford Creek. Box tiles were used in central heating systems, and I would suppose that most central heating systems were in villas, which is why I have mentioned the matter here.

Dartford Creek is another name for the stretch of the Darent between Dartford and that point opposite Purfleet where it joins the Thames, and this suggests that the two discoveries were made in the same area. If the box tiles, used in underfloor heating, were used in a building near where they were found, then the building must have been on an island or on the edge of the Roman river Thames, but in a position where there was no fear of flooding. If it was so placed, then there must have been a massive rise in flood levels here since the Roman Occupation. But for one curious fact I would reject this suggestion out of hand, and assume the tiles formed part of the cargo of a boat which foundered on the chalk ridge in the river here, or that they were dumped in the river in some other way. The curious fact is that Pieter Goos's *De Zee-atlas* published in Amsterdam in 1675 shows an island in the Thames off Purfleet, and this island is shown surrounded by a thick line such as is used elsewhere in the map to show the coastline, the river, and Canvey Island. This may have been a mistake on the part of the copyist; but when linked with the fact that hypocaust tiles have been dredged up off Purfleet it makes one wonder.

Pottery and settlements

The fact that I am lumping pottery and settlements together in this one section calls for an explanation. In the ordinary way, with one particular exception, it is reasonable to assume that concentrations of pottery mark the site of a settlement. The exception is where pottery consists of urns from burial grounds, which while often placed beside roads were not necessarily near settlements.

Nowadays, when Romano-British pottery comes from a cemetery, the fact will be made clear in reports of the discovery. In earlier years however, reports of pottery finds did not always make clear whether the find consisted of burial urns, or was broken domestic pottery of which piles can be found on any Romano-British occupation site. Among such vague reports are those of the finding of Romano-British pottery in Hall's gravel pit and at the junction of Sandy Lane and Mill Lane in Aveley; in Hall's gravel pit at Linford; and in Condover's gravel pit at Low Street. If there were any way of confirming that burial urns only were found at these sites, then years after the original find was made, and after gravel working or other factors had destroyed the site, the report of the discovery might still be of significance in suggesting the possible course of a Roman road. If it was domestic pottery it would be of significance in indicating the probable site of a Romano-British settlement. But where there is nothing to go on apart from the original literary evidence, choice between these alternatives is difficult, if not impossible.

Concentrations of domestic pottery at or below high tide level on the banks of river or estuary may also mark the site of a settlement, although the tide can move pottery and destroy other evidence of occupation, and does make orthodox excavation impossible.

That both banks of the Thames from London to the sea were once lined with Romano-British settlements is not in doubt. What is in doubt is the relationship between such pottery as is, and has been found on the banks, and more important centres of population. Today's river banks are not the banks of the Roman river: these were at or below today's low water mark, which means that the evidence of settlements on the Roman bank has now been destroyed, or still remains buried under silt. Where remains are so hidden, and are uncovered in wet silt by a high (or low) spring tide, or discovered in dried out silt by chance excavation for drainage ditches and the like, it is impossible to say whether the greatest concentration of remains, and therefore of settlement, has been discovered — or whether it still lies hidden elsewhere in the neighbourhood. In this it differs from the situation on hard ground, where the plough will tend to show where the greatest concentration of Roman remains, and therefore of settlements, is to be found.

Another reason why it is difficult to assess the pattern of riverside settlement in some areas is that during the nineteenth century both banks of the Thames were restored in places by the addition of hardcore from London, the banks at Tilbury with material excavated during the construction of the underground railway at Tower Hill, those below Gravesend and on the Medway marshes north of Upchurch with hardcore from Lambeth. That which I have seen north of Upchurch is made up mostly of pottery and other kiln material; that at Tilbury, which came from the Roman city of London, can be assumed to have contained Roman material. It has been suggested that the Romano-Greek Heraclia tombstone and two busts inscribed in Greek, found during the building of the Central Dock at Tilbury and now in the basement of All Hallows, Tower Hill, in the City of London, may have formed part of this hardcore from the Roman city, although it is unlikely that they would have been dug up near Tower Hill, carried to Tilbury, and been dumped there without being seen. (Ralph Merrifield, in his *Roman London* suggests the tombstone was probably brought by an English gentleman making the grand tour "some time in the last 350 years", but I must say I wonder why he left his luggage on the Tilbury marshes. I think these remains came from a Roman town on the site.)

The pattern of settlement along the foreshore is also less easy to define because of the vague way in which locations of discoveries were described by earlier researchers. Thus Palin in his *Stifford and its Neighbourhood* reports the finding in 1869 of much Roman pottery at the end of the track leading from Low Street across the marshes, which he calls the Manor Way, and says was thirty feet wide. There are three later references to this same discovery in the transactions of various historical and archaeological societies — the first to the finding of a large deposit of first-century burial urns on the foreshore at the end of Manor Way, West Tilbury; the second to the discovery of large deposits of first-century urns on the foreshore at the end of Manor Way, Little Thurrock; and the third to the discovery of incineration burials "opposite Low Street Manor House in Mucking Marsh". If, as I suppose, Little Thurrock is an error for West Tilbury, then the first two reports clearly duplicate Palin. I think the third report must also be a duplication, although this would assume two errors — that Manor House is Manor Way, and Mucking Marsh is West Tilbury Marshes.

Lloyd Williams, a Grays solicitor, is reported by Palin as saying that at a point on the bank of the river in West Tilbury close to the boundary between the parishes of East and West Tilbury "several pieces of Roman earthenware have been found, and small fragments of such pottery, in no inconsiderable quantity, can be to this day seen on the surface of the mud, as also pieces of brick of Roman shape, and a few pieces of stone which seem to have been tooled for either paving or building purposes".

It was Palin's opinion that these remains came from a Roman burial place since encroached on by the tide. Spurrell also reported that he had probed the mud "opposite the Low Street Manor Way" and found an urn and Samian ware at a depth of between three and four feet.

Manor Way is the track, at first metalled, which runs south from

Low Street and is covered for its later course by refuse tips. I went to the river end of it in the early 1960's and found what looked like unsquared pieces of paving stone well worn on one surface, as well as Roman bricks and a few pieces of rough and broken Romano-British pottery, but not the heaps of pottery often found on sites elsewhere.

I must now describe four areas of proved occupation on the Essex bank and foreshore of the river, making clear that it cannot be assumed that these were the only, or even necessarily the most important, settlements there.

The Victoria County History says that Roman tiles, flint blocks, bones, potsherds and oyster shells were found in excavations for the Central Dock at Tilbury in 1883 seven feet below the modern surface, scattered over "40 a." The report of the Royal Commission on Historical Monuments says that the remains were scattered over an area of forty yards or morc "lying on a mossy, grass grown surface seven feet below the modern surface". The source for these two reports is Spurrell's paper in the *Archaeological Journal* for September 1885, where he writes "In the excavations for the new Tilbury Docks, I saw in October 1883 Roman tiles and pottery, with bones and food refuse, oyster and snail shells, tiles and flint blocks. They lay in the fine alluvial grey clay, but on a mossy and grass-grown surface which could not have been unlike the surface of the marsh there at present. This layer was seven feet below the surface. The area covered with remains was about 40 yards square, but there were signs of a much wider spread".

Writing in the *Essex Naturalist* for 1912, Spurrell said that Roman relics were found over the whole area of dock excavation at Tilbury, and many were of "such excellence" that some of the workmen were able to make a goodly harvest by their sale in London. I take the Heraclia tombstone to have been found among these relics.

The probability, to be examined in a later chapter, that this was the main river crossing point below London, coupled with Spurrell's discoveries, suggests that there was here a Roman settlement of greater importance than any so far known on the lower Thames, save perhaps that at Gravesend whose discovery was reported in September 1979.

According to the report of the Royal Commission on Historical Monuments the remains of three Romano-British huts could be seen in 1920 in the river mud below high tide mark at East Tilbury, with

John Topham

Plate 8. The kinder face of the estuary: a view from Cliff Gardens, Westcliff on Sea.

A.F. Kersting

Plate 9. The Essex marshlands near Bradwell looking across the Blackwater towards Mersea Island.

A.F. Kersting

Plate 10. Rochester on the Medway in Kent. The cathedral and castle by night.

Plate 11. Grays to Stanford le Hope from the air. For further details see list of plates

By courtesy of Fairey Surveys Limited and the Greater London Council

National Monuments Record

Plate 12. This photograph of the Roman Fort of the Saxon Shore at Portchester in Hampshire gives some idea of what the walls of the estuary forts at Bradwell in Essex and Reculver in Kent looked like when in commission. The castle and church within the walls are mediaeval additions.

By courtesy of the Essex Record Office

Plate 13. Members of the Essex Field Club on the Roman Broomway near the coast of Foulness in May 1907. A feeder road is seen returning to the coast on the left.

Plate 14(a). A photograph taken inside one of the three basins of the Viking docks at Dockacres near Carnforth in Lancashire, now destroyed by gravel working. Fortified docks were built by the Danes for similar purposes in and near the Thames estuary

Plate 14(b). The Street at Whitstable in Kent, a Roman construction of uncertain purpose, is shown in this high level air photograph as a straight line under the water at right angles to the coast. By courtesy of Fairey Surveys Limited and the Greater London Council

traces of a fourth farther west. They were near the western parish boundary, and at that time the foreshore for about one hundred yards each side of the huts was littered with first and second-century potsherds. Immediately to the east of the huts was a shallow channel running north-east and south-west, with some traces of flanking stakes, which might have represented a track leading down to the edge of the river.

Farther down river there were Romano-British peasant sites on Canvey Island, at Thorny Creek on the south shore of the island, and at Leigh Beck at its eastern end. The houses were of mud and wattle with tiled roofs. A large flanged roof tile, and part of one of the curved ridge tiles which covered the joints between the roof tiles, can be seen in the Dutch cottage museum on the island. Large quantities of Roman pottery have been washed out of the mud at Thorny Creek. Pieces of roof and flue tiles have also been found here, as well as a fragment of a rubble wall which "may be Roman". At Leigh Beck, where Samian as well as local pottery has been found, the sea is at the time of writing rapidly destroying a Romano-British settlement.

Much pottery has been found on the foreshore east of Tilbury Fort. Spurrell, in the paper quoted in a previous chapter, said that at low water the shore beneath the saltings on the east side of the fort was covered with Romano-British pottery which extended for a couple of miles, that is to point some 500 yards west of Coalhouse Point, East Tilbury. Samian pottery bearing the stamps of forty-eight different makers was also found in 1912 one mile east of the fort.

First-century B.C. and fourth-century A.D. pottery has been found on the foreshore north of Coalhouse Fort, East Tilbury, at a point after the Thames has turned north into the Lower Hope. I have never found pottery here, but since the report states that it was found stretching for half a mile "five feet below the modern saltings level" it may be necessary to dig down to it.

I shall now deal with settlements inland. The Roman military sites at Orsett and Mucking to which reference has already been made later became centres of civilian settlement. Fragments of heating, roof and building tile found with "prolific" pottery in the ditches of the Roman "camp" at Mucking prove the existence of substantial buildings which may have been sited down the terrace slope closer to the water supply.

The camp (as I suppose it) at Gun Hill, which is on a pre-Roman agricultural site with field boundaries marked by ditches, returned to being an agricultural settlement in the second half of the first century. This is proved by the fact that when the ditches of the earthwork were excavated, animal bones, querns, a great deal of pottery, and the remains of ovens were found.

What may be a military camp at Stifford Clays has already been described. This camp also became the centre of a Romano-British settlement, for pottery extending to the fourth century has been discovered there, mostly coarse Romano-British pottery of the first to third centuries.

The site at the former Palmer's Girls School has already been listed among those which may have been defensive, although the suggestion is speculative. It certainly developed as a civilian settlement, for the report of the excavation is concerned mainly with boundary ditches, pottery, and the possibility of there being a villa at or near the site. Several hundredweights of broken pottery have been excavated from this site.

Among settlements which are not known to have developed round a Roman military station, the two most important in the general area of Grays and Tilbury are that at Tilbury itself, already noted, and a newly discovered site at Chadwell.

The site at Chadwell covered an area of some twenty acres. This settlement, now almost destroyed by gravel working, was on the south side of the road which runs east from the crossroads near Chadwell church to West Tilbury.

This site is just to the east of a straight north-south way which leads ultimately to the river between Tilbury Riverside railway station and the World's End. The Thurrock Local History Society Journal states that the settlement probably superseded riverside settlements at Tilbury (I would be inclined to say supplemented) and was occupied from pre-Roman times up to, and possibly beyond, the fifth century. The journal states that it was the principal Romano-British settlement in the area.

There is a further reference in 1960, in volume 5 of the journal, to a village or small town at Grays and West Thurrock in the second to fourth centuries. According to the journal, settlements at Stanford-le-Hope, West Thurrock, and Linford are suggested by the discovery of groups of Romano-British material at these places — I have myself pulled a piece of Roman brick out of the roadside verge by the road bridge in Linford. A first-century Romano-British settlement in what was the Botany at Purfleet has also been recorded. The site of a small Romano-British settlement near Bishop Bonner's Palace at Orsett is described by Mr Bannister in volume 9.

Farther afield there are a number of references to Roman sites in the Billericay area. Nathanael Salmon the Essex historian (1675-1742) writes of Blunts Wall, now a farm about one mile west of Billericay, "Here are yet Traces of a *Vallum* and Ditch including about four acres, one Part of which hath been ditched about to feparate it from the reft. There have been alfo within Memory fome Mounts, or High Ground, artificially raifed and fince levelled, within the Inclofure, which I fhall not pronounce to have been *Praetorium*, but leave for the Adept to determine." Salmon suggested it was the site of a Roman posting station.

H. Jenkins, writing in the *British Archaeological Journal* for 1863, said that Roman remains had been dug out of several tumuli at this site. In the first one-inch edition of the Ordnance Survey map the site appears as Blunt Walls, and has against it the word REMAINS. All traces of ditch, ramparts, and artificial mounds have now disappeared.

Salmon records a tradition that an old town stood in the neighbourhood of Basildon church, and mentions that the foundations of two or three buildings have been ploughed up in a field near the church called Town Field "whence the Swains collect that the Town stood there". He adds that a quantity of human bones have been dug up in the parsonage garden, "whether of Inhabitants, or the *Exuviae* of a Battel, nothing shews".

Volume III of the Victoria County History of Essex makes certain additions to the settlements shown in the Ordnance Survey map of Roman Britain. It places Durolitum at Romford, and greatly increases the number of minor settlements, particularly in the south of the county, marking "other" settlements at East Ham, Barking, Grays, Chadwell, West Tilbury, East Tilbury, Stanford and Bulphan. It adds settlements on Canvey Island, at Leigh, Prittlewell, Shoeburyness, Wakering and Barling. Other settlements added are at Rawreth and Burnham, both on the Crouch; Sandon and Danbury east of Chelmsford; and, farther north, Heybridge, Tollesbury, Great Braxted, Layer Marney, Mersea Island, Layer Breton, and others on the east of the Colne.

Burials

The Roman cemetery at the end of Manor Way, West Tilbury, has already been mentioned. Other cemeteries are at Home Farm, West Thurrock; Home Farm, North Ockendon; and at South Ockendon and Low Street. The report of the Royal Commission on Historical Monuments for Essex also records the existence in former times of a group of three second-century burial mounds 200 feet long and twenty feet high at South Ockendon. Only one now remains.

Romano-British cremation burials have been found near Ford Place, Stifford. They are on the north side of the Mardyke "gorge", on the gravel terrace just north of the fifty-foot contour line, and immediately to the north of the east-west grass avenue which leads towards Ford Place.

Romano-British burial grounds have been reported west of Bulphan Fen and in South Hornchurch. The first is said in the 1863 volume of the Transactions of the Essex Archaeological Society to be in fields which belong to Home Farm. A later report in the *Gentleman's Magazine Library* (1731-1868) gives a map reference which suggests the burial ground was a couple of hundred yards north-east of Middle Farm. The report also says the site is spread over sixteen acres — a mighty large burial ground. This must be why workmen were credited with saying that it was "the scene of a great battle". One of the fields in which remains were found is, or was, called Ruin Field.

The South Hornchurch burial ground is 300 yards east of Mardyke Farm (which is nowhere near the Mardyke) and 600 yards north of the main road to Tilbury.

Churches on Roman sites

A number of churches in Essex and Kent, as well as in other counties, are thought to have been built on the sites, or immediately next door to the sites, of ruined Roman buildings. This was done for three reasons. Such sites were less easily reclaimed for farming by the Saxons than virgin woodland or land which had at some time been under the plough; according to Bede, Pope Gregory sent instructions to Mellitus, Bishop of London, that pagan temples should not be pulled down, but should be purified and used as churches; and Saxon church builders where possible sited their churches near such sources of masonry, bricks and tiles as were offered by a ruined Roman building.

Where there is Roman masonry in a Saxon church it should be possible to tell something about the nature of the building from which that masonry was taken. Some shapes of cut stone must be recognisably Roman; and it should be possible for anyone familiar with Roman buildings and masonry to identify these masonry elements where they exist in early Saxon churches, and to speculate on their first function, and in what type of building.

This matter of re-used stone, and indeed of stone in churches generally, has received only the most general notice. It is the exception rather than the rule for those who write about churches to say what stone was used in its building, and where it came from; and concerning foundations they usually say nothing.

One church which comes to mind as an example, although far away from our area, is that at Brixworth in Northamptonshire. I have not seen the guide to this church, which may be all that it should be. But it is a Saxon church and contains a great variety of stone not native to the area, including granite. I do not know whether later additions have been made to the building, but if not then it is difficult to think that the Saxons can have brought this stone to the site. If they did not, then it must be Roman, and taken from the ruins of Roman buildings in the neighbourhood. It should be possible to identify the granite and other stones both as to source and original use; and this might teach us something more than we know at present about the movement and use of stone in Roman times.

To return to churches in Essex. When Tollesbury church was restored in 1875, foundations were discovered in the churchyard from which much Roman brick and tile used in the fabric of the church may have been taken. Roman bricks were dug up on the south side of Canewdon churchyard in about 1848, which suggests that there may have been a Roman building on the site. Laindon church, according to Palin, is "supposed by some to stand on the site of a Roman encampment". The churches at Alphamstone, Little Baddow, Belchamp St Paul, Great Coggeshall, Stansted Mountfichet and Sturmer are said in volume III of the Victoria County History to be on or near Roman sites. There are also said to be Roman foundations in the church and churchyard at Ongar.

One obvious example of a church built on or close to a Roman site is that at East Tilbury. We have already seen that tesserae were found near the church in the eighteenth century, which suggests the existence nearby of a Roman villa or building of some importance. Earthenware and pottery have also been found there. Palin reports Lloyd Williams' statement that when a trench was dug across the land between the church and river wall in the 1850's a layer of bricks and tiles, which Williams thought Roman, was found at a depth of sixteen or eighteen inches. The layer extended for over twenty feet. A coin of Vespasian and a small urn were found among the bricks.

What confirms Williams' statement that these bricks were Roman is the fact that there are Roman bricks both in the present fabric of the church and in the churchyard wall near the gate. Further, when certain alterations were made in January 1958 the material excavated from inside the church — I think while removing the floor — was piled by the road outside; and from this rubble I took away one or two Roman bricks. These facts, coupled with the earlier discovery of tesserae near the church, confirm me in my belief that there was a substantial Roman building nearby.

Although on the frontier of our area, another outstanding example of a church being on or near a Roman site is at West Mersea, where according to Miller Christy a Roman tessellated pavement still formed in his day the paving of the footpath beside the high road just outside the churchyard wall.

Roman bricks in churches

It is reasonable to assume that where Roman bricks are found in the fabric of a church there was at least one substantial Roman building nearby. Such bricks are found in the fabric of thirty-two out of the 109 described in that part of the report of the Royal Commission on Historical Monuments which deals with central and south-western Essex. Volume III of the Victoria County History says there are 106 recorded cases of Roman bricks being used in Essex churches, and two of bricks being used in unnamed secular buildings, of which Colchester castle is presumably one. This total outstrips the number of known villa sites in the county.

Miller Christy estimates that something like seventy per cent of all Norman churches in Essex are built in part of Roman bricks, although I think it might be more accurate to say "contain some Roman bricks in their fabric".

At one time the proportion of churches containing Roman bricks — and the amount of Roman material in any particular church — must have been greater. Many Saxon churches were pulled down by the Normans and their successors before they replaced them with their own churches. It is also possible that the Normans tended to reject bricks in rebuilding and to use stone where possible because bricks were associated with the buildings of a conquered race. If there is anything in this suggestion, then the Saxon churches now demolished contained more Roman bricks than the Norman churches which replaced them and, if still standing, would have provided even stronger evidence of the Romanisation of Essex.

Some churches have quoins of Roman brick, as at Mountnessing. The church at South Benfleet not only contains Roman bricks, but the walls of nave and aisles contain squared ragstone and septaria which are possibly re-used Roman material. More Roman bricks, and a well believed to be Roman, were found four to five feet below the ground surface near the churchyard here "in erecting a petrol pump" in 1926 — presumably digging the space for a petrol storage tank.

There is a footpath made of bricks "of Roman size" about two feet under the surface of Ashingdon churchyard near the south-east corner of the church. There are one or two Roman bricks in the church at Wennington, which stands on the edge of highland and marsh between Rainham and Purfleet, and can be seen to advantage from the train. There are Roman bricks in Chadwell church and in the churchyard wall, and in the church at Horndon on the Hill.

Finally, Smart Lethieullier reported in 1750 that the foundations of one of the great pillars of Barking Abbey were made of Roman bricks, while in 1876 much Roman tile, including flue tile, was seen on the abbey site.

Red hills

One Romano-British feature found on Canvey Island and other low lying areas near the estuary must be described — the red hills which are peculiar to Essex and parts of Kent. Red hills are low, level topped, wide spreading mounds of variable outline which consist of fine burnt clay with a dull red tinge. They contain small quantities of a kind of burnt ware called briquetage, which is in fact broken kiln fittings. Some 250 of these red hills are known, of which fourteen are on Canvey. They are also found farther north in Essex, for example at Langenhoe, Goldhanger, and Canewdon.

Red hills mark the sites of salt production centres which were set up in the Iron Age and continued working into the Roman Occupation. The salt was made by pouring sea water into large evaporating pans made of soft clay which were then set over a fire and heated. The water boiled and evaporated, leaving a crust of salt which was scraped away and used for cooking. Fragments of the pans used, with part of the wall lining of one of the fires and a wedge to hold the pan above the fire, can be seen in the Dutch Cottage museum on Canvey Island, as well as a piece of the green glassy slag which formed naturally in the fire as time went on. The rim of a large jar in which salt may have been stored is also on display.

In many cases the red hills of Essex, whose soil produces good crops, are given over to cultivation. The soil has also been carted away for top dressing the heavy clay of the nearby highland, and has in some cases been used for flooring farm buildings. H. Stopes, writing about these salting mounds in the *Archaeological Journal* for 1879, mentioned that one old man had for years been in the habit of carting away soil from one group of red hills which covered some thirty acres and during that time carted away many hundreds of loads.

Centuriation and the Mardyke

A glance at the 2½-inch map shows that there are two areas in Essex where roads, paths and field boundaries follow an unusual rectangular pattern — at Orsett, and at Asheldam between the rivers Crouch and Blackwater.

At Orsett there are also three parallel roads running north and south which catch the eye because they are all straight and the same distance apart. From west to east they are Blackshotts Lane, Baker Street and Rectory Road.

Further examination of the two areas will also show that many of the fields are exactly the same size, and that in Orsett the distance between each pair of parallel north-south roads is seven times that of the basic squares of fields, whether in Orsett or Asheldham.

What we have in both places is a Roman land settlement area where most of today's field boundaries and many of the roads and paths still follow the lines laid down by the Roman surveyors. Where the remains of Roman field boundaries and occupation roads show up in this way on large scale maps in the grid pattern of roads, paths and field boundaries, it is known as centuriation.

What proves that Orsett and Asheldham were Roman land settlement areas is that in both cases the basic unit of measurement is the *actus*, which was 116.05 feet. The sides of the square fields at

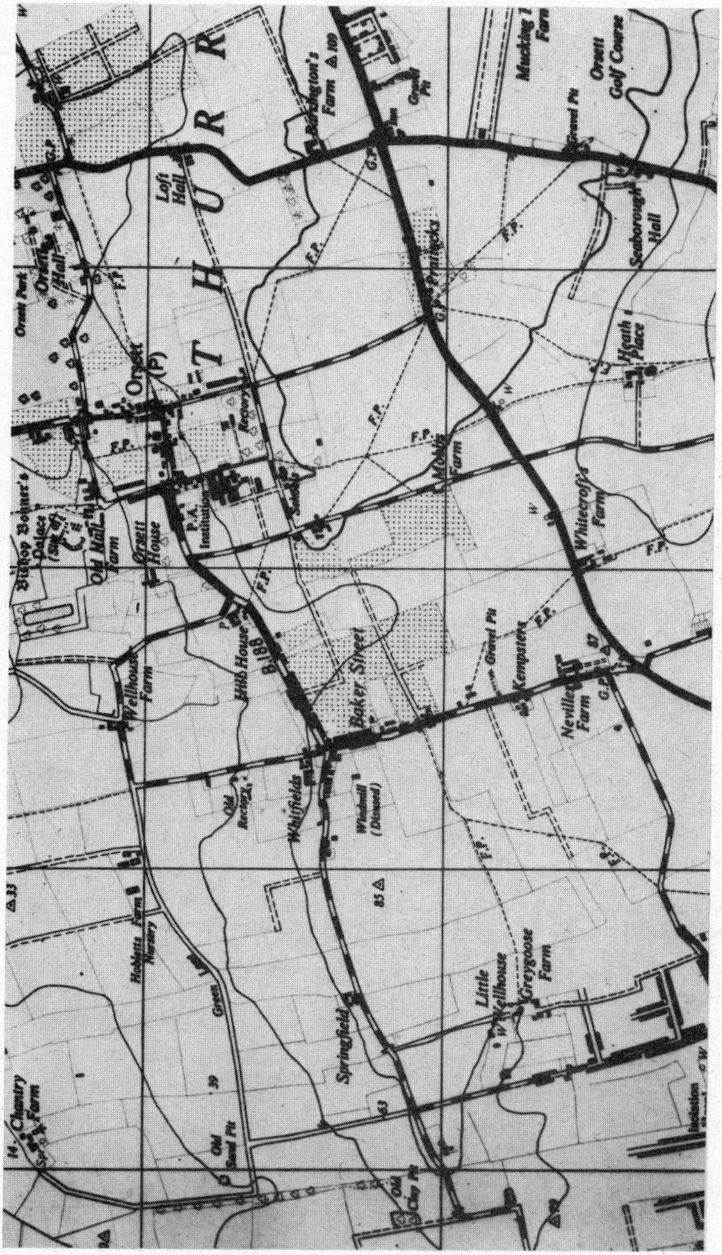

Figure 1. This map, on a scale of 2½ inches to the mile, shows the Roman land settlement area at Orsett in Essex, where many of the field boundaries and roads are five Roman actus (580.25 feet) or multiples of five actus apart. Crown copyright reserved.

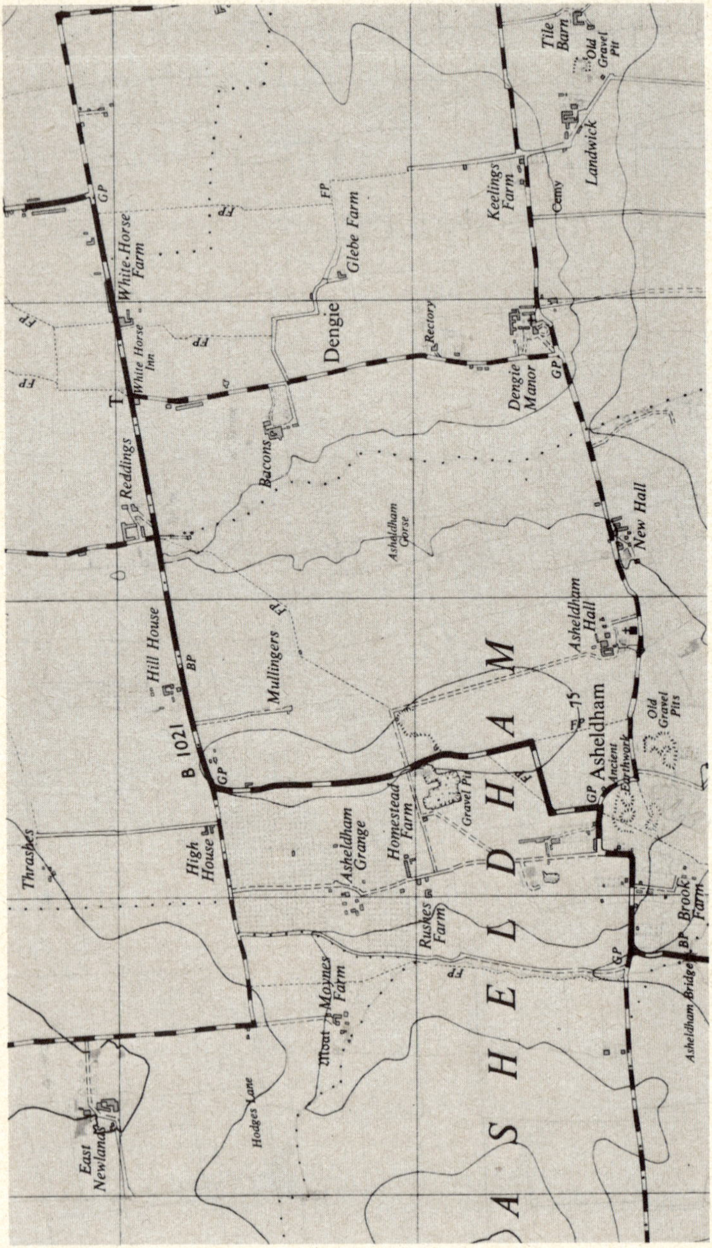

Figure 2. The Roman land settlement area at Asheldham in Essex on a scale of 2½ inches to the mile. Midlands, referred to in the text, is just off the map to the right. Crown copyright reserved

Asheldham are 4,642 feet long, exactly four times as long as the double-square rectangles at Orsett, which have sides 1,160.5 feet long, and exactly eight times as long as the sides of the single square fields there, which have sides 580.25 feet long. Wherever the Romans laid out these land settlement areas, usually for time-expired soldiers, they laid out such square or rectangular fields with sides measured in multiples, usually five or ten, of an actus — as at Orsett and Asheldham.

Square or rectangular Roman fields in these two areas are found in pairs or in blocks containing three or more; sometimes they form a series in line between parallel boundaries, as is found immediately west of the Brentwood road just north of Orsett village. Sometimes, too, today's roads form the boundaries of one or more of these fields — as do Blackshotts Lane, Baker Street and Rectory Road.

The southern boundary of the area at Orsett is the road which runs from Nutberry Corner, Grays, to that point west of Stanford le Hope where it is joined by the road from Horndon on the Hill. To the east the area is bounded by the Horndon road as far as Eastern Avenue, which forms the area's northern boundary. Of its western boundary I am less certain, but I would be inclined to take it along a line running north and south through, or west of, Stifford Clays.

The boundaries of the Asheldham area are less clear, but its central area is south of St Lawrence, west of Tillingham, and north of Asheldham. The grid pattern there also differs from that at Orsett in that it is formed by roads and paths, and hardly at all by present field boundaries; but the areas so enclosed are still interchangeable with those at Orsett as to size and shape. These areas of centuriation at Asheldham and Orsett are defined in greater detail in Appendix I.

The fact that Orsett was a land settlement area suggests that the Mardyke, which passes along the western borders of the area, and whose tributaries pass through the heart of it, may have been straightened by the Romans to make it easier to transport farm produce to London. Such straightening of rivers to provide transport canals was common Roman practice. In similar conditions in the Fens there is a network of transport canals of which some essential to that network, now dried out, have been proved Roman by excavation. The only question is whether this, or some other factor, is responsible for the comparative straightness of the Mardyke.

The Mardyke, north of Stifford, crosses the alluvium of Bulphan and Orsett Fens. In these conditions, where gradient is negligible, natural streams usually meander. The fact that the Mardyke does not — and in this differs so obviously from its western neighbour the Ingrebourne — might make one assume without question that it had been straightened at some time for transport purposes. On the other hand if the Mardyke, or its present bed, was at one time the continuation of that then larger stream the Darent, then it may be flowing along a meander which in the earlier river was some distance across. If so the Ingrebourne, which doubles back on itself every few yards, has the meanders of a small stream, the Mardyke those of a larger river.

I think, however that the present course of the Mardyke has been straightened and that its name has some bearing on this. (Reaney records in his book on the place-names of Essex that it was referred to as the *marcdice,* or boundary ditch, in the spurious 1062 charter with which Edward the Confessor gave Waltham Abbey lands in this area of Essex; but unfortunately the reference in the charter is not to the Mardyke, but to another stream, as Reaney himself makes clear in his later description of the charter boundaries.) The Mardyke was certainly known as *le merkediche* in the cartulary of the Knights Hospitallers in the thirteenth century, and was therefore accepted as artificial at that time. (Reaney has thirteenth century for the cartulary in the text, fifteenth century in the list of abbreviations; but while the cartulary began in 1442 it could still contain a thirteenth century reference.)

It is to be admitted that in 1285, and perhaps earlier, the southern part of the Mardyke was referred to as the *flete,* or *fleot,* which comes from the Anglo-Saxon word for a creek, as in the Fleet river in London; for in that year the element appears in the name Purteflyete, the equivalent then of the name Purfleet. And fleet, unlike ditch, does not necessarily imply artificiality. But Reaney gives the derivation as *mearc* and *dic.* I think the answer is that the Saxons recognised the Mardyke as artificial without necessarily considering who dug it, and therefore called it *dic*; and having adopted it as a boundary, called it *mearc*; and so the Mardyke.

The case for assuming that the Mardyke was straightened artificially by the Romans for transport purposes within their land settlement area — the conclusion to which this argument has been leading — may be strengthened by the fact that the course of the minor tributary of the Mardyke which runs ten actus west of the Brentwood road at and north of Barnards, and forms the western boundary of a series of ten-actus fields arranged in ladder formation, is artificial and Roman. This tributary may have been straightened in order to provide a land settlement boundary, but transport needs would be equally important.

As the Mardyke is today it is difficult to think that either it or the shallow ditches which now serve as tributaries could have carried transport barges. The whole area has been drained dry by efficient land drainage and wholesale pumping of ground water out of the chalk by cement manufacturers and others near the Thames. The water-courses have also been neglected as transport canals. But the fact is that until about a century ago, farms in the fen were connected with the Mardyke by these tributaries, which were then wide shallow ditches up which narrow shallow-draught vessels could be poled after sailing up the main stream from the Thames at Purfleet. These vessels brought loads of London street refuse for use on the land (road dust and horse manure forming a fertile combination) and on their return journey carried back corn and fodder for the same horses.

Mr K. Bannister, writing in volume 7 of the Thurrock Local History Society Journal, tells how his grandfather, a barge owner in 1870, took his dumpy barge up the Mardyke and then up one of its tributaries as far as Lorkins Farm just over 400 yards west of Golden Bridge on the main Brentwood to Tilbury road. No one, looking at the 1¾-mile ditch which connects Lorkins Farm with the Mardyke today, would allow the possibility that it could ever have carried anything larger than a kayak. But since the Mardyke and associated waterways were able to take dumpies in the nineteenth century I suggest they were also able to take shallow draught Romano-British transport barges, which were very like dumpies, during the Roman Occupation. Lorkins Farm is in the heart of the Roman land settlement area.

Coldharbours

One feature of Roman Britain which remains to be described is what are called coldharbours. The name, which appears in over 300 places in England, comes from an Old English word meaning "cold shelter". Subject to what may be said later, the name was applied by the Saxons to the remains of stations on Roman roads. These stations, which were known in Latin as *mansiones,* were rectangular in shape and had the road running through the centre. They existed to provide horses for official travellers and shelter for road users generally. Salmon's suggestion that Blunts Wall near Billericay was such a posting station has already been noted.

The name coldharbour is still applied to lanes, roads, and settlements, and as a study of old maps and records shows was at one time applied even more widely than it is now.

I should, however, point out that a note on coldharbours in the English Place-Name Society's publication *The Place-Names of Surrey* states that the great majority of these names have no relation to Roman roads, and that the theory that coldharbours go back to Roman roadside inns or caravanserais was founded on too few instances, and on small scale maps. I have no doubt that not all coldharbours were so named in Saxon times, and have my own doubts about that at Millwall in the East End of London. On the other hand the comments I quote were published in 1934, and since then the number of roads or stretches of roads known to be Roman, or probably Roman, has greatly increased. My own feeling is that the name is still a strong indication of the existence of a Roman road nearby; and while I would not identify a road on this alone, I would go to considerable lengths to follow up what I still regard, in the majority of cases, as one of the clearest pointers to the possibility of Roman origins.

(Thus the fact that Coldharbour Lane at Purley in Surrey is so called set me off one evening to see whether there was any evidence of a road where the line of the lane continued over the hill above Purley. I discovered the remains of a Roman road which can probably still be seen in the allotments and recreation ground on the other side of Edgehill Road, and between it and the airfield. It was in the form of what archaeologists call a hollow way, that is to say a Roman road whose stone foundations and metalling have been robbed, thus leaving an extended depression.)

I know of three coldharbours in our area of Essex, one at Barking, and two at Coldharbour Point on the Thames between the outfalls of Ingrebourne and Mardyke. That at Barking, on the site of Porters Lodge, which was immediately east of the point where Porters Avenue joins Lodge Avenue today, was known as Colharboroughe in 1555, and a field nearby was formerly called Cold Harborough Marsh. The first known reference to those on the river was in 1528.

I do not know why there should be two coldharbours so close to each other at Coldharbour Point inside the angle formed by the turning Thames opposite Erith, or why one should be called Great and one Little, but my belief that the name means there was a Roman station here is mildly stengthened by the fact that I have found Roman bricks at high water mark at the Point.

In this connection I should refer again to the coldharbour at Millwall, which is towards the north end of the east side of the Isle of Dogs by the Gun Tavern and the entrance to the West India Docks. It is today a narrow lane known only as Coldharbour, running between the entrance to Blackwall Basin and the South Dock of the West India group. It is shown in Rocque's survey of the Isle of Dogs (1741-45).

The position of the three river coldharbours, one at Millwall and two opposite Erith, is interesting. If they do mark the sites of Roman posting stations they could have been built only for those crossing the Thames. No one travelling east or west on the north side of the river at these points would make the great detour necessary to call at either unless he intended crossing the river.

CHAPTER 6

The Forts of the Saxon Shore

I now refer to what I regard as some of the most striking Roman remains to be seen anywhere in the country — the Fórts of the Saxon Shore which ring the south-east coast of England. Strictly speaking only those at Bradwell in Essex and Reculver in Kent are in our area, and some of the best preserved are outside it. But I would recommend anyone who can do so to make the trip to see that at Pevensey, which is easily accessible by train from London, and as to general characteristics may be taken as typical.

The area enclosed by the walls at Pevensey, given by one authority as "over eight acres", by another as "a little under ten acres", is so large that only one sixth of it was taken by the Normans when they built a castle in its south-east corner. Even in decay the twenty-five feet high, twelve feet thick stone walls of the Roman fort with their projecting bastions for mounting ballistas are impressive. In commission, with the defensive moat filled with water and naval vessels standing by, the fort must have been daunting indeed.

The walls were built of flint and sandstone rubble with coursed facings of green sandstone from Eastbourne, and ironstone, presumably from the Weald. Some of the stones at the base of the walls are massive. The walls themselves, like London Wall, were built in sections by gangs working to some extent independently, and the joints between the sections can be seen where some of the material has fallen away.

The foundations of wall and gatehouse, which last is the most impressive feature at Pevensey, are made of flint and chalk originally held in place by a framework of wooden beams on which the lower mortared courses were laid. The bonding courses on the outside face of the walls are of red brick, ironstone and green sandstone, and are set in a pink mortar made with pounded brick. It was Roman mortar such as this to which Roach Smith referred in 1865 as "the well known impervious mortar which helps to distinguish Roman masonry from that of all subsequent periods, and which is the wonder and despair of modern masons".

I have described the construction of Pevensey in some detail in order to give an idea of the ambitious nature and massive construction of these forts. They vary in shape from rectangular to oval, and in extent from four to ten acres. Their walls usually have rubble cores, facings of flint or stone in small regular courses, and bonding courses of brick or stone.

The forts are spread out along the south-east coast of England from Brancaster on the north-west coast of Norfolk to Portchester in Hampshire. The two forts on the estuary are, or were, at Reculver in Kent, about ten miles west of the North Foreland, and Bradwell on Sea in Essex, at the north-eastern tip of the area of land which lies between the Crouch and Blackwater.

Excavations at Bradwell in 1864 and 1865 discovered the foundations of walls fourteen feet thick which enclosed some four acres of ground. One fragment of wall showed a triple layer of bricks, four courses of septaria, and then a second triple layer of bricks. The Roman material in Cedd's nearby church of St Peter on the Wall, the only one remaining of several he built in Essex in the seventh century, is assumed to have come from the fort. It contains stone in abundance, which suggests that the Romans used squared stone as well as bricks in the fort.

I said the Roman bricks and masonry in Cedd's church are "assumed" to have come from the fort because of the slighter possibility that they came from buildings which grew up near the fort in Roman times, or may have preceded it. Henry Laver, writing in 1909, reported that many years previously he had seen the remains of houses on the mud flats east of Bradwell chapel. "Old Joe Ketcher", he added, "often told me in my boyhood that he went on the flats in his younger days, after a tremendous gale, which had lasted many hours or days, and the sand and mud was removed more than he ever saw before, and there were foundations of many houses. These were certainly Roman".

In this Laver echoes Norden, who said that St Peter on the Wall appeared to have been a town "now greatly devoured with the sea". Norden added, "and buildings yet appear in the sea". The foundations of buildings and the line of roads still appear there today at low tide after winter storms.

The title Forts of the Saxon Shore is taken from the *Notitia Dignitatum*, an official handbook of the civil and military organisation of the late Roman Empire, which listed and named nine of them. It has always been assumed that the handbook called it the Saxon shore because it was under Saxon attack in the later years of the

Empire, although it is unusual, and in the Roman Empire possibly unique, for a district to be given the name of its assailants. It has also been suggested that the south-east coast of Britain was known as the Saxon Shore because of the extent to which it was settled by Saxons in the later years of the Roman Empire. The degree of settlement, on which the theory depends, is not known, although it is accepted that some settlement did take place. At the moment, therefore, speculation on why the area was so called must be based on other considerations, which are set out among much else of value in that excellent book *The Roman Forts of the Saxon Shore* by Stephen Johnson.

The forts in Britain had their equivalents on the south side of the Channel and North Sea in a chain of forts extending north-east as far as the mouth of the Rhine. That coast was also known by the title Litus Saxonicum, the Latin form of Saxon Shore. Johnson suggests that the defences in both Britain and Gaul were regarded as one military unit, the sea equivalent of the Roman land frontier which stretched across Europe; had the title Saxon Shore developed locally as a result of Saxon settlement in Britain and Gaul one would expect the name to be in the plural, that is Litora Saxonica, or Saxon Shores.

The forts in Britain and on the Continent are clearly part of the same defence system, not only because they are listed as such in the *Notitia*, but also because of their construction, siting and position, as well as what we know of their function and the times in which they were built. Working from north to south, and with the Latin names of the forts as in the Ordnance Survey map of Roman Britain, those in this country are:

Branodunum	Brancaster, Norfolk
Gariannonum	Burgh Castle, Suffolk
Othona	Bradwell, Essex
Regulbium	Reculver, Kent
Rutupiae	Richborough, Kent
Dubris	Dover, Kent
Lemanis	Lympne, Kent
Anderita	Pevensey, Sussex
Portus Adurni	Portchester, Hampshire

One other Roman fort may have been part of the same Saxon Shore defence system, that known as Walton Castle, which used to stand near Felixstowe in Suffolk. It is now washed away by the sea. Broken pieces of its walls could still be seen on the shore at the end of the eighteenth century, while Roach Smith, writing in 1865, said parts of the fort could be traced at low water and a Roman cemetery farther inland, presumably associated with the fort, was not then fully washed away by the sea.

The forts of the Saxon Shore were heavily fortified guard-posts equipped with Roman field artillery. They acted as strongholds for the fleet defending the coasts of Britain and Gaul against Saxon sea raiders, and were defended naval bases rather than military positions. Each fort, however, had a land garrison in addition to naval vessels and their crews. This was a mobile force whose duty it was to deal on landing with any marauders the fleets had failed to intercept.

Only two forts, those at Burgh Castle and Brancaster, are said in the *Notitia* to have cavalry, but it is reasonable to suppose that other forts may also have been so equipped. It is also known that the naval vessels based on Pevensey took their name, the Classis Anderetianorum, or the Anderetia Fleet, from a variant of the name of the fort at which they were stationed. Other flotillas may have done the same.

The majority of buildings within the forts (which contained ships' stores and equipment as well as accommodation for sailors and soldiers) were probably of timber. There are fragmentary traces of long narrow timber barrack blocks, each with its own hearth, at Richborough, Pevensey, Portchester and Burgh Castle. There were stone built baths within the walls at Richborough, Lympne and Dover; and other stone buildings not further identified in the first two forts.

The forts were supported by signal stations; a number of sites for these, particularly in East Anglia, have been suggested. Rather more certain are those in Yorkshire, excavation of two sites there suggesting that they may have been added to the shore defences by Theodosius in and after 368.

One earthwork in south Essex which may be a signal station has been seen from the air near Hadleigh High Street, just over 400 yards south-west of Hadleigh church. This site, on the ridge overlooking Benfleet Creek, has good views of the Thames estuary, although unlike nearby Hadleigh Castle it is set back from the edge of the bluff. The earthwork measures some 200 feet across and has double ditches.

The warning system also relied on patrolling scout vessels, which according to Vegetius had ropes, hulls, sails, and even the sailors' uniforms painted or dyed blue-green for camouflage.

What were the circumstances which caused the forts to be built when they were? The late third century was a time of increasing attacks on the Roman Empire by tribes living east of the Rhine. These culminated in two great raids in about 260 and 276, in the first of which the Alamanni crossed the Rhine frontier and spread devastation as far as Tarragona in north-east Spain. The forts of the Saxon Shore were built to contain equivalent attacks by sea.

The forts at Reculver and Brancaster were probably earlier than the others; Johnson suggests that those at Burgh Castle, Bradwell, Walton Castle, Dover, Richborough and Lympne were built between 276 and 285, probably on the orders of the Emperor Probus (276-282).

It had previously been thought that the fort at Richborough was built later during the usurpation of Carausius, who seized power in Britain in 287; but Johnson sets out the evidence for believing that the walls were in fact finished shortly before his time.

Johnson also records the fact that Bushe-Fox found a coin of Constantinian date — that is 335 — in one of the beam holes underneath one of the external towers at Pevensey, and refers to "the vexed problem of the date of construction and occupation" of the fort in the light of that discovery. He points out that one cannot be certain that the evidence of this single coin is trustworthy, and concludes that only more comprehensive excavation can tell whether the Pevensey fort was in fact built as many as forty years after the other forts of the Saxon Shore.

Johnson concludes his review of the probable dates of construction by saying that Portchester, while one of the main group of forts, may have been built, or at least completed internally, slightly later than the others.

(If the fort at Brancaster was earlier than the other forts of the Saxon Shore the implications are far-reaching. As we have seen, Brancaster is one of a group of forts listed in the *Notitia* whose siting and method of construction suggest common function and purpose. It was massively constructed, clearly as a base for Roman warships operating against a determined, powerful and disciplined enemy. At that period of history, and with a fort in that position, the enemy can have been Saxon only — Brancaster is some 150 miles away from the North Foreland round the corner of Norfolk on the Wash, and farther still from the Straits of Dover. No one else would attack Britain at this point. It follows from its position that even were there no *Notitia*, and no sign of other Roman forts on the south-east coast today, those who built this naval base at the mouth of the Wash must have inevitably built similar forts in the Thames estuary and on the coasts nearer to the Continent — and against the Saxons.)

The forts were not built to resist large scale landings and attack by ground forces. They were all on or near the sea, and if there was a second line of defence inland we have no evidence of it. They were not built to withstand siege, were poorly connected one with another by road, and built on low rather than high ground. They were therefore not a strong cordon of heavily defended posts warding off invaders, but fortified naval bases to protect the warships whose duty it was to seek and destroy raiders. And since a fleet is a mobile extension of the offensive (and defensive) power of its base, and the ability to carry out a successful naval action depends on efficient bases, the forts were sited on inlets where maximum protection could be given the ships against weather and possible attack (and, although this is subsidiary, deny those same inlets as points of entry to raiders). It was the function of the naval vessels based on the forts to repulse enemy ships at sea, not that of the fort and its defenders to repulse invaders who had already landed, for which purpose they would be largely useless — as indeed they proved.

The way in which the forts, as a group, acted as a line of defence against attack by sea is set out clearly in *The Roman Forts of the Saxon Shore*. They were so positioned between the Channel and the Wash on the south-eastern shores of Britain, and between the Channel and the Rhine on the facing shores, that they formed a funnel-shaped trap. The farther west the Saxon sea raiders went, and the narrower the seas, the nearer and the greater was the concentration of Roman warships which could intercept them. Even if they got through the Straits and escaped forces farther west such as those at Pevensey and Portchester, they still had to make the return journey and run the gauntlet of the narrow seas a second time. It is for this reason that forts on the south coast were spaced at greater intervals than those in Kent: the former, with the fort at Boulogne, were "long stops" to catch any ships which had slipped through.

It has, however, been suggested that some of the forts of the Saxon Shore in Britain, in particular that at Richborough, were built by the usurper Carausius, who seized power in Britain in 287 during the reign of Diocletian and wanted to defend his newly won territory, not primarily against Saxon raiders, but against the power of Rome itself.

The usurpation of Carausius took place shortly after Diocletian had appointed his friend Maximian to be responsible, as a sort of junior Emperor, for the government of the west. At this time the coasts of south-east Britain and northern Gaul were under heavy Saxon attack. Carausius was put in charge of the Channel defences in 285, and so found himself in command of the forts on each coast which had been built in the previous decade, as well as of the flotillas based on them. It was his duty to prevent the raiders reaching the coasts of Britain or Gaul by attacking them at sea; if this failed he was to attack them on landing or destroy their ships as they returned. According to Johnson the almost immediate success he won against the raiders resulted from his using the bases to their best tactical advantage.

Contemporary Roman reports however claim that he allowed the raiders through and collected their booty as they returned home, keeping the spoil for himself. On discovery he was condemned to death. He thereupon revolted, and with his fleet, then based on Boulogne, occupied Britain and proclaimed himself Emperor.

Johnson points out that the suggestion that Carausius deliberately let Saxon raiders through is a rumour reported by a source hostile to him, and that had this been his policy it is difficult to see how he could have gained enough popularity to be accepted as Emperor in Britain. Johnson suggests that in capturing marauders laden with plunder Carausius might have been merely mopping up groups which had slipped through the Straits in conditions which prevented interception. (I hesitate to comment, but if, as I suppose, his position depended on the army, he could, if the rumour was true, have secured loyalty through the spoils of war. If the rumour is not true, the result is to reject a reason not entirely unacceptable, replacing it with the speculation that Maximian was jealous and wanted to get rid of a dangerous and talented rival — a possibility more than likely, but for which there is I believe no direct evidence.)

Whatever the truth of the matter, Maximian began building a fleet in 288 with the intention of ousting Carausius. It seems likely that this fleet was wrecked by storm in 289, or defeated by Carausius.

Carausius had complete control of the sea approaches to Britain and of the Continental shore to a point somewhere short of the mouth of the Rhine. There was no place on this coast where Maximian could prepare a fleet: he had to build his ships on the Rhine and Moselle.

Then if he proposed attacking Britain directly he would be forced to sail straight into the Channel trap, and probably with less experienced crews under less expert direction. If this is what happened, there is no need to seek a further reason for his failure. But whatever did take place, Carausius was left in undisturbed possession of his territory for a period during which he minted coins of gold, silver and billon (an alloy of silver and base metal) in London and elsewhere.

In 293 Diocletian appointed two more junior Emperors, Galerius to serve under him, Constantius Chlorus to serve under Maximian. Shortly after his appointment, Constantius Chlorus recaptured Boulogne after blocking the entrance to the harbour and denying naval support to the troops in the town. As a result, Carausius had to relinquish his hold on the coast of Gaul and its system of naval defences. The Channel trap became powerless, and his southern flank was wide open to Roman counter attack at any point on the length of the south coast.

In the same year Carausius was killed by Allectus his second in command, who continued to hold out in Britain for three years. Then in 296 Constantius Chlorus, having built the necessary ships, assembled two forces, one at Rouen, one at Boulogne. That at Rouen crossed the Channel in fog, landed on the coast of Hampshire, and defeated Allectus. Britain was restored to the Empire.

It has been suggested that Richborough was built by Carausius as a defence against the central Roman power because of the discovery there some years ago of a single coin minted during his reign — but found, according to Johnson, in dubious circumstances. After a detailed analysis of all the archaeological evidence from this site to date, coins included, Johnson rejects the possibility that Richborough could have been built by the usurper. He does, however, allow the possibility, on the evidence of the coins excavated there, that Carausius may have been responsible for the construction of the buildings within the already built walls at Portchester.

These are the archaeological objections to the suggestion that two specific forts may have been built by Carausius. General objections which apply to the construction by him of any forts within the group are that in and immediately after 285 he had no need to build shore defences because his fleet ruled the narrow seas; and that when he had need to defend his southern flank after the loss of Boulogne he seems to have made no attempt to fill in the gap between the south coast forts.

I do not know whether the fact that nine forts of the Saxon Shore are named in the *Notitia*, but ten at least have been identified archaeologically, justifies speculating on the possibility that others may have been washed away by the sea in the Thames estuary in addition to that farther north at Walton Castle. If regularity of spacing in this area not far from the Channel trap was of importance, then one might expect there to be another fort somewhere between Bradwell and Reculver, say at or near Shoeburyness, or on the low water edge of Foulness Sands north or east of Foulness Point.

Some support may be lent the last suggestion by the existence of the Broomway, a metalled road which runs below high water mark parallel with the coast from north of Shoeburyness to Foulness. I shall deal later in greater detail with the origins and function of this road. All I need say here is that it is unquestionably Roman; and that if there was a Fort of the Saxon Shore on the low water mark edge of Foulness Sands, then the Broomway, or rather an extension of the Broomway, may have led to it. Maps do not show such an extension; but it is noticeable that the one-inch Ordnance Survey map shows the Broomway suddenly going through a right angle bend to turn in at Fishermans Head. A Roman road would have turned in towards the head earlier, or continued in a straight line past the point of turning. If we can rely on the map — and Chapman and André do not show this right angle in their 1777 map of Essex — it therefore means that the short section leading to Fishermans Head is the last of a number of feeder roads which connect with the Broomway, and that the main road continued in the same direction. If it did, it would have struck what is now the low water edge of Foulness Sands — in Roman times the edge of the land — somewhere along the channel connecting Crouch and Whitaker Channel. If there was a Fort of the Saxon Shore at Foulness this was the place for it.

There is little doubt that sandbanks such as the Foulness and Maplin Sands, which today form extensions at low water of the Essex mainland, were in Roman times an integral part of that mainland and dry at all states of the tide. It is difficult to think that the stretch of coast so formed to the east can have been left without protection when other parts of the estuary were fortified by the Romans. It is then only one step further to speculate that the East or West Barrow, or one of the Shingles — sandbanks in the estuary probably dry at all states of the tide in Roman times — may also have been fortified by the Romans.

CHAPTER 7

Roman sites in Kent

This chapter on Roman sites and remains in Kent deals only with the area north of Watling Street, and with that part east of the Medway in lesser detail than that to the west. It cannot therefore claim to give any indication of the variety, richness, and number of Roman remains in Kent as a whole, or even in that part of the county which fronts estuary and sea east of the Medway.

Earlier antiquaries and archaeologists stressed the fact that those parts of Kent which bordered the Thames and Thames and Medway estuaries were full of Roman remains, principally pottery. Areas said to be particularly rich were the marshes near Higham and Cliffe, at the mouth of the Medway, and along the bank of the Thames itself from (say) Plumstead Marshes to the sea.

I have no doubt there are vast quantities of Roman pottery under the silt of the Thames and Medway marshes. I have no doubt that in the nineteenth century, the period during which these discoveries were described, much pottery could actually be found on the river and estuary edges of the marshes, and in the tidal creeks which seam them. But while I have come across a small amount of broken pottery in these areas, I have found nothing like the masses of unbroken pots described by Spurrell and other nineteenth-century antiquaries. I have for example been to Sharfleet Creek at the mouth of the Medway, and to the banks of the Thames opposite Dagenham, both said to be areas rich in Roman remains, and found nothing — save at the last multitudes of presumably replaced pot insulators from the southernmost of the two vast pylons which take power cables across the river here.

Roman sites in the Higham and Cliffe area seem to consist of settlements by the river, and potteries farther inland on the edge of marsh and highland. The *British Archaeological Association Journal* for 1849 describes excavations at Higham during which a great variety of Roman pots was dug up, and says that "vast quantities of similar deposits covered at least four acres". Spurrell said that the Roman potteries at Higham extended for some three miles along the southern, highland, edge of the marshes. He saw over one hundred unbroken pots dug out of a field which sloped down to the edge of the marsh south of Higham church "and such immense quantities of broken fragments that the new embankment of the railway there was in places made of them".

Payne, writing in volume 23 of *Archaeologia Cantiana*, said there were two layers of Romano-British potsherds along the ballast cutting of the North Kent Railway opposite the signal box about a mile beyond (that is west of) Higham station, while Roach Smith reported in volume 13 that newly dug graves in Higham churchyard continually disclosed Roman pottery and tiles.

These reports refer to potteries. Nearer the river the reports are of settlements, industrial sites, and burial places. At the river margin of the Higham marshes a Romano-British industrial site has been identified on the river side of the tidal wall in Higham Bight, while Romano-British cremation burials have been found in the tidal mudflats of Higham Bight itself. Volume 68 of *Archaeologia Cantiana* records that in 1953, in a trench cut for clay in the Higham marshes about 150 yards south-west of the northern end of the Barrow Hill causeway, a Roman site, nor further described, was found.

In the Cliffe area a number of Roman sites have been found in the marshes between the chalk bluff and the river. Payne has recorded the discovery of several Romano-British graves in the marsh near the cement works, now in ruins, by Cliffe Creek, close to the river wall and under some four feet of alluvium.

Romano-British industrial sites have been identified on the foreshore north of the mouth of Cliffe Creek where there are Romano-British salt pans, and at a point on Cliffe Creek some 400 or 500 yards from where the chalk rises from the alluvium. Pottery has been found at three places on the marsh: north-east of Wharf Farm, Cliffe; farther north of this site near Cliffe Fleet; and in the marsh at a point south of Mead Wall, and north-east of the central portion of Cliffe Creek.

Spurrell said he had picked up pieces of Roman pottery on the Blyth Sands, which he thought were inhabited in Roman times, "particularly near the Brimp, where lay a quantity of broken tile". The Blyth Sands are off the north shore of Hoo, and dry at low water. I have not been able to identify the Brimp.

One site in the Cliffe area which might be connected with a Roman river crossing is on the foreshore north of the mouth of Cliffe Creek. It was reported in 1966 that a group from St George's School, Gravesend, had found there a channel of hardened ooze about twelve feet wide leading from Cliffe Creek to stratified Romano-British mounds, and the outline of a boat twenty feet long. There was also a reed floor mixed with briquetage, and a chalk and gravel floor forty yards long.

Some miles to the east of the area of Higham and Cliffe, and on the other side of the Medway estuary, is the village of Upchurch. So much Romano-British pottery has been found in the marshes to the north that the commonest type, which is black, is known as Upchurch ware. Other Roman remains have been found in this area on Slayhill saltings, on the saltings between Twinney and Halstow creeks, and on Milford Hope, Ham Green and Kingsferry saltings. Greenborough, Bishop, Burntwick, Nor, Hoo West and East marshes are all said to have produced remains. These were mostly pottery, although more permanent remains are, or were, those of a Roman villa on Slayhill saltings reported by Spurrell to have been destroyed by fire. The saltings on the east side of Otterham Creek, as well as both banks of the creek itself, are said to have yielded a vast store of Upchurch ware over a long period.

I must, however, say that they have yielded none to me. Doubtless because my visit coincided with high tide, on the one occasion when I walked along the eastern bank of Otterham Creek all the way to Bayford Marsh I found nothing but half a dozen small pieces of much battered local pottery and one sherd of Samian. I was compensated for this lack of foresight in my arrangements by the fact that it was spring, and at one point where the orchards came down to the shore the fruit trees were in bloom and the grass underneath, cropped by a flock of sheep, was like a lawn lovingly tended for centuries, a long green carpet rolled out under the fruit trees and over the tidal wall as far as the sea edge. It was a pleasant experience to walk by the sea with apple blossom overhead.

The marshes north of Shoregate Creek have produced much Roman pottery in the past, but here also I have been unsuccessful save for finding flint axe heads and getting myself cut off by the tide. It is essential for anyone who tries to get down on the marshes here to make absolutely certain that he has worked out the tide tables correctly. The safest thing is to wait at the creek while the tide is ebbing and cross the moment the water is low enough, bearing in mind that the creek cannot be crossed for some hours at high water. This will give the adventurous as much time as possible between tides. Wellingtons and even thigh boots are necessary for the crossing, which at low water is difficult because of deep mud, but in itself not particularly dangerous.

I mention this because the last time I was on the saltings here I worked out the tides wrongly, and had to spend some hours of darkness sitting in the ruin of a cottage at Greenborough, assuming it was the highest point in the marshes, and hoping that breaks in the tidal walls did not mean it was likely to be under high water mark. After crossing at the next low tide I got back to Rainham at about two o'clock in the morning to find the station shut, the recreation ground with its shelter locked, and the rain falling steadily, as it had been doing since I was cut off by the tide hours before. While standing in a shop doorway wondering what to do, the impossible happened and a local hire car came by whose driver kindly drove me back to Ryder Street, St James's, in a little over an hour. It is always as well to check and double check tide tables.

So far I have dealt with sites on or near the marshes. One of the most important sites on the highland is the Roman town of Vagniacae at Springhead south-west of Gravesend, where the remains of Roman baths were found in 1814 and much else, particularly in recent years, has since been discovered. Many of these discoveries relate to roads, and are dealt with in a later chapter.

Among smaller sites is one on the highland edge due north of Shorne. It is about 400 yards west of Queens Farm, and has as its eastern boundary the parish boundary between Chalk and Shorne, which here runs in a straight line due north and south. A path which ran from the Lower Higham Road east of Filborough once passed through the site, which I believe has now been destroyed by gravel workings. The site of a substantial Roman building has been excavated about a mile to the west, on the highland edge some 170 yards south-west of West Filborough. A. F. Allen, who reported its excavation in volume 73 of *Archaeologia Cantiana*, said that he found a "well coursed" chalk wall, as well as flints, rubble, and Roman plaster and tiles. He said that the building had been demolished for the material it contained — Chalk church nearby has Roman tiles and bricks in the east wall of the chancel.

A good deal farther west a Roman site has been recorded at Stone Castle quarry, Greenhithe, about one mile south-east of Stone, and some 300 yards north of Watling Street. The 2½-inch map shows a Roman burial ground to the north of the site.

With the possible exception of parts of St Martin's church at

Canterbury, where Queen Bertha of Kent is said by Bede to have worshipped before Augustine came, and the foundations of a fourth-century Christian chapel attached to the villa at Lullingstone in the Darent valley, there are no known remains in Kent of Christian churches built during the Roman Occupation.

The chancel of St Martin's is made wholly of Roman brick, but whether any part of the fabric dates from Roman times, or all the bricks used were re-laid by the Saxons, could be decided only by a closer examination of the mortar than I have been able to carry out.

There are two churches in our area of Kent which contain Roman work not known to have formed part of an earlier Christian church on the same site — at Stone near Faversham, and at Erith. According to John Newman, author of the Penguin guides to the buildings of Kent, excavation of the ruined chapel at Stone has shown that it includes part of a Romano-British pagan mausoleum, while according to Roach Smith there is Roman work (which is not visible today) in the parish church at Erith. Roach Smith suggests that this work was connected with a Roman harbour, a suggestion I deal with in greater detail in a later chapter.

Newman says that something remains of ten churches in the county built by Augustine or his followers compared with one in Essex, that at Bradwell; and that those which remain above ground contain much re-used Roman material. None is west of the Medway, although east of this river and north of Watling Street are the churches of St Andrew, Rochester (604), Minster in Sheppey (664) and Reculver (669). According to Newman, of these three only Minster has walling high enough to impress the eye.

I now come to matters more speculative. A square entrenchment or deep ditch, which seemed to have been a fortification, was discovered at the end of the seventeenth century not far from Higham. It was in a wood then known as Chapel Wood, which took its name from the parish church of Merston, then in ruins, within the same wood. The site is on the north face of the high ground which slopes down from the crest of the Gravesend to Rochester road at Gadshill, and about 500 yards west of Hill Farm, which is on the more westerly of two roads leading from Higham Upshire to that part of Higham near the railway. I have been to the site of the church, but saw nothing worth recording. I believe it was under a crop at the time, and in any case I was not then aware that there had been a square earthwork nearby. The wood referred to in the seventeenth century no longer exists.

The entrenchment, whose discovery is reported in Pearman's *Rochester Diocese* (1897) contained about three acres, and its sides were "according to the cardinal points of the compass". Within the ditch were many irregularities which might have been the foundations of buildings.

It has also been suggested, on the basis of a reference in the Peutinger Table, that there may have been a Roman settlement known as Madus at either Higham or Cobham, or at Barming or Teston on the Medway south-west of Maidstone. The Peutinger Table is a Roman map on which places, routes, and mileages are written. It is named after Conrad Peutinger into whose hands it came in the sixteenth century. I mention the possibility here mainly because of the reference to Higham, the only one of these four places north of Watling Street.

According to Gordon M. Hills, writing in the *British Archaeological Journal* for 1878, the Table shows a road from Duroavernus (which he takes to be Durovernum, or Canterbury) to London, on which the three towns of Raribis, Burolevo and Madus are marked at distances of seven, fourteen and thirty-one Roman miles from Canterbury. (A Roman mile is slightly shorter that an English mile.) He places Raribis at Nash Court one mile north of Boughton under Blean, which is on Watling Street east of Faversham, and Burolevo one mile east of Bapchild, which is on Watling Street just east of Sittingbourne; and adds that Madus "goes 2½ miles beyond the Medway on the Roman road through Rochester". He then suggests that it could be a place beyond the Medway such as Cobham or Higham or, if on the Medway, Barming or Teston. This is typical of a certain kind of antiquarianism, for Barming and Teston are nowhere near the Roman road from Canterbury to London. With Cobham and Higham he is nearer the mark, although I think he is referring, as earlier antiquarians often did refer, to parishes and not to villages. Cobham is about a mile south of Watling Street, Higham Upshire and Higham one mile and three miles to the north. The parish boundaries of Higham and Cobham do, however, follow Watling Street for short distances, and it is to these parishes I think he must refer.

Concerning his first station of Raribis, I would have thought a more likely site was on the Roman road at Boughton under Blean itself, and not off the road to the north, although one mile east of Bapchild is reasonable for Burolevo.

The suggestion that Madus was at Barming or Teston can be ignored. If the Table can be relied on, this settlement was probably somewhere near where Crutches Lane joins Watling Street west of the Medway or, if it was 2½ miles beyond the Medway as Hills suggests, slightly farther west. This would take it to where the next side road, that leading to Shorne Ridgeway, leaves Watling Street to the north. Either site would be close to the southern boundary of the parish of Higham and the northern boundary of that of Cobham. The Ordnance Survey map of Roman Britain records that a Roman milestone was found on the north side of Watling Street at Shorne Warren, but I have been unable to find out more about it or to relate it (if relationship is possible) to the suggested site of Madus.

A writer in *Archaeologia Cantiana* for 1952 suggested that there was a Roman land settlement area in Hoo, the broad peninsula between the estuaries of Thames and Medway. If this is so, and the evidence is less conclusive than for the areas I have described in Essex, then there is an area of Roman land settlement on each side of the Thames at the point where it narrows.

CHAPTER 8

The East Tilbury crossing and Roman river crossings

I have no doubt it was possible to ford the Thames at East Tilbury in prehistoric times, not only because flood levels were then much lower, but also because of the existence of the prehistoric track which leads to the same area on the Essex bank.

The track shows up clearly on the 2½-inch map of the Tilbury district, running from the western entrance to Hangmans Wood at Grays to the church at East Tilbury. It is particularly clear in the field below the vicarage at East Tilbury, where it has the appearance of a broad Pilgrims Way. There are two mark stones in the field at this point.

There are three significant things about this track. The first is that it so clearly makes for the river bank at East Tilbury. The second is that it is older than the present road system of the area because in two cases, first north of Chadwell, and then at West Tilbury and Low Street, its course is followed by a modern road which first takes over and then leaves its line while the track continues on its way. This tendency for a modern road to take over a section of an older way, and then to leave it, happens with Roman roads. I suggest that in this case it has done so with a track, which while doubtless in use in Roman times, was much older. The third and most important thing about this track is that it makes for the last place on the river where hard ground comes anywhere near the water, and the last place where in the ordinary way one would consider fording or ferrying.

The track is not medieval, as are so many "prehistoric" tracks, although I have no doubt it was used in the Middle Ages. It is not a pilgrim road for taking travellers to the shrine of St Thomas at Canterbury: it cuts right across the main pilgrim route, which was southwards to West Thurrock, and also across the roads which lead to ferries having their northern terminals between West Thurrock and Tilbury. I cannot see it except as a pre-Roman track leading from central England to the lowest point at which the Thames could be forded.

The evidence for there being fords or ferries in the Thames below London in Roman times is slight. There is some confusing literary evidence that during the invasion by Claudius in A.D. 43 the Roman forces forded the Thames at East Tilbury. The existence of what may have been a Roman causeway leading to the north bank of the Thames at West Tilbury, together with the discovery in the nineteenth century of Roman remains where it struck the river bank, have been held to suggest that there was also a Roman ferry at this point. The Roman road pattern at the south of Gravesend, which is dealt with in a later chapter, and to a lesser degree that north of Tilbury, suggest with greater reason that there may have been a ferry between these two points. The existence of two coldharbours on the Essex bank opposite Erith, together with the fact, as we saw earlier, that the name Erith means an earth or muddy soil harbour, and appears in the seventh century, suggest there may have been a ferry here also. These are the only pointers to possible Roman crossings that I know.

I will deal first with the suggestion that there was a ford at East Tilbury in Roman times, which I first came across in Worley's book on Essex churches. Worley referred to the description of the Greek historian Dio (A.D. 155-230) of how the Britons forded the Thames when escaping from the forces of Aulus Plautius. It occurred to me, in reading Worley, that if there were a ford here in Roman times it must have been served by easily identifiable Roman roads, as were the Humber crossing at Brough and that across the mouth of the Wash from the end of Peddars Way in Norfolk to the end of the Lincoln road at Seacroft. I could not believe that the Romans, whose chief port of entry was in east Kent, and whose two most important governmental and military stations at various times were Colchester and York, would in the movement of men and goods from one to the other make the long detour through London. I was therefore surprised, on looking at the map of Roman Britain, to find that the only road marked between the Colchester road in Essex and the Canterbury road in Kent was a short stretch of road leading to the Roman fort at Bradwell. But believing that Roman crossings must have existed below London, and that roads must have led to them, I set out to find them.

When I began my researches I thought it might have been possible to ford the river at the head of the estuary, that is somewhere between Tilbury and East Tilbury on the Essex bank, and between Gravesend and Higham on the Kent bank. I still think this may have been possible in a dry summer, but now assume that any crossing which took place here regularly was by ferry. I also thought that the straight road which passes through Linford and East Tilbury was a Roman road leading to that ferry. I am still inclined to think that this may be a Roman road, but the absence of an equivalent road on the Kent side is puzzling.

In discussing a possible ford near East Tilbury three things must be considered: literary sources, on which the whole tradition is probably based; the state of the river in Roman times; and Roman sites in the area.

As far as literary sources are concerned it is Dio, described in *Chambers's Encyclopaedia* as "one of the greatest bores of all antiquity" who is the only classical authority, and that a dubious one, for the existence of a ford here in Roman times. He said the Romans forded the Thames during the invasion, and seems to suggest that this took place near the head of the estuary. Unfortunately that part of the *Annals* of Tacitus which must have dealt with the invasion is lost, so that it is impossible to check what Dio says.

Dio introduces the invasion in Book 60 of his *History* in the following words: "While these events were happening in the city, Aulus Plautius, a distinguished senator, commanded an expedition against Britain." He says three divisions of troops were sent over in A.D. 43 and made an unopposed landing, the Britons "taking refuge in swamps and forests". He describes the decisive battle of the campaign on the west bank of the Medway, and then comes this reference to the Thames. "Thence the Britons retired to the river Thames at a point near where it empties into the ocean and at flood-tide forms a lake. This they easily crossed because they knew where the firm ground and the easy passages in this region were to be found; but the Romans in attempting to follow them were not so successful. However, the Germans swam across again and some others got over by a bridge a little way upstream, after which they assailed the barbarians from several sides at once and cut down many of them. In pursuing the remainder incautiously they got into swamps from which it was difficult to make their way out, and so lost a number of men." Then, after the Romans had crossed the Thames, either by swimming or by bridge, and had lost a number of men by incautious pursuit, the Britons, so far from yielding, were the more united. Because of this, and because of the difficulties he had encountered at the Thames, Plautius (according to Dio) became afraid, and instead of advancing any farther, proceeded to guard what he had already won, and sent for the Emperor.

Claudius crossed over to Britain "where he joined the legions that were waiting for him near the Thames. Taking over the command of these, he crossed the stream, and engaging the barbarians, who had gathered at his approach, he defeated them in battle and captured Camulodunum, the capital of Cunobelinus".

If we are to take any notice of Dio at all we must accept that the Britons forded the Thames "at a point near where it empties into the ocean and at flood-tide forms a lake". The point of crossing can hardly have been above Gravesend Reach, where in our day the estuary begins, and hardly below Mucking Creek because of the width, as well as the depth, of the river below this point — that is if we accept Dio's statement.

We know the Thames was narrower and shallower in Roman times, although we do not know by how much. It may be reasonable to assume it is now deeper by the fifteen feet which the land has since then sunk compared with the sea. On the other hand I do not know how much one should allow for more recent changes, in particular for a deeper channel resulting from a greater tidal discharge, which in turn resulted from a greater mass of water pressing on the mouth of the Thames. These post-Roman changes do not, however, prevent our making comparisons between different stretches of the river. If the contours of the bed were then much the same as they are now, then in Roman times there were two stretches of the river above and below East Tilbury shallower than any other part of the river between a point above Broadness and one south of Crowstone, Southend.

The upstream shallows at East Tilbury begin just east of the Tilbury power station, and end just off Coalhouse Point. In this 1,300 yards stretch which centres on Powder Bank it is possible to plot a number of courses from bank to bank more or less at a right angle to the river which, even on a broad front, nowhere cross water deeper than thirty-one feet at low water.

This shallow stretch ends where the river is let down off Coalhouse Point to depths of up to forty-eight feet. Then comes a second stretch of shallow water in the middle of the Lower Hope Reach. At the downstream end of this second shallow stretch it is possible to plot a course in a straight line from the Kent to Essex shores which nowhere strikes water deeper than thirty feet.

If the straight track which can be seen on the 2½-inch map to run from just south of Southfields Manor Farm towards Balstonia follows the course of a Roman road, the case for a ford at Mucking is strengthened, for if this line is extended it strikes the river bank immediately opposite this shallow stretch. On the other side of the river the Strood to Cliffe road, if extended, would strike the Kent bank opposite the point where the Essex line hits the north bank. On the other hand, to cross the river at this point in a straight line it is necessary to follow one course only and not, as in the case of the Powder Bank stretch, any one of a number. This course is also not at right angles to the river, but at an angle so acute that were fording possible today its river passage would be double the length of any crossing above Coalhouse Point.

If fording were possible in Roman times, the two likeliest places would therefore be at Powder Bank or directly north of Cliffe. If we could rely on Dio's statement that the Thames was "forded at a point where it empties into the ocean" then there is no point in trying to guess at the depth of the Thames hereabouts in A.D. 43: all we need do is decide which was the shallowest place, and that is where the ford was. But we cannot, of course, rely on Dio.

For even if we accept his account we get into insurmountable difficulties over his reference to a bridge "a little way upstream". According to Dio the bridge was at a point where it was possible for German soldiers to cross and take part in the same action as those who swam the river. If the attack of those who swam was co-ordinated with the attack of those who crossed by bridge, then the bridge cannot have been more than a mile or two away. But while there may be nothing in theory against the British having a floating bridge at Gravesend, it has always been accepted without question that London Bridge, over twenty miles upstream, was the lowest point at which the Thames was ever bridged. And if the British had a bridge of boats or rafts at Gravesend, one wonders that it was not destroyed by them at the Roman advance or, if it was, that the fact is not recorded.

But ultimately one comes to a point where one questions the whole of Dio's account, not only concerning the point where the action took place, but whether fording was possible below London at all. Ralph Merrifield, for example, in his book *Roman London*, suggests that the bridge, and therefore the fording, may have been at Southwark.

It is certainly difficult to know how much importance to attach to Dio, particularly since he seems to be in conflict with a (perhaps) more reliable witness. For Caesar, writing of his campaign in 54 B.C., says that the Thames was fordable at one point only, and that with difficulty, and a good deal of interesting material has been written about where that fordable point was. Many authorities think it was at Coway Stakes between Walton and Shepperton; others at Wallingford; others at Brentford; others at Wandsworth; but all above London. Certainly the Thames was fordable at Brentford in 1016, when Edmund Ironside and his army crossed it twice during his campaign against Canute, and this was a thousand years after Caesar's expedition during which time flood levels in the Thames must have risen.

If Brentford was not the place where Caesar forded the Thames, then he was wrong in saying that the Thames could be forded at one place only, and his evidence is undermined. He certainly did not speak with local knowledge, and was not above exaggerating the difficulties he overcame. But the fact remains that what he says tends to break down Dio's story.

It would be interesting, if the Romans did cross near East Tilbury, to know where Plautius camped near the Thames to wait for Claudius, and where Claudius set up his own camp or camps near the river. Elliston Erwood, writing in volume 34 of the *British Archaeological Journal*, points out that thousands of troops were involved but not a single earthwork which could be associated with Claudius has been discovered. Where, he asks, are the rectangular enclosures with earth banks which one associates with Roman campaigning?

It is true that since his paper was published in 1923, enclosures believed to be Claudian have been discovered near the Essex bank of the Thames, but as far as I know none between Medway and Thames.

Similar questions are asked by Donald R. Dudley and Graham Webster in their book *The Roman Conquest of Britain A.D. 43-57*. Referring to the Roman crossing of the Medway, the decisive action of the campaign, they comment, "It is difficult to believe that such a violent clash would not have left some permanent mark on the landscape. The Roman army must have built temporary camps for their forces of the usual geometric pattern. So far nothing has been observed either from the air or on the ground resembling these features."

These authors' comments refer to the Medway area, but they tie in with the fact that the area between Medway and Thames seems to be equally free of evidence of Roman camps or forts; and this is the area where such enclosures would be found if Claudius and his forces had crossed the Thames at East Tilbury. The answer must be that the Romans crossed the Thames in the London area and went the whole way south of what is now Watling Street.

I said earlier that as far as I knew no rectangular enclosures suggesting Roman occupation had been found between Medway and Thames. Without suggesting for one moment that it is Roman — I have not even seen it — I must refer again to the square earthwork of about three acres whose discovery near Higham is described in the previous chapter. It it were ever found to be Roman, then it would be interesting to try and relate it to known first-century earthworks on the other side of the river, and to a possible crossing here during the invasion.

If any of the first-century earthworks in the Thurrock area listed at the beginning of chapter 5 are Roman camps set up by the Emperor's forces on his visit, this would provide massive confirmation of the suggestion that he crossed in the Tilbury-Gravesend area. Without such confirmation, and had not Dio used the phrase "near where it empties into the ocean", one would without hesitation put the whole action much higher upstream, perhaps immediately below the site of the City, or on the other side of London altogether.

We must now consider whether the Romans operated a ferry at East Tilbury after the initial period of invasion. The evidence for this is weak and indirect. The obvious need, already outlined, for such a ferry; the possibility that the Linford to East Tilbury road was a Roman road giving access to it on the Essex bank; the tradition among antiquarians that access was also given by a Roman road on the Kent bank; the fact that the medieval ferry here was mentioned centuries before any of the lower Thames ferries — these are the only pieces of dubious evidence.

I will deal first with the possibility that the Linford road is a Roman road leading to a crossing at East Tilbury. One suggestive factor here is the overall straightness of the road. A second factor calls for a slight detour into early church history. Bede, in his *Ecclesiastical History*, says that Cedd built churches in several places in Essex, but names only two, Bradwell and "Tilbury". The first church still remains: there is some doubt where the second was built, although I believe it was at East Tilbury. Both sites were near marshy ground in desolate areas not far from the sea. There were also ruined Roman buildings at

Bradwell whose material was used to build the church there, and I imagine the same was true of "Tilbury". The church at Bradwell was built at the end of a Roman road; and if, as I believe, that at "Tilbury" was at East Tilbury, then the road which leads there from Linford may be Roman too.

But to prove the Linford road Roman it is necessary to identify possible Roman roads connecting with it to the north, and in this I have been unsuccessful. The most promising clue was a fourteenth century reference, which will be taken up later, to a *herestrete* at Horndon on the Hill, *herestrete* being one of the names given by the Saxons to a Roman road. But I do not know which was the road referred to here unless it was that which runs north and south through Horndon village. South of Pump Street, itself a suggestive name, this road has widely spaced boundaries — twenty-three paces from the west fence to the east ditch — and the present road takes up about half of the area so enclosed. The width continues off and on to Horndon. Here and there some cottages and gardens seem to have encroached on the line of the road, so that its width cannot be a recent feature. But even if we assume the East Tilbury road to be Roman, there is no real evidence that Pump Street is its northern extension.

I also examined the area south of the southern terminus of the Linford to East Tilbury road to see if I could find where it struck the river, but here again I was unsuccessful. I could find no sign of a road continuing south of East Tilbury church, either across the saltings, or at or below high water mark on the river side of Coalhouse Fort.

In later researches between East and West Tilbury I did come across a metalled road leading down to the river, although it was clearly not an extension of the Linford road, had no connection with the Roman site already mentioned at West Tilbury, and could not be related to tracks known to have crossed the marsh before tipping began, or to roads leading down to the marsh today. It was, however, directly opposite the shallow stretch at Powder Bank.

To be quite fair I was told about the road, and the matter fell out in this way. It was on Easter Day 1957 that I walked for the first time westwards along the river bank from Coalhouse Fort. The tide was out, and between the toe of the river wall and the edge of the main channel there was a wide band of soft mud. After a time I came to the edge of one of the dust shoots which cover many of these lower Thames marshes, and knew I would see nothing more until I came to the other side of the tip. By that time, however, I would be well past the course of any Roman road which could lead to a crossing to Higham, the place always mentioned as the Kentish terminus of the ferry from East Tilbury.

I continued along the house-high plateau formed here by the contents of London's dustbins until I was met by a man on duty at Surridge's Wharf, where lighters with refuse from London are or were emptied. He commented that I chose a curious route for my Easter walking. I told him that I was looking for a Roman road.

"Where would it have run?" he asked.

"Down towards the river," I replied.

"It's funny you should say that," he said. "Twenty years ago three of us built this river wall. We had twenty lighters filled with rubble, and we sank them in line here, along the river edge of the marsh, to make a wall for the tip. One day when I was going over the ground I came across a road of stone going down into the river. I was so surprised that I pointed it out to the chaps with me. This is the first time since then that anyone has mentioned it to me."

My informant, Mr Arthur Young, told me that the road was paved with rough stone such as was used on river walls, and was nine or ten feet wide. I thought at once of the Broomway, the road of much the same width made of Kentish rag which goes down into the sea at Great Wakering Stairs north of Shoeburyness, and after running parallel with the coast below high water mark returns to Foulness. I have no doubt the Broomway is Roman. Unfortunately there is not, in the case of Arthur Young's road — as there is in the case of the Broomway — documentary evidence of its existence as a metalled causeway in the fifteenth century.

Arthur Young's road is about three-quarters of a mile west of Coalhouse Point and completely covered by the tip and river mud. Elated by my discovery, I went to some trouble to try to dig down to it through the mud, but without success, and the road is still there waiting for its exact line to be discovered. Arthur Young told me that along this particular stretch there were only two hards — where the road was, and at Coalhouse Point. The note I took of our conversation at the time states that he recognised the causeway for what it was while making up the river wall, and pointed it out to the chaps working with him as a road "going down into the river". He added that the road was at the only point where one could walk well out, and that it might be more easily identified at the edge of the main channel, where the mud would be scoured away by the flow of river and tide. Mr Young was not certain whether his road was a continuation of any of the tracks which crossed the marsh at this point before the area was used for tipping. I went to the northern edge of the tip where these tracks came out from under the refuse, but found nothing which seemed likely to be the road's northern extension. I also followed the former parish boundary between East and West Tilbury which continues in alignment across the highland, but found no sign of metalling on the surface of the soil.

On the Kent side of the river I searched for an equivalent road above low water mark, as well as on marshes and highland, but without success. At this point the Kent bank is an area of mild erosion corresponding to the area of accretion on the Essex bank, and little foreshore is exposed at low tide. There is also a stout river wall of Kentish rag which is set farther out in the river than that on the north bank, so that at low tide less of the foreshore stands revealed than on the Essex bank. Whether for these reasons, or because there was no crossing here in Roman times, I have never seen, from the bank, any suggestion of tile, pottery, masonry or the other remains one associates with a Roman site, although I have walked along this stretch of river for years at all states of the tide.

The difficulty in identifying any comparable road on the south side might suggest that what Mr Young saw was not a road, but the top of a stone jetty for loading and unloading. Until recent years there was such a jetty going down into the river at the World's End inn by Tilbury Fort which was used for embarking and disembarking sheep fattened on the marshes for the London trade. Had it been decided to build a similar jetty in the East Tilbury area it would have been built on a hard, as would a Roman road leading to a ferry. So short are memories that a jetty might have been made here a century or more ago for loading sheep, and then fallen into disuse, become silted over, and forgotten after a period of agricultural depression which made fattening here uneconomical. But Mr Young saw it, said it was a road, not a jetty, and was made of stone.

I turn now to literary evidence. The case for a ferry (as opposed to a ford) at East Tilbury in Roman times depends almost entirely on references by Salmon and Hasted to Higham Causeway, the road which is said to have led to the ferry on the Kent side. Salmon's *History and Antiquities of Essex* — according to Gough, Salmon's "last shift to live" — was published, unfinished, in 1740. Salmon's reference in it to the causeway appears in the section dealing with East Tilbury and is at least thirty-eight years earlier than that of Hasted in his *History of Kent*.

Salmon first refers to "the ancient ferry over the Thames" at East Tilbury, then adds, "The famous Higham Causeway from Rochester by Higham, yet visible, points to the place of the old ferry".

Hasted picks up Salmon's reference, and relies also on the evidence of two Kentish antiquaries, Dr John Thorpe (1682-1750) and Robert Plot (1640-1696), that the crossing was from East Tilbury to Higham.

It may be that Thorpe refers to Higham Causeway in his *Registrum Roffense*, which deals with the history of the diocese and cathedral of Rochester; but a good deal of the book is in Latin, and I have not read it. There may also be a reference to the causeway in the records he left to the Society of Antiquaries, which I have not studied either.

Plot, in addition to his books on Oxfordshire and Staffordshire, "made a discourse" on Roman ways in Kent in 1690, and part of his collection came into the hands of "the late Mr Thorpe" of Bexley. If this Mr Thorpe had any connection with that earlier mentioned, it may be that Plot's discourse also found its way to the Society of Antiquaries. Subject to these comments, references by Thorpe and Plot to Higham Causeway have not to my knowledge been published.

I give Hasted's reference in full. "At the east end of the parish, in the road from Frindsbury to Cliff, is the estate of Mockbeggar, and on the summit of the hill southward, the mansion of Hermitage, below which, in the flat country, at an equal distance from the church, is the manor and hamlet of Higham-ridgeway, a name plainly derived from the ancient causeway through it, leading towards the river. Plautius, the Roman general, under the emperor Claudius in the year of Christ, 43, is said to have passed the river Thames from Essex into Kent [*sic*], near the mouth of it, with his army, in pursuit of the flying Britons, who being acquainted with the firm and fordable places of the river, passed it easily. This passage is considered to have been from East Tilbury, in Essex, across the river to Higham. Between these places there was a ferry on the river for many years after, the method of intercourse between the two counties of Kent and Essex for all these parts, and it continued so till the dissolution of the abbey there; before which time, Higham was likewise the place for shipping and unshipping corn and goods in great quantities from this part of the country to and from

London and elsewhere. The probability of this having been a frequented ford or passage in the time of the Romans, is strengthened by the visible remains of the raised causeway, or road, nearly thirty feet wide, leading from the Thames side through the marshes by Higham, southward to this ridgeway before-mentioned, and thence across the London high road on Gads-hill to Shorne ridgeway, about half a mile beyond which it joins the Roman Watling Street road, near the entrance into Cobham Park."

Let us for the moment ignore Hasted's reference to Higham Causeway and consider his suggestion that there was a ford or ferry at Higham in Roman times. If there had in fact been a Roman crossing here it would have been for the convenience of those travelling between, on the one side, the Channel ports and the highly developed area of Kent in and east of the Medway valley and, on the other side, central and eastern England. If the crossing were an established feature, then a Roman road would lead to it, a road which in the other direction would lead to the Roman bridge at Rochester, either directly, or by way of Watling Street to the south.

If we are to find such a road we must seek it first in a direct line between Higham Bight and Rochester, or failing that between Higham Bight and Watling Street. But we must not be satisfied that we have found this road unless it has all the characteristics, including ruthless directness, of a Roman road — it should drive as directly towards the Thames as Peddars Way drives towards the ferry station now lost on the north-east shore of the Wash. There is no such road on the highland here, where straightness would be most in evidence; nor is there such a road crossing the marsh, unless it is buried under the silt which covers the whole of the Roman horizon.

Hasted does, however, refer to a highland road called Higham Ridgeway which runs across the hard ground from the south end of Higham Causeway to Gads Hill; and we must now consider this road with his comments in mind. I have the feeling that the Ridgeway is a pre-Roman track, a feeling which is strengthened by the fact that there is a mark stone on the corner at Gads Hill. It is true that the name Ridgeway is sometimes applied to a Roman road, and that this road has an overall continuity of direction; but Roman roads are straighter than this. Neither I, nor as far as I know anyone else, has ever found any physical evidence of it being Roman.

We must now turn to Hasted's reference to Higham Causeway, the marshland course of the road which connects with Higham Ridgeway. What is important here is that Hasted claims that it was in existence and could be seen in his day; if it could be seen then, some vestige at least should be visible today. But he does not give the slightest effective indication of where the causeway ran, which makes one wonder whether he ever saw it — whether, indeed, he might not be in error over its very existence.

There are three tracks or footpaths which cross the marshes near Higham today: that which runs from Higham church to the head of Higham Creek, and in its northern stretches runs along the top of a floodbank; the causeway which runs west of Barrow Hill; and the floodbank which leaves the Beckley Hill track to the west of where it turns into the Barrow Hill track and thereafter runs north-west and ultimately west to the main Thames floodbank.

It is generally assumed locally that the Higham Causeway to which Hasted refers is the second of these, the now gravelled track which runs just to the west of Barrow Hill today. (Barrow Hill is neither a burial barrow nor a ship burial, but a naturally weathered mass of Thanet sand pushing up through the silt.) A former vicar of Higham told me that there was a local tradition about the causeway, but no one knew for certain where it ran, and all the literary references were copied from Hasted. He also thought it probably ran by Barrow Hill.

We must now consider the evidence of maps. The map published in Hasted marks as a road the path which today continues the road from Higham Upshire past the church and across the railway line, although Hasted does not take it as far as Cliffe Creek, and after a time makes it shoot off to the east. I have followed this path, and seen no evidence of road or raised causeway. Hasted's map also marks a road or floodbank which leaves the Beckley Hill track (now, in part, the road from the Uralite factory) somewhere near where it runs under the railway line today, and after running between north and north-east strikes the Thames floodbank near the head of Cliffe Creek. No other roads are marked north of Higham, and neither of the two which are marked is identified as Higham Causeway.

The first edition of the one inch Ordnance Survey map for Kent is no more help than Hasted's map in identifying Higham Causeway. Like Hasted's map it does not mark the Barrow Hill causeway, nor does it mark the path which leads from Higham church to the head of Higham Creek. It does, however, show the third and most westerly track, which ultimately runs north-west to the main floodbank of the Thames, but describes it as an Old Wall (that is an old floodbank) although it has also been used as a footpath or track.

Spurrell, in the map which accompanies his article in the 1885 *Archaeological Journal*, does show the three ways which cross the marsh today. That to the west, the floodbank which leaves the Beckley Hill track and runs north-west and ultimately west, he marks but does not name; that which begins in the driftway south of Higham church, and becomes the causeway west of Barrow Hill, he calls Ferry Road throughout; the eastern way, which continues the road east of Higham church to the north, and by later branching towards the north-west leads to the head of Higham Creek, he calls Public Way as far as the branching; thereafter he calls it Causeway to Ferry.

What is interesting is that Spurrell's map takes the Barrow Hill track — which he calls Ferry Road — right over today's tidal wall to the site of the blockhouse built in 1539 by Henry VIII on the edge of what used to be Higham Saltings, at a point where Tudor bricks and roof tiles can still be seen today. Higham Saltings have been almost entirely eroded by the tides in recent years, but when Spurrell drew his map they stretched from today's tidal wall almost to the edge of the fairway.

I shall restrict further comments on the possible course of Higham Causeway to the Barrow Hill causeway; for although Spurrell, in the text accompanying his map, gives an incorrect reference which would identify as Higham Causeway the unnamed floodbank which leaves the Beckley Hill track and runs north-west, careful reading of the text shows that he is in fact referring to the Barrow Hill causeway. I have no doubt that this is in fact Higham Causeway.

I am confirmed in this belief by Roach Smith's comments in volume 13 of *Archaeologia Cantiana* where, in describing the course of Higham Causeway, he writes, "If, instead of passing Higham church, towards the marshes, the road on the left be taken, and followed in front of the houses and past them, the causeway will be found at a short distance. The last of these houses, the Sun beershop, bears also the significant name of Old Ferry House."

Spurrell says that the causeway loses itself abruptly on reaching the present river wall, but lies beneath the saltings about a foot deep. He adds (writing in or shortly before 1885) that its course could be traced for some distance out in the saltings by the ditches, the gravel washed off it, and the plants growing on its surface, which differed from those on either side.

Gravel can still be seen today on the east side of a short creek leading to the site of the fort. It is on the river side of today's tidal wall, and runs across tide-washed mud; but it is in line with Higham Causeway, and clearly marks a continuation, or perhaps an integral part, of it. This gravel is presumably the remains of the metalling Spurrell saw in 1885, but when it was laid is anyone's guess; and whether this last section of the causeway was made in the sixteenth century to lead to the fort, or the fort was built at the end of an already existing metalled road, cannot now be decided.

The course of Higham Causeway across the marshes is not straight. I assume it to have been decided by the (as I suppose) partly natural watercourse on the western side, which is referred to as a boundary in an eighth-century Saxon land charter in the words *marc fleot* — although this again does not necessarily mean the road is that old. There is certainly no sign of a ditch on the east side of the road, as there might be were the road Roman.

The fact that the gravel metalling on the causeway is clearly an extension of that used on the road leading from the Uralite factory does not mean the causeway was in earlier centuries an extension of this road: it was, as Roach Smith implies, an extension of the driftway from Higham, which in its northward course passes under the disused railway line to join the causeway at the point where it turns through an angle at the gate. The present metalling was put there by the river board after the 1953 floods, and I suspect that it may have been added to metalling laid during the latter part of the war for the invasion of France. I do not think it can have been obviously metalled before the war, because it is not marked even as a track on my 2½-inch map of the area which was compiled from six inch sheets last fully revised between 1906 and 1931, and with other partial systematic revision in 1938 and one-inch road revision of 1946 incorporated.

I have pointed out that the course of Higham Causeway is not straight. This fact does not necessarily deny it Roman origins, for Roman roads crossing alluvial soil often weaved, as the Roman Fen Causeway does. But whether it is Roman or not, its extension south of the gate already referred to seems unlikely to be Roman because it goes through two abrupt changes of direction, the first on entering the drift way, the second when the drift way connects with the road which leads south from Higham.

It is now necessary to deal with the suggestion by nineteenth century antiquarians that there was a crossing farther west, at West Tilbury, at a point where Roman remains have been found at the end of what has been seen as a Roman causeway. (This causeway is farther west than that seen by Arthur Young.) Palin stated that a raised causeway thirty feet in width (now under refuse tips) led to that point on the bank where the remains were found, and said this causeway was the extension of the Low Street Manor Way. This is the track which today runs south from Low Street, and can be seen clearly from the train just south of the highland edge. Palin also quotes a suggestion by Lloyd Williams that there was a Roman ferry from a point in West Tilbury close to the boundary between the two parishes of East and West Tilbury. Williams came to this conclusion because of the quantity of pottery, brick and stones tooled for paving or building on the shore at this point, and commented, "The foreshore also, at this point, is much harder than elsewhere along the river's edge, and an old roadway (at present used only for farming purposes) leads from here in almost a straight line to the group of houses known as Low Street, whence it continues as a bye-road in the direction of Horndon-on-the-Hill." Williams seems to imply that this road was Roman.

It might be thought surprising, if there was a ferry between Higham Causeway and the Essex bank in Roman times, that no evidence has come down to us of settlement on each side. But any Roman ferry would have connected the two edges of what is today's central river channel. The ferry stations, and settlements near them, would have been at or near these edges, and so would have been washed away centuries ago by rising flood levels and fiercer tidal incursions in the same way that Henry's blockhouses at Higham and East Tilbury have been washed away. Lesser developments away from the edge of the Roman river — or what remains of them — would also now be buried under feet of silt.

CHAPTER 9

British and Roman roads

O.G.S. Crawford, writing in *Archaeology in the Field*, says that most attempts to reconstruct in detail the network of minor pre-Roman tracks are foredoomed to failure "nor can one do much more than guess the main thoroughfares that we assume to have existed before the Romans came". This is largely because of the difference between British roads — which developed from individual men and animals making their way across country as best they might — and Roman roads, which were planned, built, and maintained. As Crawford so clearly points out, natural tracks were first formed by animals. They were then followed and varied by humans, who chose a route combining direction with the avoiding of natural obstacles. The best route between two places, Crawford explains, was not discovered at once. It was the result of a long process of trial and error, during which difficult passages were gradually eliminated, and short cuts discovered. A natural track was therefore a product of evolution, of accumulated acts of artificial selection, chiefly performed by human beings, but to which animals made many contributions.

Natural tracks were much wider than made roads because when travelling over open country a group of people tended to spread themselves out — as, of course, cattle did and still do. Individual travellers, carts and herds also moved farther and farther out to avoid bad going where the track was rutted and muddy after wet weather. For these reasons, and in order to avoid wet or flooded bottoms, they kept mostly to higher and more open ground, on which most pre-Roman settlements in any case are found. As a result their movement formed ridgeways such as are found in the Cotswolds, and along chalk ridges throughout the south and east of England.

As far as I know it has never been suggested, except as later quoted, that metalling was ever used on pre-Roman tracks, although a correspondent quoted by Alfred Watkins in his much-abused book *The Old Straight Track* asked a series of questions which have also occurred to me. "If the roads in pre-Roman times were negligible, of what use were the horses and chariots which bulk so largely in Celtic poetry and in Roman and other descriptions?" he asked. "It is manifestly absurd to deny the capacity of making roads to the people who carted the enormous masses of stone to erect at Stonehenge and elsewhere from far away sources, carried their tin from Cornwall to the Isle of Wight, prepared those dewponds which still serve upon a thousand hills, and raised up earthworks which must have required labourers by the thousand and garrisons as great." He may have been mistaken in some of his examples, but the general question is one worth asking.

I would not suggest the British — I use the word, here and elsewhere, to describe the inhabitants of this country before the Romans came — metalled their roads as a regular practice, but I would have thought it necessary to metal fords or places where their tracks could not avoid a boggy crossing. I suspect that someone, somewhere, has dealt with this matter of pre-Roman road metalling apart from Watkins, and if so then this book is the poorer for my not knowing of it. I can only say that a number of causeways were built during the Bronze Age across the fen to the hard ground which formed the island on which Ely cathedral now stands. This was a more difficult construction job, and one carried out at an earlier period of history than that in which roads leading (say) to Colchester might be required to be metalled before the Roman Occupation. It is also true that the Romans, on whom we rely for our knowledge of the British, would never let it be said that their roads were any good, any more than the Normans would have praised Saxon building. Although professional archaeologists do not allow for the existence of metalling anywhere except round the gates of hill forts, I would be surprised if those who produced the gold coins of Cymbeline did not at some points metal their roads. How else could they have dealt with mud? (A note inserted in proof. The *Daily Telegraph* reported in October 1979 that a metalled road with several layers of flint cobbling, which dated back to the fifth century B.C., had been found inside the Iron Age hill fort at Danebury in Hampshire.)

I have referred to Watkins as the author of a much abused book. It is true that his main thesis, that pre-Roman Britain was covered with a series of straight tracks which he calls leys, is untenable. But this makes no difference to the evidence he produces of things he has seen. He was an unreliable interpreter, but he seems to have been an accurate observer. Thus he observes, correctly, how surface boulders were moved from their original positions in prehistoric times to mark tracks, crossroads and fords, as well as the centres of settlements and meeting places; and since this observation has some connection with pre-Roman roads, I shall make a slight diversion to say something about it here.

Watkins calls these boulders mark stones, and among many which he mentions is the Tibble Stone where six roads meet at Teddington Cross near Tewkesbury. He also mentions, and illustrates, mark stones by the English Bridge at Shrewsbury, and in Wye Street, Hereford.

When I was a child there was a mark stone of mountain limestone, glassy with age and the affectionate attention of children, where the path to Crag Bank left the Lancaster road in Carnforth. It is there no longer. Similar mark stones, there called waystones, are said in *Lancashire Lore* published by the Lancashire Federation of Women's Institutes to mark a prehistoric trail across the Furness district north of Morecambe Bay.

In Essex there are boulders at the crossroads in the centre of Brent Pelham, two in a field below the vicarage at East Tilbury, and one by the vicarage itself. These last probably mark the prehistoric track which followed the crest of the bluff down to the river here. In some cases mark stones are also found at fords, as at Linton in Cambridgeshire, just over the Essex border.

Among boulders which mark tracks or crossroads north of Watling Street in Kent are those at the corner of Forge Lane and the Gravesend-Rochester road opposite Gads Hill; on the north side of the Higham Upshire to Higham Hill road where the track goes down to Allotment Gardens past the first row of houses out of Higham; and on the top of the hill which leads from Gads Hill to Higham, where the path leads off into the woods by the gate on the east side of the road.

To return to the matter of pre-Roman roads. We know that many old tracks were straightened and metalled by the Roman engineers, and I cannot help thinking that they may also have relied on them in places for a rough foundation as well as general direction. We also know that when these natural tracks were taken over, a great width of way was no longer needed. The space which remained each side of the metalled road was therefore retained within hedges, and used as a grass verge. In later centuries squatters built wayside huts and cottages on these verges. Roman roads not based on British roads were also given wide verges to reduce the possibility of surprise attack from wood or undergrowth. As a result of these arrangements, many Roman roads still have wide verges today in spite of land grabbing and later power farming.

A natural track with wide verges is not, however, necessarily British, for with few exceptions all newly created medieval roads were natural and wide ranging. For this reason many roads thought to be British are in fact medieval market tracks. Thus where one gets a series of narrow and more or less parallel paths crossing open chalk on a wide front, the chances are that they were made in medieval or even later times by cattle being moved to market on the hoof. This is true also of the courses of known British roads, for example that of the Icknield Way over Royston Downs. Although this way is known to be British, the narrow parallel paths which mark its course were probably made by cattle being driven in to London at the time that granite cattle troughs were being put up in the streets to slake their thirst.

These things mean that while British tracks, where they still remain in their original state, are wide, wandering, and unmetalled, this alone is not enough to identify them. Nor can excavation help to prove or disprove their origins, simply because it cannot produce, or as far as I know has not so far produced, pre-Roman road metalling. On the other hand there are certain pointers which may be of value, as for example the track's destination, the way it chooses to get there, and its possible relationship to known pre-Roman and even Roman sites. In addition, pre-Roman tracks have two characteristics, one little shared by medieval tracks, one which is unique.

The characteristic of pre-Roman tracks seldom shared by others is that they made their way along the main watersheds. In this way, by making detours to avoid springs and the waterlogged ground in the upper reaches of rivers, as well as the rivers themselves, they were able to cover much of the country with the minimum of river crossings. The second characteristic, which is shared by no other ways, is that many pre-Roman tracks, in particular those from Avebury to the Channel, Avebury to the Wash, and along the Cotswolds, have contour forts spaced out along their courses from ten to twelve miles apart. In places they also have burial barrows just below or beside the crest of the ridge which can be seen in profile against the skyline by those walking slightly lower down the slope. One place where barrows can be seen in this way is on the Icknield Way where it crosses Therfield Heath just west of Royston.

As far as official sources are concerned we start with a clean sheet. The Ordnance Survey map of Iron Age Britain shows camps on both sides of the Thames, but no tracks between the Icknield Way to the north and the North Downs trackway to the south, both of which are outside our area.

I have, however, already drawn attention to the Hangmans Wood track which led to a crossing at East Tilbury at a time when the river was fordable. It is the only trackway in our area of Essex and Kent which I would describe without hesitation as pre-Roman. I suggest it was still in use in 4000 B.C., when the Channel bridge to the Continent was still in existence, and when according to borings earlier described the land at Chatham was thirty-six feet higher than it is now. I also suggest the Thames was still fordable at this point during the period of sea sinking which took place after 2800 B.C. If I am right in this speculation, then the track is certainly Neolithic. I have found a number of Mesolithic and Neolithic flint tools along its course between Chadwell and East Tilbury; and Kenneth J. Barton points out in the autumn 1958 volume of the Thurrock Historical Society Journal that of Neolithic finds in the Purfleet, East Tilbury, Grays and Stifford area, several come from near the Mardyke bridge at Stifford. This is an obvious point for the track to have passed in its westward extension.

Glyn H. Morgan, in his *Forgotten Thameside*, describes a feature on this track near East Tilbury known as the Soldiers' Graves. While I think it has no connection with the trackway I shall deal with it here. Morgan says the Soldiers' Graves are a natural scarp which runs roughly parallel with the river for about half a mile west of the church and has been accentuated by human agency and heightened by the digging of a ditch along its base. Volume 4 of the report of the Royal Commission on Historical Monuments for Essex says the Soldiers' Graves are an abrupt and partly artificial scarp with a ditch and external rampart at the foot, but were probably not a defensive work.

I was told by the Vicar of East Tilbury in 1973 that the Soldiers' Graves were at the bottom of the vicarage garden and almost impossible to see. I examined the gravel terrace west of the vicarage and could find no evidence of it being artificially added to, although at the time the area was covered with undergrowth. Nor could I recognise a continuous excavation at the foot of the bluff. What I did see, however, were three places where pits had been dug in line at the base of the terrace, each having the floor area of a good sized house. Whether or not these are the Soldiers' Graves — and they look more like graves than the other features described — it may be possible to learn more of their function by taking account of the geology of the area. The bluff which runs along the northern edge of the marshes here is formed by the forty-five foot gravel terrace, and between this terrace and the silt which runs parallel with it from east of Bowaters Farm to near the vicarage at East Tilbury there is a narrow strip of chalk. The Soldiers' Graves (if they are the Soldiers' Graves) are limited to this chalk strip. My own guess is that they were dug by soldiers to get chalk to make the foundations, in waterlogged silt, of the blockhouse built by Henry VIII at East Tilbury. I am confirmed in this speculation by the fact that 200 tons of chalk were used in another of Henry's blockhouses, that on the site of what is now Tilbury Fort.

I think it is possible that the Hangmans Wood track was taken over by the Romans and metalled for part of its course. Where it crosses Terrels Heath west of Chadwell, now a recreation ground, its line is followed by a fairly high bank and, towards the south end of the heath, by a clear stretch of gravel where the grass is stunted.

The banks still in evidence in Terrels Heath Wood suggest that the road was originally up to thirty feet wide. Dr Derham, an Upminster man, referred to it in 1706 as a highway leading from Stifford to Chadwell and then a road of some importance. Salmon, in giving measurements he had taken of the depth of deneholes in Hangmans Wood, also said they lay "near the highway leading from Stifford to Chadwell". It is clearly shown as a road in the first edition of the Ordnance Survey map.

If the Hangmans Wood track was in use in the Iron Age it might, in its westward extension, have passed by the Iron Age camp at Uphall, Barking. This camp extended over fifteen acres. Its site can be seen from the train as it crosses the river Roding between West Ham and Barking stations. The site, north of the railway line and east of the Roding, has for some time been the property of a chemical company, and I understand that no sign of the earthworks now remains.

There are Iron Age sites at Mucking and at The Park on Langdon Hills and, I believe, at East Tilbury. Farther north and east there were Iron Age camps, or hill forts as archaeologists call them, between three and fifteen acres in size at Witham; at Danbury, half way between Chelmsford and Maldon; and south-east of Fossetts Farm just north of Southend. This last is marked on the Ordnance Survey map of Iron Age Britain as Grove Field Camp, but the name Grove

Field does not appear on my 2½-inch map of the district. The map of Iron Age Britain also marks a camp of under three acres in extent at Asheldham half way between the Crouch and Blackwater estuaries.

As far as pre-Roman tracks in Kent north of Watling Street are concerned, Crawford suggested that there must be Bronze Age tracks in north Kent leading to points on the estuary where many hoards of late Bronze Age work have been found. He suggested they led from the British road from Salisbury Plain to Canterbury, which in its passage across Kent follows the southern escarpment of the North Downs. I believe that in pre-Roman times this track was called Sarn Gwyddelin or, if my Welsh does not fail me, the Irishmen's Causeway. It is now known, in part, as the Pilgrims Way. It runs south of Watling Street, and is therefore outside our area.

A second pre-Roman road ran along the north side of the North Downs on the general line of Watling Street. According to volume 1 of the Victoria County History this road was connected by a series of tracks with camps on, or near, the more southerly road.

Payne referred to two roads in north Kent which he thought were prehistoric. The first is a track which in his day ran, and may still run, from Thong to the river bank in Higham Marshes. He regarded it as prehistoric because it led from a pre-Roman, possibly Bronze Age, burial ground which is about 1,000 yards north-west of the summit of Shorne Hill in the acute angle formed by the footpath from Ifield Place and the Shorne parish boundary. Payne's account is confusing, because he says at one point that the track ran from Thong northwards to the marshes below Chalk, and at another from Thong to Higham Marshes. A course from Thong through Chalk to Higham would form two sides of a triangle, and take the course of the track well away from the burial ground. Payne also says the track is followed by a parish boundary — and the only boundary here goes nowhere near Chalk. For these reasons I think he must have meant to refer to the marshes below Chalk *church*, which is well east of the village. If so, then his track would have gone northwards from Thong to some point on the Shorne parish boundary, and then along that boundary to Shorne and Higham Marshes.

Payne says that although immediately north of Thong the track crossed ploughed fields its course could still be traced, and towards the Gravesend to Rochester road it could be seen more clearly in the form of a worn channel. He claimed that from the point where the track crossed the Gravesend to Rochester road its course could be traced across Higham Marshes to the Thames. I have not examined the course he describes, but it may well be one of the Bronze Age roads to which Crawford refers.

Payne believed another prehistoric track ran from Brewers Gates, Cobham Park, through Shorne village, east of the old windmill, and then past the Crown Inn to Green Farm and (Old) Kings Farm, and so to the main Gravesend to Rochester railway line and the Thames and Medway canal. It then followed what is now a raised causeway with a deep ditch on either side, which still skirts the marshes for nearly a mile to Higham church. Payne said this causeway was known as the Land Way, and was the old way from Higham to Shorne. It can be seen today in the gravelled track which leads from the Uralite works to the south end of Higham Causeway, then in an unmetalled stretch which bears right, passes under the now disused railway line to Allhallows, and by a drift way almost impassable in wet weather leads to the crossroads south of Higham church. Many years ago I formed the impression that there was some sort of an earthwork on the top of Shorne Hill; Payne also suggests that there may have been a camp at this point. If so, then it might have had some connection with this track.

I have no doubt that some of the borstals on the northern slopes of the North Downs are prehistoric. Borstals are sunk tracks formed by the movement of men and animals up and down the side of a chalk hill. Traffic kills the turf, and breaks down the crust of chalk underneath. Rain then comes and washes down the path so made, bearing away the powdered chalk as slurry. In time the path turns into a deep gully, broad at the surface and narrow at the bottom, in section like a letter V. When one of these gullies became too deep and narrow for comfort another would be started beside it, until in time there were a number radiating, like the sticks of a fan, from the upper point of entry. Hence the borstals of north Kent, which gave their name first to a village and then, because of what was then a prison nearby, to the system of corrective training introduced there.

* * *

Roman roads existed to connect military camps and stations, civil and military settlements, ports, fords, ferries and bridges. When they could do so the Roman engineers took their roads in a straight line from one objective to another. More commonly, because of intervening high ground or other conditions which made overall surveying difficult, they took their roads in a direct line, not from objective to objective, but from an objective to one or more intermediate sighting points, and from the last of these to the objective. This meant that while the overall direction of a road was fairly direct from objective to objective, there would be slight changes in alignment at sighting points. There is therefore a distinction to be made between changes in direction at an objective, which may be considerable, and changes in alignment at a sighting point, which will be slight. It should also be clear that changes in direction at an objective are related to the road's next objective, changes in alignment between objectives to the terrain over which it is necessary to pass to reach the next objective.

In the ordinary way sighting points, and therefore changes in alignment, were for obvious reasons on high ground, often on the side of a hill from which sightings could be taken in both directions, and often in unpopulated areas. It follows that roads which change alignment on low ground are not usually Roman.

I have made a distinction between changes of direction which relate to an objective, and changes in alignment which relate to the terrain over which the road passes to reach that objective. I also included fords, ferries and bridges under the heading of objectives. For the sake of accuracy I must now point out that while some river crossings are objectives — and any changes in direction which take place there are conditioned entirely by the position of the objective — some crossings were neither objectives nor sighting points, but simply obstacles to be overcome, and at such points changes in direction resulted from the terrain.

It is now necessary to consider two other important classes of obstacle: variations in gradient; and fen and marsh.

The question of whether Roman roads turn aside because of gradient is a difficult one. They do this much less than other roads, and for this reason there are cases where a Roman road can be recognised as such because it continues to climb an obstacle which British or medieval roads would avoid. There are, however, cases where the straight course of a Roman road does vary because of gradient. For this reason the tendency for a Roman road to continue in a straight line in spite of increased gradient is a relative and, as I have suggested, a

Plate 15. It was in open boats such as this that the Saxons came into the Thames estuary after the end of Roman rule in Britain. The vessel shown was preserved in waterlogged alluvial soil at Nydam, where it was discovered in 1863. It is now on show in the Schleswig-Holsteinisches Landesmuseum fur Vor- und Frügeschichte, by courtesy of whose director, Dr Karl W. Struve, this photograph is reproduced.

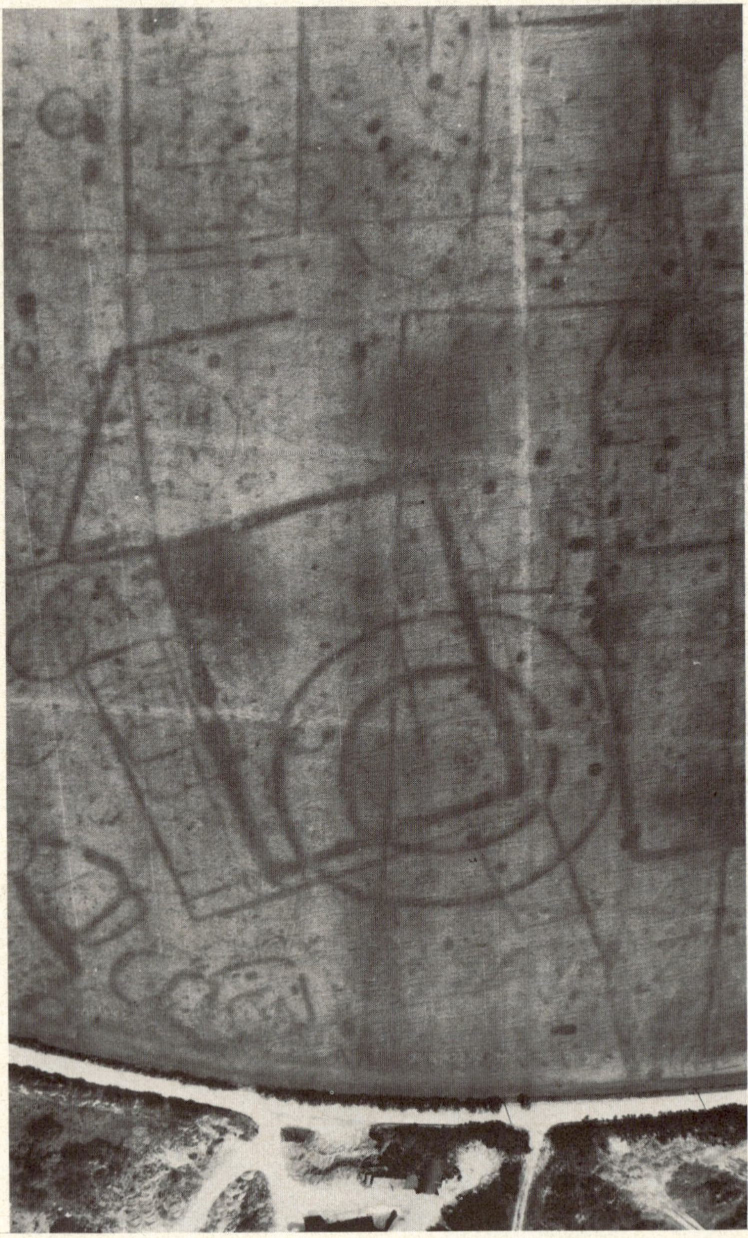

Cambridge University collection: copyright reserved

Plate 16. Crop marks in barley showing a double-ringed Iron Age enclosure, rectangular Romano-British enclosures, and Saxon hut sites at Mucking in Essex. A photograph taken from the air in June 1962 before excavation began.

W.T. Jones

Plate 17. This cast bronze belt set, inlaid with silver, was found on the Saxon site at Mucking in Essex. It was probably worn by a German mercenary in the Roman army. Note the swastikas.

Plate 18. Gravesend to the Medway from the air. For further details see list of plates

By courtesy of Fairey Surveys Limited and the Greater London Council

John Topham

Plate 19. The largest ship ever to come up the Thames. The *Mauretania*, 36,000 tons, in Long Reach in 1939 on her way to the King George V Dock in London.

By courtesy of P. & O. Steam Navigation Company

Plate 20. Tilbury in the days of its glory. The *Strathmore*, 28,400 tons, at the landing stage in September 1935, with the Tilbury Hotel in commission and three other liners and a sailing barge in the docks.

John Topham

Plate 21. Conrad lives. The Gravesend waterfront in days gone by. A collection of ships' figureheads can be seen to the right.

difficult matter.

There are at least two types of changes in gradient which may cause a Roman road to go out of alignment. The first is a single deep and narrow valley; the second is the series of valley heads which may be encountered if a road is taken in a straight line along a hill or mountain ridge. As for the first, where a sectionally aligned Roman road comes to a single valley, particularly among chalk downs, it may make a semi-circular detour to go round the head of the valley. I do not suggest that the road at Great Hermitage due east of Higham Upshire in Kent is necessarily Roman for this reason, but the road does in fact make such a detour between two straight sections to go round the head of a valley here.

Where a Roman road makes such a single detour the chances are that it was laid out from scratch, and owes nothing to an earlier British road. Where a Roman road varies its course to avoid dips caused by the heads of valleys along a ridge or watershed, then the chances are that it is following the course of an earlier British road or ridgeway. Here the question of whether a Roman road running along a ridge does or does not follow a British road is secondary; what is important is that such roads, while showing signs of Roman metalling and construction, do vary in alignment in order to keep to the ridge. High Street, the Roman road which runs along the top of the mountain chain bearing that name in the Lake District, and probably follows the general course of a British track, does not keep to strict alignment. Certain ridgeways in north Kent which are held by tradition to be Roman, and Higham Ridgeway in particular, also do not keep to strict alignment; but this does not automatically prove that they are not Roman.

It is now necessary to consider barriers caused by marsh or fen. While it is true, subject to what I have already said, that a Roman road passing over hard ground takes the shortest course either to its objective, or to the next of one or more points on the way to that objective, a road passing over an area which is part hard ground and part marsh or fen may not do this. Such a road will not necessarily take the shortest overall course; it will often take the shortest course over marsh or fen, even if this means taking a longer course over hard ground, and a longer overall course over both hard and soft ground.

Thus when the Romans took their roads across the southern peat Fens from the highland on one side to the highland on the other, and crossed islands of hard ground on the way, they did not always go in a straight line. In the case of the Fen Causeway, which connects the Northamptonshire highland with the Norfolk highland, they took the road from the containing highland to the nearest point on the nearest island, then across that island in a straight line to the farthest point on the other side; then across the next stretch of fen at its narrowest point; and so to the next island. They repeated this process from island to island until they reached the highland on the other side of the fen, even if this meant going out of their way to do so.

This means that while on ordinary mineral soil Roman roads usually took the shortest distance between two points, in the peat Fens they took the shortest route between two points on hard ground — which is not the same thing at all. The result was that a Roman road crossing highland, island, and fen soil had its overall fen distance reduced as much as possible, even if this meant increasing the distance it travelled over highland and island soil; even if it meant, as it did, that the overall distance from highland on the one side to highland on the other side — across highland, fen, island, and highland soil — was thereby increased. I am not suggesting that Roman roads in our chosen area necessarily change alignment because of the two types of physical obstacle I have described, although we shall see later that Watling Street does so immediately west of the Medway to reduce its passage over marshy ground.

Subject to everything I have said, it is still a fact that the straightness of Roman roads is their most outstanding feature. Even so, this should not allow us to assume that a modern road whose course continually diverges slightly from an overall straight course is not therefore Roman. Many Roman roads went out of use after the Romans went, and stayed out of use until the eighteenth and nineteenth centuries, when modern road construction began. If at the end of that period of disuse a road was laid along the course of the Roman road, then the modern road would today be as straight as that laid out by the Roman engineers. But where a Roman road has been in use ever since the Romans left, and travellers have over the centuries turned away at times from the rutted and miry central section to try and find easier going to either side, then today that road may diverge throughout its course from a straight central line. I do not say the road through East Tilbury is necessarily Roman for this reason, but it does show the characteristic I have described.

There were three main types of Roman road in Britain: military, civil, and agricultural. Military roads were made to help in the subjugation of the country. Peddars Way in Norfolk, laid after the revolt of the Iceni, is an obvious example. Civil roads were laid for trading purposes. While built in the same way as military roads, there was less rigid adherence to long straight alignments, and short lengths between a greater number of sighting points were used more often to fit irregularities in the ground. The roads which connected London with the iron mines of the Weald are examples. Agricultural roads planned by central authority were laid out in land settlement areas, which were usually set up for retired soldiers. They formed the boundaries of the regular gridiron series of fields which have already been described under the heading of centuriation.

The metalling of the average Roman road varied in width from fifteen to twenty-four feet, although in some cases it was only twelve feet wide. In other roads, and these the most important, it was up to thirty feet wide. One authority has given road widths as ten to twelve feet, fifteen to eighteen feet, and thirty feet. Another has stated that normal standard width was twenty-one feet between ditches.

Roads were usually built on raised embankments made by scooping out material from each side. On Stane Street, which ran from London to Chichester, and on more important roads generally, the ditches so formed were often eighty-three feet apart. This width is not necessarily related to the width of metalling, for at one point on the Roman road from London to Lewes where metalling was eighteen feet wide, the ditches were fifty-two feet apart.

Where local stone was obtainable the Romans took their metal from a large number of pits beside the road. But they were prepared to bring metal from some distance if none was obtainable locally. The Fen Causeway at Eldernell had foundations of limestone brought eight miles from Peterborough, and possibly farther. Hoggin — gravel containing clay — was widely used, and even brick dust and oyster shells, brick dust from ground Roman tiles, and oyster shells from one of the Romans' favourite foods.

Details of the construction of the roads hardly concern us. They were soundly built, although in general side roads were not made so well as main roads, so that their metalling was soon destroyed and their courses lost. Where roads crossed fen or marsh they were built very soundly indeed. Watling Street had the following layers under its six to eight inches-deep paved surface where it crossed low lying ground west of the Medway at Rochester: first nine inches of small pebble gravel mixed with "black earth", presumably alluvium containing peat, which was rammed. Beneath this were seven inches of finely broken flints on top of five inches of rammed chalk and, underneath this, yet another layer three feet six inches deep made up of whole large flints, rough pieces of Kentish rag, and fragments of Roman brick. This lowest layer of metalling was laid on marsh mud, which contained oak piles about four feet long with pieces of wood laid, or perhaps nailed, at intervals across them. The causeway was about fourteen feet wide; a six-feet square section of the pavement found under the post-Roman surface metalling when the road was dug through in 1897 was cut out, and can be seen today in the courtyard of Rochester Museum. (So George Payne. In fact this metalling is medieval, but it is still to be seen in the grounds of Eastgate House, the former museum.)

Roman camps and forts set up during or after the invasion — the first as temporary, the second as permanent, fortifications — were often sited on or near roads at irregular intervals. These can usually be identified only by excavation, possibly following the examination of photographs taken from the air.

For the sake of completeness I should mention that water troughs were often sited by Roman roads. One in Grevatts Wood on Stane Street near Bignor in West Sussex measured twenty-four feet by twelve, and was built of flint, sandstone, and pieces of Roman brick. According to Palin, in his time the ancient well at the bottom of Chadwell Hill known as St Chad's Well, which has now disappeared, had "more the appearance of a tank, wide and shallow, large enough to walk into", so it is likely that it was Roman, and the road beside it. It is presumably the *cold well* which gave Chadwell its name.

I suspect that wells, as well as tanks, were sometimes set near Roman roads, although I know of no authority for this. Mr Cattermole of Cliffe believes that Lipwell Hill well, just north of the road from Cooling to High Halstow in Hoo, may be Roman. The way in which wells are set beside roads in the Cooling Street area of Hoo is certainly striking.

On the other side of the Thames the schoolhouse at East Tilbury, on the straight road from Linford, had a well inside the kitchen; there is another in a front garden on the other side of the road. Another well is marked north of Hob Hill. This is on the series of footpaths, tracks, roads, and field boundaries which form a straight line driving south from the point near Old House Wood north of Chadwell to the double ditched track which leads to the west end of the saltings just east of Tilbury Riverside station.

Perhaps I should conclude this review of features which may be found near a Roman road by recording that burials frequently took place by the side of roads, temples were usually close to them, and villas seldom far away.

It is now necessary to describe some of the characteristics of Roman roads as they exist today, for it is only by recognising these in the field that one can usually hope to identify roads which have been lost to history.

I have mentioned the continuation of Coldharbour Lane, Purley, as a hollow way. If metalling has been removed, as was the case here, a wide shallow hollow, ragged in outline, may mark the course of a Roman road, particularly on a slope where the action of water has deepened the course. Sometimes, when a hollow way has become waterlogged, a new road will have taken its place alongside. In other cases a straight length of stream bed may be a hollow way; but I know of no example of this, and imagine it to be rare.

Cottages have sometimes been built on the crown of Roman roads to take advantage of solid foundations; and such cottages, or their successors, remain today. Sometimes a line of cottages can be seen built on the embankment of a Roman road, with a modern road running to the side. Even more common as a sign of Roman origins is the enclosing of the wide verges of a Roman road. A series of long narrow plots, or possibly a cottage with a long garden, may have been carved out of space beside the road. Such robbing can cause the Roman road, or a modern metalled road on its course, to snake a little while maintaining overall alignment. Narrow enclosed plots alongside a road which run, not at right angles to the road, but as a long strip beside it, also suggest Roman origins.

In some cases parallel ditches or large scoops which have provided material for the embankment may still remain. I think one is not likely to encounter these in Essex, where so little physical evidence of Roman roads can be found. The course of a road may sometimes be shown by a band of flints running across a ploughed field, as on the east side of the London to Cambridge railway line immediately north of Great Chesterford station, on the east and west sides of the

Cambridge to Ely road near Denny Abbey, and on the course of the Fen Causeway east of Peterborough. Flints, where they appear in the bank of a hedge or in the sides of a ditch, may indicate the passage of a road. A grain crop is often sparse and stunted above the course of a road, and fruit trees above a Roman road may "do badly". In late autumn or summer after a dry season, grass above a road may be brown because of shallow rooting and lack of deep moisture, while stunted growth in a hedge may be caused by stony soil which retards growth at that point.

As a result of trying to trace Roman roads I have drawn up a series of what I regard as operating possibilities, and one or two certainties. The first certainty is that the Romans knew what they were doing. The second certainty is that Roman roads always go somewhere. They do not stop in mid-air; and if they are going to a certain place, they do not continue to point somewhere else after a change in alignment becomes unlikely. These two factors are so reliable that if a road behaves in a way inconsistent with them, then either it is not a Roman road, or the assumptions on which the search is based, and the interpretation of such evidence as has been obtained, must be in some way unsound.

I know of only one exception to the two principles I have outlined. Edmund Vale told me that one place where the Roman surveyors made a mistake was on Watling Street, of all roads, near Oakengates in Shropshire. He said that two gangs working towards each other, one from the west and one from the east, missed each other in the forest and ran parallel for some distance before the mistake was discovered. He describes the error in his book *See for yourself*, although for understandable reasons he refers to one of the gangs "coming up from the south" at a point where Watling Street runs due east and west. He adds that it is, or was then, bad and crooked going between the ends of the two roads. I am not familiar with the roads or with that section which connects them, but I have no doubt Vale knew what he was talking about. We have no such topographers nowadays.

There are other principles which while not always reliable, can be helpful. The first is that of all natural features which mark the course of a Roman road, a hedgerow is the commonest. The second is that if a Roman road turns through an angle of more than (say) ten degrees for no obvious reason, then it may be that another road leaves it at the point of deviation in a balancing direction. The third is that one Roman road does not generally join another Roman road at an angle of ninety degrees or near it without continuing on the other side, unless there is a settlement or military station at the point of junction. The fourth is that if a fairly straight road crosses right over a Roman road, then that straight road may be Roman also. The fifth is that where a modern road, track or footpath turns through a right angle to right or left and, shortly afterwards, through another right angle to left or right, then continues for some hundreds of yards parallel with the extension of its previous course, and finally goes through the same movement in reverse to continue in alignment with that previous course — then the two separate sections in alignment, particularly if they are connected by a hedgerow or footpath also in alignment, are probably Roman. The sixth is that where a fairly straight road runs into another road at right angles, turns either right or left to follow the second road for a short distance, and then turns through a compensating right angle to continue its passage in the same overall direction, then this road will be of more recent use or construction than that whose course it has temporarily followed. The seventh is that evidence of Roman roads given by amateur observers should always be taken seriously. The eighth is that road metalling known to be older than 1800 on a path or track, or a road no longer used by wheeled traffic, which might seem to connect with a known Roman road system, should always be considered with the possibility in mind that it also is Roman. This is because metalling installed before about 1800 was usually a good deal less uniform and consistent over a distance than it was in Roman times, and in and after the nineteenth century. This is particularly so where consistency of material and construction is maintained over stretches not now regarded as part of a continuous thoroughfare. (Thus the stretch of metalled path leading from Bowness to Ferry Nab on the east side of Windermere, where it crosses the stream shortly before it joins the road leading immediately to the ferry, is similar in material and construction to the metalled path on the other side of the lake between where it leaves the stile on the road below Cunsey, and the footbridge over the first beck. This is the sort of similarity, on what is now an entirely broken thoroughfare, which *might* make one wonder whether it was Roman.)

These principles are, I think, sound; but I should add that when the open fields with their individually held strips were enclosed, the roads which were then made tended in places to follow the medieval rights of way which divided one cultivated strip from another. They therefore take a completely straight course for about quarter of a mile and then turn through a right angle bend, follow this new course for perhaps a hundred yards, and then turn through a compensating right angle to resume their previous direction. What is missing here, however, and what is essential if Roman origins are to be considered, is a second double movement which restores, not only direction, but also alignment.

Most of the principles I have outlined can be tested in practice. The matter of reports by amateur investigators, particularly in earlier centuries, calls for further comment.

It is widely assumed that evidence offered by observers who lived before the age of archaeological enlightenment is unreliable, particularly if it conflicts with what is now regarded, in the light of present knowledge, as inherently probable. The assumption, as it stands, may be open to argument; what is not arguable is its frequent result, which is wholly bad — the failure to carry out fieldwork.

It is true that modern archaeologists know more about the Roman invasion and Occupation of Britain than antiquaries of a century or more ago. They know more about the economic and industrial state of the country, have a greater familiarity with the spirit, feelings, and details of the daily life of Roman and Briton as well as of Saxon, Dane and Norman. This information, not all of which was available to earlier observers, often allows present day students to pass judgment almost instinctively, and correctly, on historical and archaeological problems. It certainly makes it easier for them to assess what might be called inherent probability in the field of archaeology.

As far as Roman roads are concerned present knowledge is even more precise. We know more about their courses, and hundreds of miles unknown to our predecessors have now been traced and mapped with accuracy. We know more about the way they were built, the materials used in building them, and the sources from which those materials were obtained. We know a good deal more about the other characteristics of Roman roads, both when they were in use, and now that they are in advanced decay; and in this chapter I have already touched on a number of these. Perhaps most important of all, we are now able to use the evidence of place names, aerial photographs, and certain electrical and other techniques to good effect.

On the other hand the archaeology industry has now become a vested academic interest rather than the interest of the educated layman; and academic jealousy, which is to some degree inevitable whenever those in a circumscribed community are paid because of their knowledge, sometimes tends to minimise the importance of work done by those outside the union, either because they are amateurs, or because they are dead. It is likely that academic jealousy cannot prevent, for too long, the acceptance of the easily verifiable work of contemporary amateurs. On the other hand I think it can, and does, have an influence on the importance attached to earlier evidence. It can rate more highly recent literary evidence than the evidence of fieldwork, or of one's own eyesight. Worst of all, it can discount the evidence of those who have seen and described something which has now been destroyed, simply because those observers lived before archaeology became a science.

It is true that earlier observers did not always identify correctly what they saw. But the degree of their unreliability varied, and they were more likely to identify a Roman road correctly than, say, a burial chamber. Indeed, where Roman roads are concerned, there are reasons why we should take careful note of what earlier observers recorded, reasons which apply only to Roman roads, and to no other antiquities. The first is that it is only since about 1800 that roads have been properly metalled. This means that the older the evidence concerning the existence of road metalling, the more reliable it is as evidence of Roman origins. That is why descriptions of Roman roads provided by earlier antiquaries must be treated in quite a different way from descriptions of burial chambers or camp sites.

There is a second reason why we should take careful notice of what earlier antiquaries said concerning alluvial areas such as the Fens and the Thames estuary — that we do not always know how wet or dry these areas were in Roman times. Flooding in these flat lands near the sea has always depended on the relative levels of land and sea. We may believe that certain areas in the Thames estuary, now submerged at high tide, were dry land in Roman times; but we still do not know for certain how high and dry they were. Nor do we know, with certainty, to what extent low lying areas inland were subject to freshwater flooding, how high flooding was, or how long it persisted. Yet these factors bear immediately on the siting of Roman roads in the estuary; and it is our ignorance concerning them which may undermine all theories of inherent probability in the area — and, at the same time, increase the value of earlier eyewitness reports. Those witnesses were there. The chances are that they saw what they said they saw. Most important of all, if we take their evidence seriously and go and look, it is possible that we may still find enough evidence there to confirm their account. That is why I try not to allow my own theories about Roman roads to override the direct evidence of earlier researchers, even when their identification may be at fault, or related to theories now known to be false. In other words, responsible eye witness accounts of any period of history must not be rejected because they lived before the foundation of archaeology schools.

But even more important is it that one should go and look. It takes a lot of time and money. It is often inconvenient, and sometimes uncomfortable. In academic circles it is sometimes rated as secondary in importance to library facts and documentation. But in the case of Roman roads there is no substitute for it.

It is now necessary to consider other vaguer and more peripheral clues to the possible existence and courses of Roman roads. Two of these clues, the first general, the second specific, concern churches. The general principle is that nearly all Saxon monastic foundations were put on Roman roads. The specific clue is that if a Saxon or Norman church has Roman bricks in its fabric or scattered below the surface of the churchyard, then the church may have been put on or near the site of a Roman building, and therefore possibly near a Roman road. As we have already seen, a number of churches in Essex are thought to have been built on the site or immediately next to the site of a ruined Roman building, so that bricks and (possibly) masonry from the ruin could be used in building the church.

Place names can be helpful. When the Saxons came they tended to avoid Roman roads and Roman settlements, but they did recognise the difference between a road made simply by the movement of men or cattle, and one made artificially. Artificially made roads, which were of course Roman, they called by the word *straet* or *strate*; and where the word Street is now used as part of a place name it may be derived from the Saxon word, and there may therefore be a Roman road nearby. This is even more likely where the name Street appears, in open country, as part of the names High Street, Green Street, or Old Street. In areas settled by the Danes the word *gate* can also indicate a Roman road, the Fen Causeway where it passes through Peterborough being referred to as Fengate; but this hardly concerns us in Kent or Essex. The word *straet* can also form the first syllable in a place name. It appears in the names Streatham, Stretham, Stratton, Stretton (meaning in these cases the village on the *straet*), in the names Stratford, Stretford (meaning the ford on the *straet*) and in other names where Stret- is the first syllable. The prefix Stan- meaning stone, and referring to the stone metalling of a Roman road, appears in such words as Stanford and Stansted — and, of course, in Stane Street and Stone Street. These names also indicate Roman roads, or paved Roman fords.

Other names which refer to the raised embankments on which Roman roads were built include Ridgeway, The Ridge, The Causeway or Causey, Long Causeway, and Devil's Causeway. The endings -cester and -caster refer to a Roman military station, and it may be assumed that settlements so called are on Roman roads. The same remarks apply to Chester, Castor and Caister, alone or in formation. The possible significance of the name Coldharbour has already been observed.

Local government boundaries, particularly parish boundaries, are of value in tracing Roman roads. Those who marked out the first parish boundaries in Saxon times often took advantage of continuous features in the landscape such as streams or ditches. They also took advantage of artificial as well as natural features, and of these the most commonly exploited were the raised embankments of Roman roads.

This is why parish boundaries, or former parish boundaries, can help us in tracing Roman roads today. When the church adopted the line of a Roman road as a boundary, the road became an extension of the church itself, and so remained until such time as charters or maps could record it. It did not matter if the metalling was robbed, buried, or broken by frost and ploughing; it did not matter if it was lost in later road building, or if the raised embankment on which the metalling was laid was carted away. The line of the road had been recorded for ever.

So far so good. The real problem is whether a straight stretch of boundary seen on the map to follow a road, or the line of a possible road, is Saxon, medieval, or recent. Parish boundaries were first marked in England in the time of Theodore of Tarsus, a seventh-century Archbishop of Canterbury. If it could be assumed that all parish boundaries were laid out by him or his immediate successors, and have remained unchanged ever since, then parish boundaries would be proof in themselves of Roman origins, rather than pointers to where proof might be found in the field. The trouble is that we know very little about the origins of parish boundaries anywhere. Some, we know, have been altered in recent times, particularly in the Grays and Tilbury area of Essex; but concerning most of them we do not know how they were laid out, or how first recorded; nor have we usually any means of confirming whether or not they follow the same course as they did in Saxon times.

To some extent, of course, certainty is not essential. It is fieldwork, not boundaries, which proves a road to be Roman. But it may save a few wasted journeys if one can eliminate the boundaries known to be modern, and rely as far as possible on those which stand a good chance of being Saxon or Norman. This is best done by working, wherever possible, on older maps or, in the case of Essex and some other counties (but not Kent) on the map of parish boundaries published with the place-name book for the county.

When one is getting down to things as far as maps are concerned it should be remembered that the original manuscript plans from which the first edition of the Ordnance Survey map was engraved are still in existence, and that these mark the courses of Roman roads sometimes omitted from the engraved maps (and other forgotten features such as the Cromwellian fortification under Peterborough isolation hospital). Other helpful maps are the reprints of the first Ordnance Survey maps now being published by David and Charles of Newton Abbot, tithe maps at the Ministry of Agriculture, and enclosure award maps in County Council offices.

As we have seen, all parish boundaries have been changed or done away with in the Grays and Tilbury district of Essex in recent years, so that in this important area modern maps cannot be relied on. But if one can work with a map having what are regarded as the "original" parish boundaries, or can mark these on the modern 2½-inch map, then it is sometimes possible to pick up useful hints about the courses of Roman roads. In particular, where a straight stretch of boundary continues the line of a road thought to be Roman, or where two or more straight stretches of boundary are seen on the map to be in broken alignment, the fieldworker will then go and look for the physical evidence of a Roman road along the line of those boundaries. The fact that a straight modern road is followed by one or more parish boundaries also hints strongly that it is Roman, although here it will be more difficult to find physical evidence of Roman origins.

These remarks apply also to county boundaries, although any

Roman roads followed by straight stretches of county boundary are probably now known. Here again there may have been boundary changes in recent years, and it is better to work with older maps.

There is another pointer to Roman roads, and that is references to *straets* and *herestraets* in Saxon and medieval land charters. As we have already seen, the Saxons called metalled Roman roads *straets. Herestrete* (the spelling varies) or Hare Street in its modern form, was the same word *straet* with the prefix *here*, meaning army. A *herestrete* was therefore a Roman road used by the Saxons for the movement of armies — most important battles in Saxon times took place near Roman roads.

Saxon land charters sometimes refer to the course of a *straet* or *herestrete* in describing the boundaries of manors, estates, or parcels of land conveyed from one person of authority, often the king, to another, often the church. Sometimes the boundaries as set out in the charter coincide in part with parish boundaries, and this can help us to trace them and identify other features mentioned, such as streams or valleys — and *straets.*

A number of these land charters, supposedly Saxon, were forged in the twelfth century to justify claims to land in dispute between various landowners. Such disputes, and such forged charters, were common in the Fens, where undrained land subject to yearly flooding was not enclosed or cultivated. In these conditions boundaries were marked with difficulty, and rights to outlying property never decided save by years of occupation. Landowners in the Fens — and they were nearly all monasteries — therefore commissioned forged charters to justify tenancies brought into question, or to bolster claims to property in someone else's occupation. Many Kent and Essex land charters are also clearly forged, and in some cases the name of the forger is known. Centres of proved monastic fabrication are Westminster, Evesham, Winchester, Chertsey and Malmesbury.

Having said this, I must make equally clear that a reference to a Roman road in a forged land charter is even more reliable evidence of the existence, or possible existence, of that road than if it had appeared in a genuine Saxon charter centuries before. In forging a charter, while the central fact of rights to possession may be in question, the claim must be accurate where it concerns physical features within the knowledge of all concerned, or features which can be checked by reference to charters whose authenticity is not in question. For these reasons, and because the final test of the genuineness of a Roman road lies, not even in a genuine Saxon land charter, but on a number of other factors of which fieldwork is the most important, where later I make reference to the evidence of Saxon land charters, I generally ignore the question of whether these charters are genuine or not.

There are two main collections of Saxon land charters: the six volume *Codex Diplomaticus Aevi Saxonici* published between 1839 and 1848 by the English Historical Society and edited by J. M. Kemble; and that published between 1885 and 1899 by Whiting and Company Limited and edited by W. de Gray Birch in three volumes under the title *Cartularium Saxonicum*. Saxon and medieval land boundaries which may contain references to Roman roads are also to be found in the cartularies, or records, of the great monasteries such as Ramsey; and, unpublished, in manuscript form in various libraries. As far as Essex charters are concerned a useful publication is *The Early Charters of Essex: The Saxon Period* by Cyril Hart, which is published by the Leicester University Press, and contains a valuable list of general works on Saxon land charters.

In the two main collections of Kemble and Birch the charters are printed in Latin or Anglo-Saxon, and are untranslated. In some cases the whole charter is in Saxon, including the boundaries. Sometimes the main text is in Latin, with the boundaries in Saxon. This is commonest. Rarely, the whole charter and boundaries are in Latin. The cartularies of the monasteries are also published in Latin, and have not in general been translated. Since only a handful of the charters for Essex and Kent have been translated, either in (for example) *Archaeologia Cantiana*, the transactions of the Essex Archaeological Society, the Victoria County Histories, or such works as that of Dr Hart, those who propose to search through Anglo-Saxon land charters for pointers to Roman roads must be prepared to deal with Latin and Saxon texts as best they can.

I felt I should undertake this task in spite of having little Latin and no Anglo-Saxon, and for the sake of those inclined to take up the same burden I must therefore say what I have done, and what I have not done. Although historians seem to prefer to deal with Birch's collection of charters rather than with Kemble's, I chose to begin with Kemble because his collection was the earlier, and I intended to deal with Birch later; because Kemble had a larger collection; because I was not concerned then, and for reasons already given am not concerned now, with the fact that Kemble was less "reliable" than Birch, and therefore more likely to publish the spurious; and because Kemble had an index, and Birch had not.

But Kemble has great weaknesses. The convention of numbering charters in Latin numerals imposes a strain on the researcher. There is no indication of what areas the land charters cover. There is, at the end of the third volume, a series of boundaries taken from charters in that and the preceding two volumes, and bearing the same numbers as the charters to which they relate; but they are not listed at the beginning of the book with the other contents, so that the unwary, in finding no boundaries in one of the original charters, might overlook the possibility that those boundaries were in fact elsewhere in the six volumes. There is also a second series of boundaries at the end of the sixth volume some of which, although not all, are listed at the beginning of the same volume. These also cover charters appearing in the first three volumes. The greatest difficulty with Kemble, however, is his index, which is painful. Even so it is an index, and better than none.

Since there was no indication in Kemble of what areas the land charters covered it was a matter of going through the index and noting all those places which were south-east of the Colchester road and north of Watling Street. That, at least, was my first intention; but I soon found that Kemble had identified with certainty only a small proportion of the places mentioned, and that in many places he had guessed at what the modern form of the Saxon name might be. He also seemed to have drawn up the index without reference to map or gazetteer. I therefore had to list, from the index, all the places in Essex or Kent, with the numbers of the charters in which they appeared; and then ran through the charters looking for references to a *straet*, *herestrete* or *via publica*. I rejected charters without boundaries, or those with boundaries which did not as far as I could see relate to Roman roads.

I also rejected charters which referred to land outside the area described. This last, because of the failure of the index to list names in the form in which they appeared in the charters, or in alphabetical order, and in some cases with no attempt at identification, was the most tedious task of all. In the end I reduced to sixteen the number of charters in Essex and Kent which I thought might refer to Roman roads between the Colchester road and Watling Street; and these I deal with in later chapters. They do not include some charters which seem to refer only to the Colchester road, or Watling Street; nor do they include one or two charters which may refer to streets, probably Roman, within Rochester itself. I have not concerned myself with charters covering Thanet, and for reasons earlier outlined have dealt in less concentration with such charters as may cover the north Kent coast east of Sheppey.

I have explained in some detail the attempt I made, through Kemble and Birch, to obtain pointers to Roman roads. When I had completed this work I discovered by chance that I could have saved myself weeks of work had I been aware of P. H. Sawyer's outstanding work on Anglo-Saxon charters. It has an index which far outclasses Kemble's, and which for the first time brings some order and accuracy into the topographical details of Saxon land boundaries. The ultimate work of going through boundaries for *straets* and other Roman roads would still have had to be done; but had I been able to consult Sawyer before doing this I would have had to run through a couple of dozen charters instead of many hundreds. If any follow the course I have taken, here or elsewhere, let them for the sake of their sanity begin, and not end, with Sawyer.

* * *

Palin refers to certain "ancient" roads and tracks in the Thurrock area in his two books. Some of these roads and tracks were clearly used by pilgrims going from East Anglia and Essex to the Thames crossing at West Thurrock and, ultimately, Canterbury. Others are of unknown, and possibly even of recent, date.

Palin says that the Stifford district was "constantly traversed" by Canterbury pilgrims "their tracks being still traceable to some extent, all converging on West Thurrock, whose ferry, the key to the Kentish shore, received the great mass of pilgrims from the whole eastern counties". (The great majority of these pilgrims must have crossed the Mardyke at Stifford, where there were a track and a ford before any pilgrims went to Canterbury. This is proved by the appearance of the name Stifford, which means *path ford*, in 1086.)

Palin says there were two fords across the Mardyke. One was on the site of Causeway Bridge, the road bridge to the west of the village. It was presumably this western ford which gave Stifford its name, because according to Reaney the bridge which replaced it was already in existence by 1364; and this implies that there was then, and probably in earlier centuries also, enough traffic to justify building a bridge at this point. The name Causeway Bridge is also significant in that it might suggest the existence of a made road leading to it.

According to Palin the other ford was on the site of the footbridge half a mile to the east, and higher up the Mardyke. Palin had an idea that the western ford was that used by Canterbury pilgrims, that is for north-south movement, and the eastern ford for east-west movement. I do not know on what he bases his assumption. He also states that the pilgrim tracks in the Stifford area "will be shown on the road map, and described under the several parishes", but no road map appears in his two books, and as far as I can understand it he describes the course of only two pilgrim roads. The courses of these two pilgrim roads and of other "ancient" roads in the area are described in greater detail in Appendix II.

CHAPTER 10

Roman roads in Essex

The obvious lack of any physical evidence of Roman roads in Essex puzzled earlier antiquaries. Camden, speculating on the position of Durolitum (which was somewhere near Romford) commented "but 'tis beyond my abilities to determine the exact place: for (to speak once for all) the ancient places of this County are so strangely obscure and puzzling, that I, who in other parts have made some discoveries, must here freely own my self in the dark".

Salmon, in the first volume of *A New Survey of England* wrote "Of all the Counties in England, I don't know one in which our Antiquaries have taken more Pains to trace the Roman Ways than this; and no where more unsuccessfully". Smart Lethieullier, quoted by Morant, says, "Camden, and since him all Antiquaries acknowledge, that both the Roads and Stations throughout this county are more obliterated and difficult to settle than any other County in England".

It is not only Roman road metalling which is rare, but also embankments, hollow ways, widely spaced hedges, and all the other less easily defined physical signs of the passage of a Roman road. Miller Christy claimed that there was little or no sign that Roman roads in Essex were laid on an embankment as they were elsewhere. This may be open to doubt, because the same physical factors which led to the disappearance of Roman road metalling may also have led to the disappearance of embankments. Laver, for example, stated that embankments ran down and disappeared sooner in a clay district than in areas of gravel or even sand. Morant also reported that the embankment of the Colchester road could still be seen at Ingatestone in his day, while Christy pointed out that the Essex village of Ridgewell south-east of Haverhill was said to be named after the ridge or embankment of a Roman road. Christy also quoted a certain Thomas Walford, who said that in 1790 the ridge extended for thirty or forty rods northwards, and that in that year he saw a farmer carting it away for his own use. Doubtless other embankments elsewhere in the county were similarly treated.

In spite of the fact that physical evidence of Roman roads in the field is rare, I believe that Essex had one of the most concentrated Roman road systems of any area in Britain. I think this because of the way in which roads, footpaths, field boundaries and parish boundaries run time and time again for miles in straight lines on the 2½-inch map. An idea of how widespread these "lines" are may be obtained from the fact that one particular example, which runs from north of Langdon Hills to the river east of Stanford, is outstandingly clear on the 2½-inch map, but would not be noticed on the one-inch map. Lines, as I shall now call them, are therefore even more widespread in south-east Essex than the one-inch map suggests.

Many lines run north and south, a number of them showing up clearly in the area between Billericay and Stanford on the west, and West Hanningfield and Tarpots on the east. One runs past Ramsden Crays church, another near South Hanningfield, another through Rettendon. These lines sometimes have other straight roads, paths and boundaries at right angles; and because the squares and rectangles which result are measured in multiples of five actus, it is clear that the lines are in this case the boundaries, internal or external, of a Roman land settlement area. Most of these boundaries would be followed by roads, even if only farm roads. And while the rectangular pattern of roads, paths and boundaries is seen most clearly at Orsett and Asheldham, the whole area between Blackwater and Crouch, from Latchingdon in the west to Tillingham in the east, shows signs of rectangulation.

These lines and rectangular patterns suggest Roman planning; straightness and right angle bends are rare in ways and boundaries which develop naturally. One has only to compare the footpaths in this part of Essex with those in parts of the west of England to see the difference. A footpath through virgin country wanders according to the lie of the land, woodland, marshy areas, streams, fallen trees and other, pioneering, reasons now unknown to us. Only paths which are laid out, or follow the boundaries of cultivation areas which have been laid out, are so consistently straight. I suggest that these straight lines are evidence both of Roman field boundaries and of a Roman road system much wider than has yet been accepted.

Why the physical signs of the Roman road system have disappeared in the field is a more difficult matter to explain. Like Camden, if the comparison may be allowed, I also in other parts have made some discoveries; but in south-east Essex I have followed lines which I am convinced mark the paths of Roman roads without seeing any of the signs which in other areas would give evidence of their passage.

Earlier observers, seeking to explain why so little evidence of

Roman roads had been found in Essex, pointed out that any metalling found was usually at a considerable depth; but I am not certain that such findings as have been made are, to use a fashionable phrase, statistically significant. Of eight references in all which I have come across to Roman road metalling in Essex, in only two cases was there a reference to the depth at which the metalling was found — at four feet, and at four feet six inches, below the surface — and the first was so hard that it had to be broken up with pneumatic drills.

Those who reported these finds did not say whether they were in open country or in an area which had been occupied for some time: they did not say what was the soil in each area, and whether or not the sites were on low ground. In the absence of this information it is difficult to draw any conclusions from the discovery of Roman road metalling at two depths out of eight.

There is certainly a tendency for the London clay which covers a good deal of Essex to absorb material such as gravel placed on its surface. In a wet season, when clay becomes plastic, stones and other material which are heavier than the clay sink down through it, a process which one writer has referred to as "slumping". Even so, clay would not absorb road metalling unbroken: the discovery of metalling which required pneumatic drills to break it down, if in open country and not in a hollow, takes some explaining.

The most important constructional factor about Roman roads in Essex is that they passed over land virtually free of building stone. Flint is found in some parts where the chalk surfaces, but it is difficult to work, and far from abundant. Clunch, or deep mined chalk, is available in greater quantity, but cannot be used for exposed corners of buildings. In later centuries this dearth of good building stone led to many houses in Essex being built of wood or, in the Saffron Walden area of north-west Essex, of unfired mud bricks.

The Romans overcame the lack of building stone in Essex by making much use of bricks. The Saxons, ignorant of brick manufacture, later showed their hunger for building material at (for example) Alresford near Colchester by removing from the Roman villa there the bricks of the hypocaust and the walls down to the footings. Presumably they also took the bricks from the Roman posting stations, of which no physical signs have been identified with any certainty in Essex.

Stronger evidence of this hunger for building stone is the extent to which Roman bricks were used in Essex churches built in the first two centuries after the Norman Conquest. It is customary for most of these churches to contain whole courses and arches, even parts of walls, of re-laid Roman bricks. Further, it must be remembered that for every church built in Essex in these two centuries, probably one Saxon church had been pulled down. This means that if Roman bricks were used so widely in Norman churches, they must have been used even more widely in the Saxon churches they replaced.

It is reasonable to suppose that there is some connection between the shortage of stone in Essex and the fact that so little Roman road metalling remains; but the precise nature of the connection is difficult to decide. I do not know whether stone was brought in by the Romans for their roads and was later robbed for building by the Saxons; or whether Roman roads in Essex were made of gravel and flints only, and therefore broke up sooner. The Romans did not use stone in the massive walls of Colchester. These were made of bricks, septaria, flint and chalk. If the Romans did not bring in stone for the walls of their first capital one wonders whether they would have brought it in to provide a foundation for their roads.

On the other hand stone metalling has been found in the London area on three roads crossing Hackney Marshes on their way into Essex; it may be reasonable to assume that the roads were so metalled for the rest of their courses.

One of these roads was described by Defoe, who had lived at Hackney, in *A Tour through the Whole Island of Great Britain*, which was published between 1724 and 1726. He said that the remains of a great stone causeway were "lately" found in the bottom of Hackney Marshes between Old Ford and a place called the Wyck, and that the causeway "landed again just over the river, where now the Temple-Mills stand, and passed by Sir Tho. Hickes's house at Ruckolls". He thought it was the Colchester road. In fact it ran north of the Colchester road and on a diverging course, and is therefore outside our area. All the same it is still an example of a paved road crossing Hackney Marshes and leading towards Essex.

The second stone causeway was also discovered in the eighteenth century a little under a mile north of the Temple Mills crossing, where Marsh Lane, or an extension of it to the west, crossed the Lea in Leyton. This also was north of the Colchester road, and did not connect with it.

The third stone causeway in Hackney Marshes was the original Roman road from London to Colchester. It was found at what is now Iceland Road.

The Roman Colchester road (but not today's Colchester road) arrived at the Lea crossing by way of what is known today as Roman Road and then, after a gap, followed Iceland Road, which continues the line of Roman Road in alignment down to the Lea. I think the original Roman road then crossed the river at or near the east end of Iceland Road, possibly by bridge in Roman times, but in Saxon and early Norman times by ford. It was this ford, which became "old" after Bow Bridge was built on the southern loop road, which gave its name to Old Ford Road. Confirmation that this was where the road crossed the Lea is the fact that before the First World War masonry blocks thought to form part of a causeway were dredged from the river some forty yards south of the southernmost part of Iceland Wharf.

Further possible evidence that Roman roads in Essex were paved with stone is the fact that the Roman road from Braughing to Colchester was known to the Saxons as Stane Street, or Stone Street — unless, of course, the Saxons ever referred to a gravel surface as "stone".

More to the point is that one road which I am convinced is Roman — the Broomway, which runs along the coast below high water mark from south of Pigs Bay, Shoeburyness, to Foulness — is made of Kentish rag. If this road is indeed Roman then it is difficult to believe that other and perhaps more important Roman roads in the county were not made of stone. But if they were, where has the stone gone to?

I think there are two possibilities here: that the stone (if stone was used) was taken for use in building by the Saxons; or that all road metalling was broken up, scattered, and ultimately absorbed because of the particular nature of the soil in Essex. I regard the first possibility as a little less likely than the second, and shall deal with it first.

I have already referred to the use of Roman bricks in Essex churches as an indication of lack of building stone in the area. The curious thing is, however, that the churches which contain Roman bricks also contain Kentish rag, which is used as random rubble walling in churches at (for example) Great Burstead, South Weald, Wennington, Leigh, Prittlewell, Rayleigh, Rettendon, Runwell, and dozens of others. It is therefore a possibility that the Kentish rag used in early medieval churches in Essex side by side with Roman bricks was not brought directly from Kentish quarries, but was robbed from Roman buildings or Roman roads.

The second explanation for the absence of road metalling is that the Romans used local gravel, chalk, flint, and possibly imported ragstone, which had to be based, over large areas, on Essex clay; and that this clay so "worked" that it broke up and ultimately absorbed the shattered fragments of the metalling, with the result that the physical evidence of Roman roads disappeared more swiftly than on other soils elsewhere.

We saw in an earlier chapter that London clay is a stiff clay which soaks up a good deal of water in wet weather, and shrinks and cracks in dry. It does this, strangely enough, although it is impervious to water below a certain depth. Much of the water which falls on unworked clay remains at the surface until it evaporates, but some is absorbed, and where the surface has been broken, for example by ploughing, the amount absorbed is greater. Water can also fall into cracks formed in clay in times of drought. But movement resulting from expansion as a result of absorption in wet weather, and contraction as a result of evaporation in dry, takes place mainly in the surface layers. This process continues in time of frost, when wet clay will expand on freezing, and contract on thawing.

The working of London clay has two main results. The lateral pressure on the foundations of a building gradually destroys the stability of the walls, and ultimately makes them in danger of collapse. Since the area within the foundations is not subject to movement resulting from alternate wetting and drying, pressure is on the outside of the wall only, and the tendency is for the wall to move as a unit rather than for it to be disintegrated within itself. With a road, however, there is inward and outward pressure at the same time on each side of the road, and in time some movement underneath the road as well. Here the effect is to disintegrate the road metalling.

This is the first result of the alternate shrinking and expanding of London clay as a result of drought and wet weather. The second result is that the smaller disintegrated particles of wall or road will in drought fall through the cracks in the clay, while in wet weather larger stones, heavier than the plastic clay, will tend to sink down slowly through it.

The existence of stone metalling in a now waterlogged Roman road such as the Broomway, and its absence in roads which cross dry land, may help to confirm this argument. Metalling is protected if it is always covered with wet mud and silt, but where it crosses clay and is exposed to the atmosphere it is destroyed by movement resulting from frost in winter, and alternate expansion and contraction following alternate wetting and drying at other seasons of the year.

In conclusion I would suggest that where stone formed part of Roman road metalling it was doubtless picked up for re-use in Saxon building; but I am inclined to think that the labour of breaking up the foundations of a Roman road not already broken by natural causes might have been too much for Saxon builders — who in any case might even have preferred a road to remain in existence. For these reasons I am mildly inclined to think it was clay rather than robbing which destroyed the Roman roads in Essex.

Roman road metalling has been found on the course of the Colchester road at two places in addition to Iceland Wharf — at Romford Road, Stratford, and at Feering Hill, Kelvedon. At Stratford it was in the form of a thick bed of flint pebbles with side ditches; at Feering Hill the metalling, found "in or about 1948", was that to which reference has already been made — four feet below the surface, and so hard that it had to be broken up with pneumatic drills.

According to the Victoria County History, road metalling six inches thick and ten feet wide has been observed in the bank of a lane just west of the main road from Warren Farm to Writtle village, although no road on this line appears in the third edition of the Ordnance Survey map of Roman Britain. Roman road metalling was also found at a depth of four feet six inches near Bishops Stortford in 1949 on the line of Stane Street, the Braughing to Colchester road.

Metalling proved Roman by excavation has been found at Orsett, although the course of the road each side of the excavation is not known. Metalling which may be Roman, but which has not been proved so by excavation, is to be found in the causeway going down into the river west of Coalhouse Point at East Tilbury, and metalling which I have no doubt is Roman in the Broomway off the coast of Foulness. Since the road leading to Bradwell is marked as Roman on the Ordnance Survey map of Roman Britain I assume metalling has been found here also. Salmon reports that "the Trace of a Road" was seen near West Horndon church and in Warley, and this may refer to Roman road metalling.

These are the only references, or implied references, I have come across to Roman road metalling on or near the Roman Colchester road, and in the area to the south-east of it (and on Stane Street).

Now for the courses of Roman roads in Essex. It looks as if the road from London to Colchester, which is known south-west of Brentwood as Brook Street, may have been taken first to Marks Tey and connected there to Stane Street (the road which ran from Braughing through Stortford, Dunmow and Braintree to Marks Tey and then Colchester — and according to Miller Christy to the sea at Hamford Water). If this is so, then Stane Street was built before the London to Marks Tey road — had the Romans intended taking their road from London to Colchester in one operation they would have avoided the change of direction necessary at Marks Tey. On the other hand one might have expected the London-Colchester road to be built before the Braughing-Colchester road; and the Ordnance Survey map of Roman Britain does show a spur leaving the Chelmsford-Colchester section before Marks Tey which points in the direction of Colchester.

I have already said something about the course of the Roman Colchester road near London. Once across Hackney Marshes, it crossed Stratford Broadway in front of West Ham Town Hall, and finally joined what is today's Romford Road, where Roman road metalling has been found.

According to the map of Roman Britain the road passed through the Roman station of Caesaromagus (Chelmsford) and not far from that of Canonium (Rivenhall) before arriving at Camulodunum (Colchester). The Victoria County History suggests that the station of Durolitum should be placed at Romford, although it admits that the exact site of this station is unknown. It also suggests that the Roman station of Canonium was more likely to have been at Kelvedon, and not at Rivenhall, although both sites are said to be possible.

The map in the Essex Record Office publication *Highways and Byways of Essex* shows a road from Brentwood to Maldon which passes Stock on the way. This road is in our area. A spur road leaves it on the south side at Stock and points due south. I know nothing of this road or of the evidence for its existence.

I have already referred to the stretch of road proved Roman by excavation at Orsett. This road is in line with, and to the north of, the path which runs north and south just on the west side of Orsett church. It is also on the north side of Malting Lane, and about 120 yards east of the earthwork known as Bishop Bonner's Palace. I assume it was either a section of road running from the Colchester road down to the

Thames or, more likely, a road having some connection with the Orsett land settlement area.

Salmon's reference to a road near West Horndon church appears in his description of an old road called Green Lane which he said went "anciently" through Hornchurch, Upminster, Cranham and Warley and then passed "near the Place where the new Church of West-Thorndon stands [West Horndon church, whose site has been ploughed down]; thence between Ingrave Church and Ingrave Hall to Hutton, so to Fryerning. In levelling the Ground near the new Church for the Improvements of the Right Honourable the Lord Petre, the Trace of a road appeared. The like was some years ago observed in Warley, through which this Road led."

Salmon is presumably referring to Roman road metalling here, although it was left to Muilman, who wrote some thirty years after Salmon, and copied the passage concerning Lord Petre's improvements word for word, to say so.

Salmon implies that the two sections formed part of the same road, but on the face of it the course he suggests from Cranham through Warley to West Horndon church is unlikely. Whether the road went through Great Warley Street or Little Warley, it would have to pass through something like a right angle if it then went to West Horndon church. The name Great Warley Street is, or might be, significant, but I still cannot believe a Roman road connecting Cranham and a point near West Horndon church would pass through Great Warley Street or Little Warley.

If Salmon was referring to parishes and not settlements, then it would be possible to take his road in a straight line through the parishes of Hornchurch, Upminster, Cranham and Warley, and still take it past West Horndon church. But while other antiquaries sometimes described the courses of Roman roads by reference to parishes, to do so here is meaningless. Like so many parishes in south Essex, those of Hornchurch, Upminster, Cranham and Warley are long, narrow, and run north and south.

The only material of value in Salmon's evidence is his reference to an old road, or perhaps two old roads, of which two sections were seen, one near West Horndon church, one at "Warley"; and that according to Muilman these were Roman.

I have looked for signs of a road near West Horndon church, but without success. Perhaps time will tell us more about where it ran.

I referred earlier to the absence in Essex of the physical signs of the passage of a Roman road — metalling, embankment, hollow way, width of track between hedges, and other less easily described variations in the ground which are picked up by the fieldworker. It is the following, and losing, and later re-discovering the course of a Roman road according to these indications which in other parts of the country so often prove Roman origins. Indeed, it forms a technique whose results can sometimes be as reliable as excavation. But in Essex, because of the absence of physical indications in the field, it is a technique with which I have been entirely unsuccessful. I know of only one case where it has been used to any effect, and that is with the Roman road from Colchester to East Mersea. Laver, in the Essex Archaeological Society's Transactions, describes tracing this road on the line Colchester-Langenhoe-The Strood-East Mersea by the finding-losing-finding technique, and I find his account convincing.

I have already stated that my own efforts at fieldwork in Essex have been unsuccessful. I have in fact come across only one short stretch of road whose appearance suggests it might be Roman, and that is east of Blunts Wall near Billericay. It is known that there was a Roman site of some kind here, and this alone justifies the suggestion that the road may be Roman.

I have been to Blunts Wall, and although I did not go over the whole area, could see no sign of earthworks from the road which passes through it. On the other hand the road in its passage westwards passes over a small stream draining to the north. East of this stream the road is metalled, and runs between hedges not far from each edge of the metalling. West of the stream the road is metalled only with gravel; and from this point the southern hedge suddenly moves back, leaving between hedge and road a narrow strip of ground as wide as, or wider than, the road itself. This strip continues until the road turns right into the farm. There may be a simple and modern explanation for the fact that at this point today's road takes up only a third of the area between the two hedges; but Roman roads are often so laid out — Mere Way north of Cambridge, and Via Devana east of it, are two examples which spring to mind. If this is so, then at some time in the past the border of the Blunts Wall road east of the stream was incorporated in the neighbouring field while that west of it, although it was cultivated after a fashion at the time of my visit, was still separated from the neighbouring field by hedge and ditch. Such lines as appear on the map in this area run east and west, so it is possible that an east-west road may have passed through Blunts Wall and along the stretch of road I have described.

One road thought to be Roman on the basis of air photographs has already been mentioned, that which runs northwards from the Roman camp on Gun Hill between Chadwell and West Tilbury. A. G. Trusler suggests in the autumn 1968 volume of the Thurrock Local History Society Journal that it led to the Roman camp near the Cock at Orsett. Its parallel ditches show up quite clearly in an air photograph in the 1971 volume of the same journal. I have little doubt that this was a short lived Roman road. The site has now been destroyed by gravel workings. (I refer here to Roman camps although it would be safer to call them enclosures of first century date.)

Another road proved Roman by air photography is that which the County History in its map of Roman roads takes from Heybridge near Maldon through Layer Marney and Stanway to Colchester. A photograph shows this road with its two ditches running to the east of the Gosbecks Farm site and pointing directly to Colchester.

I must now deal in detail with the Broomway, to which I have already made a number of passing references. This is the metalled road which runs down into the sea north of Shoeburyness, turns north, and travels parallel with the shore for eight miles to a point off Fishermans Head near the north-east corner of Foulness Island. It then turns inland, its landward extension leading to Foulness village. For the whole of its course below high water mark the road runs in a straight line anything up to a quarter of a mile from the shore. Its course is covered by the tide at high water, and for much of its passage by silt at low water. This last may be a fairly recent development: the road is marked on John Norden's map of 1594 as well as on that of Chapman and André. It was called the Broomway because its course was marked by sprigs of "broom-like plants" stuck in the ground on the seaward side.

The area between the Thames and Crouch estuaries is in its seaward section veined with tidal creeks. These creeks, running inland and connecting with each other two or three miles back from the coast, create a series of low-lying islands at high water; at other times the sea goes out for miles, leaving dry the Maplin and Foulness sands which form the seaward extension of mainland and islands. It is along the south-eastern shore of these islands, where they meet the north-western edge of the Maplin Sands, and at a point slightly off shore where the channels of the tidal creeks shallow out, that the Broomway takes its course.

Modern maps mark the Broomway beginning in the south at Wakering Stairs. In fact it originated south of Wakering Stairs, at a point on the shore north of Shoeburyness where the road from Dangers ends, and is so shown on Chapman and André's map of 1777.

I have said that modern maps mark the Broomway beginning at Wakering Stairs. The section which can be seen today running down into the sea at this point is the southernmost of seven feeder roads which connect the main course of the road with the shore — whether (as at Wakering Stairs) that shore is on the mainland, or on the islands of Havengore, New England, or Foulness.

According to the Ordnance Survey map there is almost a right angle bend where the Broomway turns in at the north to finish its course at Fishermans Head, which suggests that the road continued farther north. Chapman and André's map, however, shows no such right angle — they have the road running directly to Fishermans Head.

The feeder which can be seen so clearly leaving Wakering Stairs before it goes under the silt is about twelve feet wide and made of rough pieces of Kentish rag. I have been unable to examine the main section so do not know how wide it is, but I assume that it is also made of Kentish rag.

The very existence of such a stone road leading out into the sea and travelling parallel with the shore for such a distance is curious, and in this country I think unique. The Street at Whitstable (which is artificial and Roman, and may be a road) leads down into the sea at right angles to the shore, but has not to my knowledge been investigated beyond the point where it reaches low water mark. The "road" across Morecambe Bay, best known and most used of such roads in England, is not metalled.

What makes the Broomway unique is that it is made of stone brought across the estuary from Kent, and that it was referred to in the Ministers' Accounts in the Public Record Office in 1419 and, in the following words, in Holinshed's *Chronicle* in 1577 ". . . at a dead low water a man may (as they saie) ride thereto, if he be skilful of the Causie". On the basis of these two facts alone — that it is made of Kentish rag and was in existence in 1419 — I have no hesitation in describing it as Roman.

The real question is not who built this road, but why they built it; and to answer this question it is necessary to consider the problem first from a physical and then from a functional point of view. As to the first, it has been pointed out that it is often easier to ford rivers where they empty into the sea than at places higher upstream. This does not apply to rivers falling into the open sea on an exposed coast; but it can apply where a river crossing a low-lying area enters the sea at a point where the tide goes some way out. In such areas the cut channel of the river may end at a point above low water mark so that its waters spread widely, and in spreading become fordable.

Such conditions are found in Morecambe Bay, where the Keer, Kent and Leven, which higher up can be killers, can at low tide be forded at points where they have lost their identity. It was this which made the cross-sands road there possible. It has been suggested that the Broomway was built to take advantage of similar conditions, and to make it unnecessary to ford the muddy and probably dangerous tidal creeks which separate the islands of Havengore, New England, and Foulness. I later question whether this was the case, but at the moment this is probably the most widely accepted theory.

The second question, that is the function the road was built to serve, is more difficult to answer. If, as I believe, it is a Roman road, then the answer depends on three things: the nature of the hinterland; the history of Roman Britain, and particularly the history of this section of the province; and whether the Maplin and Foulness sands were then dry land or not. I will deal with these in turn.

The eastern part of the area between Thames and Crouch has always been sparsely populated, remote, free from monastic settlement, and of little commercial significance. But if the number of feeder roads leading to Havengore and Foulness islands is any indication, this area was the one the Broomway was built to serve.

It is possible to be more specific about the area in Roman times. There were no Roman settlements of any importance, no quarries and no industries. The road could therefore have been built only for military or agricultural use.

I believe that Essex was covered with Roman roads and that many of these roads, as in the Orsett area, were farm roads. We do not know how well built these agricultural roads were, and whether stone was brought from Kent to make them; but if the possibility is allowed that even minor Roman roads in Essex were made of stone, then it could be accepted that the Broomway, and its feeders, were constructed simply to serve an agricultural district; and because they were laid in what later became a continuously waterlogged soil, did not break up under the influence of frost and alternate wetting and drying as did roads laid on Essex clay.

This is the case for thinking that the Broomway was an agricultural road. It is not a strong one, if only because it is not proved that agricultural roads elsewhere in Essex were made of stone. Further, the ambitious nature of the Broomway system both in layout and construction; the small size of the area served, which amounts to little more than a sort of broken promontary between the sea and the estuaries of Crouch and Thames; the possibility that any produce from the area would have been moved to the nearest market of London by water — these all suggest the road was not made for farm use.

If it was a military road it is difficult to see what possible use it could have served in the early years of the Occupation. It is more likely that it was built later to move men and horsemen along the coast to points attacked by Saxon raiders. This does not, however, explain why so many feeder roads were made — five in a matter of three or four miles into Foulness island alone. The fact that Chapman and André mark only three feeders, that at Wakering Stairs and two into Foulness, suggests that some of the others at least may be of later construction. It hardly affects the main issue, which is that of the road itself.

The road passes just to seaward of the points where the channels of Havengore and New England creeks finally shallow out to seaward today. The immediate line of the rôad was therefore decided by the extent of the creek channels.

This fact can be looked at in two ways. If the Maplin and Foulness Sands were covered by high tides as they are today (which was not, I think, the case) then the road was made to move men along the coast to resist landings from the open sea, and passed the mouths of eastward flowing creeks at their lowest points. If, as I believe, the sands were dry land, then the road was built mainly to move men and supplies to naval stations on Roach and Crouch, and passed the headwaters of what were then westward, not eastward, flowing creeks at their highest points — just east of where they came to an end "inland" in the Maplin Sands. In later centuries tidal erosion ate right through the Maplin and Foulness Sands so that the tides came right up to, and captured, the headwaters of the formerly westward-flowing creeks.

Flowing in and out of the upper reaches of these creeks the tide so widened them that it now enters from the sea to the east, as well as from the Roach and Crouch to west and north.

To bring these speculations to a conclusion, I suggest that the Broomway and its feeders were built at the same time as the Forts of the Saxon Shore, and against the same enemy or enemies, to provide service roads to defences on what are now the low water edges of the sands, and warships stationed in Roach and Crouch. The beacon on Plumberow Mount, Hockley, an artificial mound which has been excavated and found to contain Romano-British sherds, wood charcoal and some evidence of a large central post, was probably the site of a warning beacon for shipping, lit when it was necessary to man the warships.

I have no idea how the Broomway connected with the rest of the Roman road system in south-east Essex, although Chapman and André's map suggests it may have been the extension of a road which ran along the northern shore of the Thames west of Shoeburyness.

Those who study the map of the area will notice how the Broomway so clearly connects at Fishermans Head with the only main road on Foulness Island, that which passes through Foulness village. The two roads seem to describe an extended loop covering the whole area between Wakering and the north-eastern part of the island. The inland road was built towards the end of the First World War, although this does not dispose of the possibility that it followed some sort of a return road built at the same time as the Broomway. This theory is not supported by Chapman and André's map.

I said earlier that many through roads which have the word Street in their title, for example Watling Street and Stane Street, are Roman. For that reason I now propose to say something about two "Streets" in south Essex, Bredle Street at Aveley, and Weald Street near Upminster. I have come across no references to these streets earlier than the eighteenth century, and precious few facts about their supposed courses; but they must be investigated for what they are worth.

Bredle Street is mentioned by Morant in his description of the Manor of Bretts in the parish of Aveley. He says that the high road which runs through the parish was "anciently" called Bredle Street in deeds then in the possession of Lord Dacre, and from the latter part of the name he infers that it was very probably a Roman road "especially as there could not be a better way than this from the Havering quarter of the County to the Thames". Morant suggests no derivation for the name, and it is not listed in Reaney. Perhaps it is taken from the moated fourteenth-century farmhouse of Bretts a mile north of Aveley or from a local family of that name.

The only road to which Morant's reference could apply is that which runs northwards from Aveley past Kenningtons Cottages and then Kenningtons. If this was Bredle Street, its course would have continued to the north by the same road, which is followed by the Upminister parish boundary north of the Common Sewer today. This section of the road, which on the map has the appearance of a Roman road north of the Common Sewer, is followed by the boundary all the way to the Hacton crossroads, where the road ends. The boundary then continues in alignment to the Ingrebourne, and I have no doubt a road formerly followed this course too. But if it did, it led, not to Havering, but to somewhere south of Romford.

One difficulty (if we take Morant literally) is that the part of this road which on the map seems least likely to be Roman is that which actually "runs through the parish" of Aveley south of the Common Sewer. That which on the map seems most like a Roman road, because of parish boundaries and alignment, only borders the parish, and later leaves it altogether.

We must now consider the course of the road south of Aveley, and this calls for a reference to Palin. In his first book about Stifford, Palin refers to Bredle Street "as anciently called", and says that from the latter part of the name it very probably was a road in Roman times "especially as there could not be a better way than this from the Havering quarter of the county to the Thames ferry at West Thurrock". In a note he adds, "It is conjectured to have been continued in a direct line to the west side of the church, from which it is traceable to the ferry, crossing the Mardyke by a bridge still known by a second suggestive name, the Causeway Bridge."

In his second book about Stifford he says of the ferry at West Thurrock, "This, of pilgrim fame afterwards, was used by the Romans, who constructed a road leading from it west of Aveley to Weald."

It will be seen that in his first statement Palin has made an addition to Morant. Morant took Bredle Street "to the Thames". Palin now takes it to the ferry at West Thurrock; and in his final statement makes

Weald its northern destination instead of Havering.

There are three difficulties here. The first is that Palin refers to Bredle Street as a possible Roman road, and then takes it to a ferry concerning whose existence in Roman times there is no evidence whatever.

The second difficulty is that if Bredle Street were a Roman road and did in fact "run through the parish of Aveley" it must, as we have seen, be the road which passes Kenningtons and Kenningtons Cottages today; and I would have thought this too westerly a course for a Roman road to take for West Thurrock, or even Causeway Bridge. I think we must leave the southern destination of Bredle Street as Morant had it: "the Thames".

The third difficulty is Palin's adoption of Weald instead of Havering as the northern destination of Bredle Street. On the map the northern continuation of the road which runs through the parish of Aveley looks more like a Roman road than its southern section. If it is part of Bredle Street, then Bredle Street did not lead to Havering, and still less to Weald.

If it were possible to see the deeds once in the possession of Lord Dacre it might be possible to know something more about this road. At the moment we can hardly identify its course with any certainty, let alone regard it as Roman.

I do not know that the evidence for Weald Street is any more reliable, although it is certainly more involved. It is based on a charter in which Edward the Confessor invested Waltham Abbey with certain lands in Essex (Kemble 813, Sawyer 1,036).

The passage in question is that which describes the boundaries of land at Upminster. It reads as follows in Kemble's version:

> **Ðis synd ða landgemæ̂re intô Upmynstre. Ærest at Tigelhyrste sûð tô ðâre marcdîce; of ðâre dîce west in ingceburne; and of ðâre burne norð intô beccengâre; and of beccengâre norð andlang ðâre strâte wald intô stângâre; of stângâre norð intô mannes lande; of mannes lande eft intô Tigelhyrste.**

In translation it reads: These are the boundaries of Upminster [Hall]. First at Tylehurst south to the mark ditch, from the ditch west to the Ingrebourne, from the Ingrebourne north to Beccengare; from Beccengare north along the street wood to Stangare, from Stangare north into Mannes land, and from Mannes land east to Tylehurst.

It will be seen that the charter, which is based on a copy in the British Museum, refers to *strate wald*, that is *street wood*. The version of the charter given by Dugdale in volume II of the first, 1661, edition of his *Monasticon Anglicanum*, which is said to be based on a copy in the Public Record Office as well as on that in the British Museum, has *waldstrate*, that is *wood street* or *Weald Street*, and not *strate wald* as in Kemble. Salmon, copying from Dugdale, has the same. Morant, copying from Salmon, the same.

Dugdale says Weald Street is meant, and adds that it led "to Weald Camp from Tilbury or thereabout". Salmon says under the Hundred of Chafford, "A Road led from the Thames about Purfleet, or Tilbury, to Upminster, which before the Conquest was called Wald-street, as going to Walde or Weald; this came from Upminster Common to Brook-street, where the Ford was, and goes up Spital-lane to the Camp. We find this Name of Wald-street as a Boundary of the Lands of Upminster Hall belonging to Waltham Abbey." Morant also quotes the Upminster antiquarian Dr Derham as taking the boundaries, in part, along *Waldstrate*, "the Street which leads to Weald Camp from Tilbury or thereabout". I have not checked that Dugdale copied his two charters correctly. Subject to that, this is the evidence for the existence of Weald Street.

Kemble, as we have seen, gives it as *strate wald*. This Reaney takes to mean *street wood*, that is the wood on the Roman road from London to Colchester, now known as Harold Wood after Harold the last Saxon king of England.

It is possible to trace the boundaries as given by the charter, which are much the same as the parish boundaries of Upminster today. This fact suggests that they are reliable, as does the fact that the charter was forged after the Norman Conquest.

The boundaries suggest that Weald Street (if that is the correct reading) ran from the neighbourhood of Upminster Common towards Weald. The only road to do this is Nags Head Lane, which is not followed by Upminster parish boundary for any part of its course, and on the map has little of the appearance of a Roman road. Nags Head Lane also runs through the centre of the parish, equidistant from its eastern and western boundaries. If the boundaries in the charter mean anything at all, this cannot at one and the same time be Weald Street and a Roman road.

Further, for reasons which need not be given here, *waldstrate* (or *stratewald*) was on or near the Ingrebourne, and was mentioned to make clearer the course of the boundary at this point. This in itself almost rules out the possibility that the reference can be to Weald Street: there is no road between the Hacton footbridge and the three-parish boundary stone anywhere near the Ingrebourne showing signs of Roman origins, or any disposition to go to Weald. Harold Wood, and not Weald Street, must be the boundary point intended, and whether it appears in the original as *strate wald* or with these two words transposed (like *Cnut king* in the old jingle) the translation must be *street wood*, that is the wood on or near the Roman road from London to Colchester.

The boundaries of certain land at South Weald, also given in the forged charter, have been held by Salmon, incorrectly, to refer to a Roman road. The boundaries are taken past a point known as *there gemythe*, concerning which Salmon comments, "And, answerably to this, there is on the North side of the Parish of Weald another street known as *there gemythe*, that is Via Militaris, pointing towards Ongar". The word *gemythe*, which I take to be from the same root as *mouth*, however refers to the narrow valley between Havering Plain and Weald Side, where two streams meet to form Weald Brook. Although I believe there was at least one Roman road in the South Weald area, the boundaries of South Weald as given in the charter and glossed by Salmon therefore give us no help in tracing them.

The road which I believe to be Roman leaves the Kelvedon Hatch to Brentwood road today at Pilgrims Hatch, and drives due south to cut through the middle of the Iron Age camp at Weald. The Saxons or Danes would have gone round the camp: the Romans would have driven a road through it on principle.

We must now consider two other Anglo-Saxon documents which refer to Roman roads in Essex south-east of the Colchester road. These are the will of Leofwine which refers to land on the east side of the *straete* at Purleigh south of Maldon; and the charter by which Edgar granted land at Vange.

The Leofwine and Edgar charters differ from that of Edward the Confessor in two ways. They do not mention a named road, as Edward's is alleged to do in the case of Weald Street; but there is no doubt (as there is doubt with Weald Street) that they do refer to roads, and there is no doubt that these roads are Roman.

The will of Leofwine describes land at Purleigh "on the east side of the *straete*". Since no circle of boundaries is given, and this is the only reference, identification of the road is not easy. It will probably run north and south, and if it is not a road running through the centre of the village it may be that from Maldon to North Fambridge, which Miller Christy has suggested on other grounds is Roman. Whatever its exact course, it may be an extension of the road from Colchester to Heybridge recently identified from the air. The reference is contained in the sentence

And ic gean of Purleâ intô Nutleâ healfere hîde landes on câsthealf strǽte for mîne sâwle ðâm Godes þeôwan.

The Vange charter, which was made by Edgar in 963, refers to two separate *straets* and one *herpath*, that is two Roman roads and one main road not necessarily Roman, and the boundaries given can be identified. That part of the charter which refers to boundaries reads as follows:

Đis syndon þa land gemæra to fænge . ærest of rúm fleotes muðan oð bifleot þonne andlang ælfƿenne mearce oð ða stræte þonne east andlang stræte oð alfƿoldes mearce norð ⁊ lang alfƿoldes mearce oð done herpað þanan east andlang herpaðes oð ða brycge fram þære brycge norð andlang stræte oð duddes hyrnan þonne east on cyneferðes mearce suð ⁊ lang mearce oþ byrhtferðes mearce andlang mearce suð innon þone fleot be eastan þon ǽsc hus and lang fleotes ꝥ eft on rúm fleot . ⁊ se ƿuda æt tettincgleage .

The junction of Vange Creek and Parting Gut, from which the bounds are taken in a clockwise direction, is easily identified on the 2½-inch map. The boundary thereafter runs north-west along Parting Gut and the natural stream of which it is an extension (both of which were followed by the parish boundaries of Vange before these were changed) until they reach the Fobbing road.

The first *straet* mentioned in the charter then takes the boundary east. The first possible road to run east is the main road to Pitsea and Southend, but it is unlikely that this was the *straet*, and for three reasons. It is not straight; the way in which it crosses over the Fobbing road, which is straight, suggests that it was the younger road; and it is not followed by the parish boundary.

None of these objections applies to Clay Hill, parallel with it to the north. Clay Hill is straight. It has a western extension in the footpath towards Fobbing Farm; and it was followed by the parish boundary. I suggest this may have been the first *straet* mentioned in the charter. If so, then Alfwold's boundary would have begun where Clay Hill and Timberlog Lane meet near the railway, and continued to the *herpath*, which like the first *straet* also ran east and west. The *herpath* was perhaps the section of Timberlog Lane nearly 500 yards south of Craylands, which with its eastern and western extensions runs more or less east and west and parallel with Clay Hill. Timberlog Lane and Clay Hill also run twenty actus apart all the way from the east end of Clay Hill to the road east of Fobbing Farm, which suggests they served a land settlement area.

The only difficulty is that the charter refers to a bridge at the second bend, at a point where one would think a bridge unnecessary. If this difficulty could be ignored (and of course it cannot) then the road from this point to Craylands, which Reaney suggests as the second *straet*, could well have been part of a north-south road connecting with the straight line of field boundaries which leads north to Woolshots Farm, Ramsden Bellhouse and so, perhaps, to Chelmsford. I must leave the matter of the bridge in doubt.

One possible weakness of this interpretation is that the parish boundaries of Vange, which Reaney assumes to have coincided with the charter boundaries, may have varied since; but this is a hazard which faces anyone feeling his way with boundaries. It is also curious that of two parallel roads both possibly Roman — Clay Hill to the south, and the unnamed line of roads and paths to the north taking in the east-west section of Timberlog Lane, the first is referred to as a *straet*, the second as a *herpath*. In spite of these difficulties, the charter refers to Vange, and does show that somewhere in this circumscribed area there are two, and possibly three, separate Roman roads whose possible courses I have suggested.

One final piece of documentary evidence concerning Roman roads in this part of Essex, already noticed, is that a *herestrete* at Horndon on the Hill is mentioned in the Leger Book of St John's Abbey at Colchester in about 1350. The reference appears in Reaney under

Romford Rural, but is not taken up under Horndon on the Hill. I have been unable to identify this road.

I now deal with Street names in our chosen area. One is that which according to Reaney formed in 1309 an element in the earlier name of Southend-on-Sea — Stratende. The *straet* referred to here ran from Prittlewell Priory to Milton and the shore, and was presumably Roman. The first use of the present name Southend to be recorded by Reaney is 1481.

Other Street names which may or may not indicate Roman origins include the former Green Street at Upton Park, Baker Street near Orsett, and Low Street near East Tilbury.

Green Street, formerly a small hamlet, is now part of Upton Park in the built-up area of east London. The street runs from the Colchester road nearly half a mile south-east of Forest Gate station southwards to the London to Barking road, passing Upton Park station on the way. It may be significant that its continuation south of the Barking road is called Boundary Road, and where Boundary Road peters out into the alluvium north of the Royal Victoria and Royal Albert Docks, it is called Boundary Lane.

We have already seen that Baker Street near Orsett follows one of the internal boundaries of the land settlement area there, and therefore the line of a Roman farm road. Whether the word Street was first used here in Saxon times is therefore immaterial. According to Reaney the name Baker comes from a William Bakere de Luggestret, who is mentioned in the 1402 Court Rolls; so although the line of Baker Street is Roman, the name may be medieval, and late medieval at that, given at a time when roads in villages were already being called streets.

The name Low Street, like Baker Street, applies today to a crossroads and the settlement round it; but while in the case of Baker Street the road which gave the settlement its name is known, in the case of Low Street there is less certainty. I take it to be the north-south road which leads ultimately to the marsh, and therefore connects with the Manor Way to which reference was made earlier. There can be little doubt that this southern extension, at least, was a Roman road. It was referred to in the Essex Archaeological Society's Transactions for 1873 as a "raised road". Palin said it was some thirty feet wide; and if, as I suppose, he was referring to the metalled portion, then this was a major Roman road.

There is one specialised name which although not including the element Street does suggest the existence of a Roman road, and that is Stanford. This refers to a stone paved ford, and may be compared with Stane Street, the name of the Roman road from Bishops Stortford to Colchester. The only example I know in our area of Essex is Stanford le Hope. I think we may accept the fact that a Roman road forded the Hassenbrook here, but it is impossible to suggest its course on either side with any confidence.

It is now necessary to consider the work of earlier writers who claim to have identified the courses of Roman roads in Essex, and particularly that of Miller Christy, whose findings are described in detail in Appendix III. Christy has done more, and better, work on Roman roads in Essex than anyone. His speculations, which are generally sounder than those of other writers, demand serious consideration. Unfortunately, where some individual roads are concerned, the evidence he provides for their being Roman is sometimes not enough for proof.

This statement calls for some elaboration. Evidence of Roman roads is at three levels. There is first the evidence of metalling, embankment, double ditches — the actual physical evidence of a road which can be seen by the eyes, with or without excavation. This is the most reliable evidence of all. Then there is the secondary evidence of alignment, the existence of road or field boundaries which relate here and there to the width of the whole Roman road band, the fact that part of the edge of the band has been robbed by cultivation or the siting of cottages. In addition there will be suggestions to the eye, which while less definite than the existence of metalling, embankment or double ditches, have some significance: the suggestion of the remains of an embankment crossing a hill, stretches where the crop in a field is of a different colour from the rest, or less well developed. This evidence results from fieldwork, not excavation. It does not, at least in Essex, produce evidence of metalling, of embankment in its original condition, or of double ditches, but it does provide evidence which is vastly more reliable than can be obtained from the third level of evidence — that which results from map reading alone.

One would not expect Christy, in identifying Roman roads in Essex, to describe metalling or embankment, for these do not now seem to exist. But he does not, where perhaps he could, record evidence at the second level which might confirm his speculations. In nearly all cases, apart from saying that such a line "looks like a Roman road" — and in spite of having walked over many, or perhaps all, of the roads he describes — he still seems to rely largely on map evidence to justify his claims. As a result his case often appears weaker than it may be. For although map evidence can lead to the discovery of other evidence, it is itself, save in one particular only, always evidence at the third level. It cannot usually be accepted without confirmatory evidence.

I have referred to one piece of map evidence which is not at the third level. This is where the map shows that a footpath, track or road forming part of a line does not make a detour round a hill or bluff, but goes right over. This is evidence at the second level; and it must be said that such evidence is produced in one or two cases by Christy.

In general, however, Christy relies on aligned series of paths, hedgerows and boundaries as shown on maps, but takes matters no further. He does not seem to have seen the need for the next step in identification, that of examining the line yard by yard for more concrete evidences.

I can illustrate this by reference to the road which he believes ran from Chelmsford to Canvey Island. He takes a series of footpaths and boundaries in alignment near Rettendon to be part of this road, and has clearly followed this section on foot. But he has not reported on what he found, in particular at the southern terminus of the road, in terms of the evidence required. All he says is "During this stretch its Roman origin becomes particularly obvious. As one proceeds one sees the road on ahead topping transverse ridges, several of which it crosses, falling into the depressions between them and there becoming invisible as one approaches, exactly as one sees in the case of other Roman roads elsewhere."

This in itself means nothing apart from the fact that Christy says it — which is in itself of importance. But if we are to regard this line as Roman solely on map evidence, and on the fact that the road is straight and can be seen on ridges ahead, then there are other lines which could be Roman. I have no doubt that this line is a Roman road, as are many other lines in south Essex; but we must be quite clear concerning the lack of physical evidence provided by Christy, which is not really enough for proof.

I must complete these comments on Christy's speculations by giving a warning. I believe he was mistaken in thinking, as he did, that there were any Roman roads in Essex left unfinished and hanging in the air; I also doubt his suggestion that any short stretches of Roman road whose connection with roads in broken alignment on either side has not been confirmed were ever built for use as a sighting line, and never put to use as a road.

I now turn to matters more speculative. I have already suggested the possibility of a Roman crossing between Great Coldharbour in Essex and Erith in Kent. There is a track which leads from the Great Coldharbour site (now under a refuse tip) towards the Purfleet rifle ranges, and a second track which leaves it one or two hundred yards away from the river bank. This second track, which I regard as more promising, leads in a north-easterly direction to Southall Bridge, half way between Rainham and Wennington. For much of its course this track is followed by the parish boundary between the two.

Its course was clear on the occasion I visited the area, but I was unable to follow it because of firing. I did, however, examine its northern end south of Southall Bridge, and decided that if there were a Roman staging point at Great Coldharbour connected by road with the rest of Essex then this track, which has double ditches, and is slightly raised above the ground to each side, would be worth further examination.

I have always wondered whether the Romans had any main east-west road running south of the high ground at Horndon and north of the Thames. Since so many Saxon monasteries were built on Roman roads, the fact that Barking Abbey was founded where it was in 666 encourages speculation on the possibility that an east-west road ran here. But whether or not a through road ran eastwards from Barking depends on Roman flood levels in the area, about which we know very little.

Concerning such an east-west road farther east it does seem possible that the Hangmans Wood track was metalled by the Romans west of Chadwell. If so this is the only straw of evidence suggesting that a road may have followed the line Stifford-Chadwell-West Tilbury-East Tilbury.

The name Stanford, with its reference to a paved Roman ford, might suggest that a road was taken from here to Southend. But today's Southend road can owe nothing to the Romans. Between Moore Place, a mile or so along the road from Stanford, and Pitsea, the road goes through eight right-angle bends, four to the left and four to the right, left and right alternately. In some cases a left and right-hand bend are within one or two hundred yards of each other, as at a point just north-east of Williamsons, and at Vange. The meaning of this is clear: the road between Stanford and Vange was made by those who had to find their own way across country at right angles to a series of parallel roads already in existence. Even though these roads at right angles to their direction of movement took them out of their way, what they lost in distance was made up in ease of movement along a made road. They therefore followed such a road, either until they felt they must break away and pick up their original direction by crossing trackless country; or until some subsidiary cross-road appeared which helped them to continue on their way. This happened near Williamsons, when travellers followed the Corringham road northwards for nearly a mile before breaking away to the east. It happened also west of Vange, where for a shorter time travellers followed the Fobbing road northwards before again turning east. The road to Southend must be medieval, and where it was diverted for a short time and followed a cross-road, as near Williamsons and at Vange, that cross-road was an older road, possibly Roman, possibly serving a land settlement area.

These considerations suggest that if the Romans had a road running from London to Southend it was north of the present Stanford to Pitsea road. As we saw earlier, Edgar's charter suggests that Clay Hill, which runs east and west to the north of the Stanford to Southend road at Vange, and a series of roads and paths running east and west about half a mile to the north of it, are Roman. If Clay Hill was a through road, then its course westwards is clearly on the line Lee Chapel, Doesgate Lane, Fen Gate, Blankets, Corner Farm, Fen Lane and North Ockendon. Its further course westwards is less obvious, although it would presumably have joined the road which runs past Bluehouses and Hacton crossroads and forms the south-western boundary of the parish of Upminster today.

CHAPTER 11

Roman roads in Kent

Roman roads in Kent north of Watling Street, possible, probable, or certain, include those at and near Springhead; the series of roads which converge on Gravesend; the almost fabled Higham Causeway; the roads which lead to river crossings above Gravesend; and such roads as are mentioned in Saxon charters.

The roads at Springhead are proved Roman, and some of those mentioned in charters are almost certainly Roman. Concerning the others my ideas are less formed. I think it probable that at least three of the roads leading to Gravesend are Roman, and I have little doubt that a Roman road led to a crossing or harbour at Erith. As we have seen, the name appears in a charter of 677 which is probably authentic — authenticity being of value here because it shows the name, and the harbour, were in use so early. It is therefore possible that the name may refer to the remains of a Roman ferry station or harbour of which, according to Roach Smith writing in volume 16 of *Archaeologia Cantiana*, some evidence remains in brickwork in Erith parish church. When the church was enlarged and restored in 1877 part of the south-west wall was exposed to the core and found to be built of rubble embedded in mortar containing pounded tiles, which Roach Smith said was Roman. He added that a very strong and great wall lay buried in the ground in a line running from the south-west corner of the church to the ancient creek "which may readily be taken as the site of the [Roman] harbour".

While it is possible that Erith may have been the terminus of a Roman ferry from Essex, I do not know that the discovery made by Roach Smith justifies his further suggestions that a pagan temple may have stood on the spot, and a lighthouse to guide vessels "into the then existing haven".

Concerning the possible Roman origins of Higham Causeway I have already written. Concerning Roman roads which may have existed in Hoo, and roads east of the Medway, I shall not write in detail; but in concentrating on roads farther west I wish I could do so to better effect.

Before dealing with the roads already mentioned it is necessary to define the course of Watling Street, our southern boundary, and to consider where and how it crossed the Medway. The plaque on Rochester Bridge, set up by the bridge engineer John J. Robson, allows of no room for doubt. "The Romans built a bridge of masonry on this site during their occupation of Britain" it begins; and in volume 35 of *Archaeologia Cantiana* Robson defends his position with a forthrightness unusual in antiquarian disputation.

The general history of the bridge seems to be this. The earliest documentary evidence was in the reign of Edgar in 960, when it was recorded that the ancient bridge, having become unsafe, was pulled down and rebuilt. In 1115 the new bridge was said to have ten openings, and nine stone piers forty-three feet from centre to centre. It carried a timber superstructure ten feet wide. In 1264 this bridge, or its wooden superstructure, was set on fire by Simon de Montfort, and in 1281 the whole bridge apart from its foundations was borne down by ice and snow in time of flood. A wooden bridge which was built to take its place was weakened by increased road traffic which followed the capture of Calais in 1347, and a stone bridge was built between 1387 and 1392. This was removed in the nineteenth century, when the present bridge was built.

The question of whether the earliest bridge on the site was built by the Romans depends on one fact only: whether anyone but the Romans could have constructed such foundations as were laid bare when the present bridge was built. These foundations have been described at least twice, by John Hughes who superintended the foundation work for the nineteenth-century bridge, and by John Ross Foord, the contractor whose firm had the job of removing the foundations of the earlier stone bridge. Hughes described the original foundations in a paper given to the Institution of Civil Engineers in 1851, but I find it difficult to follow, and rely on Foord as reported by Robson.

Foord said in 1863 that the foundations of the earlier bridge were made by driving piles, mostly of elm shod with iron, into the bed of the river. The piles were twenty feet in length, and were driven close together to form rectangular platforms forty by forty-five feet. Starlings outside the platforms were made of half timber piles, and secured by ties enclosing spaces measuring about forty by ninety-five feet. The intervening cavities were filled with chalk, and top and sides were planked with elm. A course of flat bedded Kentish rag was then laid over the platform, on which solid masonry was built. Foord said that in removing the foundations of the old bridge over 10,000 piles, amounting to some 250,000 cubic feet of timber, were taken from the bed of the river.

Commenting on Hughes' and Foord's reports, Robson said it was safe to infer that in building the bridge a heavily timbered open excavation was filled up solid with dry rubble masonry of Kentish rag. He believes that the timbers were piles driven round, and below, the area of the proposed foundation to hold up the sides of the excavation. He said they would be set close together or, if at short intervals, would be sheathed with stout planks to allow timber work to extend upwards to form a coffer dam. The cross timbers built in the masonry were struts to hold the piles in place, and the heavy timber platform laid over the bottom of the foundation would be to ensure uniformity of settlement and to keep down the water. The fact that the pier foundations were taken down from thirteen to twenty-five feet below the bed of the river showed that the original bridge was built of stone — a timber bridge would need piled foundations only.

Robson suggests that the arches and superstructure of this stone bridge had decayed by 960, but that the piers and foundations remained sound. The arches were therefore removed, and a timber roadway built on the already existing piers and abutments. The floods of 1281 carried away this wooden superstructure and the old masonry piers above the bed of the river, but the foundations remained until they were discovered by Hughes.

Robson says that once the Romans had gone, the art of sinking bridge foundations in river beds remained unknown until the invention of the steam engine, and the introduction of temporary pumping engines and mechanical methods of excavation. The sinking of pier foundations extending twenty to thirty feet below the bed of the river at Rochester could therefore be attributed to the Romans only.

The western end of the Roman bridge gave on to a causeway which crossed the flood plain of the Medway at its narrowest point. This meant taking the road out of alignment; but had it been taken in a straight line from the west end of Rochester bridge to the crest of the high ground west of the Medway its overall course would have been shortened at the cost of almost doubling its passage across the flood plain. The details given in an earlier chapter of the complex way in which the causeway was constructed explain why the Romans preferred a slight overall diversion, and an increased overall course, to a shorter course which included a longer causeway.

The course of Watling Street east of the Medway, and in particular through the built-up areas of Chatham and Rochester, has been dealt with by Payne in some detail. In the case of Chatham and Rochester it is largely a matter of deciding which more or less parallel roads in present use mark the course of the Roman road from the centre of Rochester to the east of Chatham. Those interested may read what Payne has to say on the subject in volume 23 of *Archaeologia Cantiana*, taking care to turn upside down the pre-1719 road plan on page 20, which has the south at the top.

The main problem with Watling Street is not what happens to the road in Rochester and Chatham, but what course it takes on approaching London. It seems to be assumed in the Ordnance Survey map of Roman Britain that the road bows to the south at Greenwich. This course has been justified because it avoided low-lying ground liable to flooding. If so, then it is curious that the whole line of the road was not taken on a more southerly course beginning at a point well east of Greenwich — say at Dartford. But liability to flooding, one assumption, implies a second which is here, I believe, an incorrect one — that flood levels in Roman times were as they are now. It is on the basis of this incorrect assumption that the report of the Royal Commission on Historical Monuments for London says the main objection to taking Watling Street directly to Westminster is that this would involve the "tidal" passage of Deptford Creek. But we have general reasons for supposing that the Thames, and therefore the creeks leading into it, were less tidal, and perhaps completely non-tidal, when Watling Street was laid out; and these have been set out, particularly as they affect the Walbrook, in chapter 3. If the Walbrook was not tidal, then Deptford Creek was not tidal and (within the terms of the Commission's statement) can have had no effect on the siting of the Watling Street crossing. My own inclination is to assume that Watling Street originally carried straight on, and that the southern bow is a later addition made necessary by rising flood levels towards the end of or after the Occupation.

Perhaps at this point I should warn against the assumption that because of a shared name Watling Street in Kent and Watling Street which led from London to the north formed part of the same through road from Dover. There is no evidence that this was the case. Watling Street north of London began at what is now Marble Arch and ran along Edgware Road, past St Albans, and so to Wroxeter and possibly Chester. It was referred to as Watling Street in the treaty between Alfred and Guthrum in 879. The Kent Watling Street was not so called until after the Norman Conquest. It was certainly known as Casincg Street in 814, in which year it appeared in the charter by which Coenwulf, King of Mercia, granted land in Bexley to the Archbishop of Canterbury. In any case whoever changed the name from Casincg Street to Watling Street cannot have known whether the road so called was regarded by the Romans as a southern extension of Watling Street on the other side of London. For these reasons speculation on the course of the Kentish Watling Street west of Greenwich, the nearest point to London to which it can be taken with any certainty, must be free from any need to extend it automatically to a point where it could connect without difficulty with Edgware Road.

What is known about the course of the Kentish Watling Street near London is this. In 1713 the remains of the road, four feet high, forty feet broad, and a quarter of a mile long, could be seen at Green Common on the London side of Shooters Hill. But the course it took in and west of Greenwich Park is not at the time of writing marked on the Ordnance Survey map of Roman Britain. Beryl Platts, in her book *A History of Greenwich*, however says that the road continued across the park to the bank of the Thames and the area in Greenwich known as Billingsgate, to which Watling Street east of the Royal Standard so clearly points. She reports that J. M. Stone, President of the Greenwich Antiquarian Society in 1912-13, came across a document in the Public Record Office which referred to an old road closed by Humphrey, Duke of Gloucester, when he enclosed Greenwich Park in 1433. Then in 1965, when a trench for gas pipes was dug across the park, the road was found in alignment, four feet thick at the deepest point.

The frontispiece to Mrs Platts' book shows the course of this road imposed on an early map of Greenwich and continuing down in alignment to what is now the Billingsgate area just east of the mouth of Deptford Creek. I have no doubt this is where the road originally ran; but it is what happens to the road at or after Deptford Creek which is the problem.

I cannot believe it stopped at the Greenwich Billingsgate. This could only mean that the whole of Watling Street traffic crossed over the river to the Isle of Dogs by ferry before connecting with the Roman road system of London. The Isle of Dogs is mostly alluvium, and to have taken a road across it might have called for a causeway as expensive as that at Strood, and longer. I doubt if the Romans would have taken this course for this reason; in any case I do not know that the remains of a Roman road have ever been found in the Isle of Dogs, where there were extensive excavations for docks in the nineteenth century.

Gordon M. Hills, writing in the *British Archaeological Association Journal* for 1878, suggested that Watling Street led to the south bank of the Thames at Rotherhithe, whence a ferry carried traffic across the river to the Roman road system of London. If his suggestion is correct, then Creek Road, Evelyn Street, and Lower Street in Deptford and Rotherhithe could be regarded as the western extension of Watling Street.

Hills' suggestion allows me to refer to my own speculation that a branch road might have left Watling Street somewhere in Woolwich and have led to a ferry whose far station was where Coldharbour, Millwall, now stands. If the coldharbour here is authentic, it can only have been on a road leading to a ferry. But even were this highly speculative suggestion accepted it would not help us to trace the course of Watling Street west of Greenwich. I must leave the matter open.

An interesting point about Watling Street is that by the eighteenth century it had gone completely out of use as a road between Park Corner, Swanscombe, and Sandy Lane, Betsham, as a result of traffic being diverted between Dartford and Strood to the more northerly loop through Gravesend.

This break in Watling Street in Swanscombe Park can be seen quite clearly in the first edition of the one inch Ordnance Survey map; and it was not until the present Dover Road was opened as an arterial road in 1924 that the link was restored. Donald Maxwell, writing after the construction of the arterial road in his *History with a Sketchbook*, says that a section of "the old road" could be seen running beside the new about one mile on the Dartford side of Telegraph Hill, and that the "original road" could still be seen as a path in the woods at the top of the northern embankment of the arterial road near Telegraph Hill. In both cases he is referring to the Roman road. But when Roach Smith, writing before the construction of the arterial road, says in volume 17 of *Archaeologia Cantiana* that Watling Street could be traced parallel to "the old road" which led by Cobham Park and Singlewell to Springhead, then I think he must be referring to what he believed was a British, pre-Roman, road. I find it difficult to follow him with certainty because it is not clear, when he uses the word "it", whether he is referring to the British or the Roman road. But I think he is suggesting that where the British road could be seen it ran slightly to the south of Roman Watling Street, and was particularly well developed west of Springhead in Swanscombe Wood.

The course of Watling Street between Swanscombe Wood and the Medway flood plain is described by Roach Smith in volume 17 of *Archaeologia Cantiana* and George Payne in volume 23 of the same publication. Payne says Watling Street ran from Strood Hill in a direct line to the northern edge of Cobham Park "where within its fence its channel is distinctly visible, running parallel with the modern road with which at times it merges. Just beyond St Thomas's Well and nearly opposite Thong Corner the road passes through a shaw, its course being marked by a deeply worn channel far below the level of the present highway. At the bottom of the hill both roads amalgamate and pass on by Claylane Wood." But A. F. Allen, writing in volume 79 of *Archaeologia Cantiana* refers to the supposed course of Watling Street at the northern boundary of Cobham Park on the east side of the Cobham road as "probably an old bank on which the deer fence of Cobham Park probably stood". It will be noticed that Payne refers to a channel, Allen to a bank; but if, as I suppose, the course suggested by Payne is that followed by the Cobham parish boundary today, it would mark an unusual variation in the alignment of the Roman road at this point.

There are two, or possibly three, roads which ultimately connected with Watling Street immediately west of the Medway. Payne said that a Roman road sloped diagonally from the causeway of Watling Street down to the river, and that it probably led to a riverside landing place from which wagons could convey material brought by boats. He did not say on which side of the causeway this second road was found, or at what point it would have struck the river.

In 1819 a paved way which might ultimately have led to Watling Street was found running east and west across the site of the Strood dock of the Gravesend and Medway canal. Extended in alignment to the west it would not have struck Watling Street; but Watling Street changes direction west of Strood Junction Station in a way which suggests that another Roman road, on a principle earlier outlined, might have left it at this point to the north. If it did, then the east-west road would have joined it.

There is a reference by John H. Evans in volume 66 of *Archaeologia Cantiana* to a Roman road on St Mary's Island on the opposite side of the Medway. St Mary's Island is that area north of Chatham and north-west of Gillingham which is enclosed in the acute bend in the Medway between Upnor, where the river flows north, and north of Gillingham Pier, where it flows somewhere between south-east and south. It is no more an island than the Isle of Dogs — although here, as in the Isle of Dogs, waterways and docks cut across the peninsula have created something like an artificial island.

Evans comments, "Hoo St Werburgh not only had communications with Watling Street and Rochester but also with the Gillingham lower road by way of Upnor Ferry and St Mary's Island; the paved Roman way through this island leading towards the ferry was uncovered in part many years ago". Perhaps he is right, but I do wonder whether he is not referring to the paved Roman way found on the western, Strood, side of the Medway, rather than to one on the Chatham side.

Fifteen Roman roads or paths are marked on the plan of Vagniacae, the Roman settlement at Springhead on Watling Street, in volume 80 of *Archaeologia Cantiana*. These include Watling Street itself, and certain town roads with which we are not concerned. Two roads which leave Watling Street on the north side must, however, be mentioned. One is a branch road, twenty-five to twenty-seven feet wide, which leads towards Swanscombe and would, if extended, strike the river; the other is really a town road in that it does not go outside the area. But it is of importance because it leads to the harbour, the spring head of today's settlement, from which the watercourse later known as Ebbsfleet led through Northfleet to the Thames west of Tilbury Ness. This was a natural waterway widened by the Romans and navigable as late as 1939; the harbour has since been filled in. When excavated it was found to be surrounded on all sides by metalling which formed an extension of the approach road.

Anglo-Saxon charters refer to many roads in Kent, but as far as I am able to judge few north of Watling Street, and of these, fewer still west of the Medway. Some refer to land actually inside Rochester, or to land immediately to the south of Rochester which has Watling Street as its northern boundary.

One charter with clear topographical references is that whereby Offa King of Mercia granted land at Higham to Jaenberht, Archbishop of Canterbury (Birch 213, Kemble 121, Sawyer 110). This charter refers to a *via* which leads "ad eohinga burh in terram sancti Andreae" — that is to some sort of an earthwork or fortified place on land owned by the cathedral priory of St Andrew, Rochester.

According to R. F. Jessup writing in the 1942 volume of *Archaeologia Cantiana* the boundaries of the land ran from "the neighbourhood of Maedham along the boundary of Ac leage, and so next to Waeterlea, from there to Colling, then along the road which leads to Eohinga burh in the land of St Andrew, and then along the boundary of Mersc tunes to Bulan ham and so into Merc fleot".

Maedham is not known, but is presumably low-lying water meadows somewhere between the highland at Higham and the Thames. Ac leage is the present Oakleigh about half a mile east of Higham church, and Waeterlea a field immediately to the west of the site of Lillechurch Priory. Jessup suggests with reason that the next point on the boundary, Colling, was Cooling Hill about a quarter of a mile north of Lillechurch, and not Cooling Street away to the north-east.

There are certain difficulties in identifying the course of the boundary on the information given, and to discuss these would call for more detailed examination than is possible here. But it is Jessup's conclusion that the earthwork mentioned is on the north side of Chilton Hills, on the north side of the Rochester to Gravesend road and near the third milestone from Rochester. Jessup says there are traces of a disturbed earthwork scarp at this point, particularly in the gardens of the bungalows on the north side of Walmer Avenue, and that according to a survey in 1862 the earthwork was much more prominent, while in the enclosure was a mound of some size.

Jessup regards this earthwork as Saxon or earlier, and suggests it is the *eohinga burh* of the charter. He suggests that the *via* or road which is our main consideration ran from Cooling Hill by Gore Green in a south westerly direction by a track called the Land Way and the forerunner of the existing bridleway to Higham Upshire. If, as I suppose, the Land Way is the unmetalled road which runs due north and south immediately to the east of the entrance to the railway tunnel by Higham station, then things become interesting. Years ago, long before I knew of the existence of the charter, I was looking for a Roman road from the Medway crossing at Rochester to Higham, and so to a Thames crossing at East Tilbury. I therefore examined this stretch of road, and others in the area, for suggestions of Roman origins. I noticed that just south of the Lower Rochester Road, where it crossed a hollow, the road was built up almost as a causeway, which seemed unusual in a road of this kind. There are certainly too many "ifs" in this matter, but if *via* had the same significance in the charter as *straet*, and if this straight north and south section of road is the *via* referred to, then the possibility must be allowed that this is part of a Roman road from Higham to Strood, possibly by Great Hermitage and Little Hermitage.

Jessup thinks that Merc fleot — mark fleet, or boundary stream — is the natural stream which starts from the skirtland track north-west of Beckley Hill, crosses the marsh west of the old tidal wall which is itself west of the Barrow Hill causeway, and finally hits the Thames flood bank near the light at the south end of Higham Bight. This stream is followed today by the boundary of Higham and Shorne — which as a boundary, first of ploughlands, then of parishes, is in this stretch as old as, or older than, Offa's charter of 774.

A grant by Swithwulf, Bishop of Rochester, of land at Haddun (Haven Street, a small settlement on Lee Green road two miles due north of the west end of Rochester bridge) with meadows at Beckley Hill and Strood, refers to an *ealden strete* at the end of the boundaries (Birch 562, Sawyer 1,276). Without suggesting that there is necessarily any connection between this Roman road, as I assume it to be, and the Street element of Haven Street, which is a late addition, it is necessary to suggest where the road may have run. There is a footpath crossing Lee Green Road at right angles by Haven Street; and an interrupted extension of this footpath to the north-east passes through a wood called Haven Street Wood. The *ealden strete* might perhaps have followed the line of this footpath, which takes a fairly straight course here, rather than Lee Green Road, which does not. I have not visited the area. Here are the boundaries which relate to Haven Street:

> bisceopes mearc an norðan east be hun'e'sbiorge oð ciolmundes mearce ⁊ ðes lan`des' `mere sƿe suð ober haddune middéƿearde ⁊ ober ðane ealdan tunsteall oð cinges mearce ⁊ suð be cinges mearce oð ðane myclan del norðan ⁊ ƿest be cinges mearce oð ciolmundes pioda ⁊ ƿest be ðy ƿioda andlanges ðare rode oð ðane pyt ⁊ east fram ðy pytte ðurh ðane ƿioda ƿið suðan hunesbiorge . . . . . . ⁊ ƿen ƿeg `. . . . ðy lande' ober ciolmundes land to ealdan strete.

The charter of 814 with which Coenwulf King of Mercia granted land near Bexley to the Archbishop of Canterbury refers to a *straete* north of Watling Street (Kemble 204, Birch 346, Sawyer 175). This is the charter, to which I referred earlier, which calls Watling Street *Casincgstraet* or *Casingstraet*. It refers to Bexley as *byxlea*, the river Cray as *craegean*, and to an unknown stream as *auene*, or Avon, the Celtic word for a river. The *straete*, used to describe part of the boundaries of the land in question, ran northward from Watling Street to a point then known as Lytlanlea — in effect, from Bexleyheath to Abbey Wood. A. H. A. Hogg, who refers to this road in volume 54 of *Archaeologia Cantiana*, says its line, followed at the time he was writing by a track, was also followed, in the 1898 edition of the six inch Ordnance Survey map, by East Wickham parish boundary. This boundary was lost when East Wickham parish was absorbed in Bexley on October 1st 1902 (local government order 44,211). I have not identified this *straete* on the ground but we may assume that it was a Roman road. Here are the boundaries:

Ærest up of crægean on fulan riðe . andlang riðe oð þone fæstendic ⁊lang dices oð þaet gebyhte . of þam gebyhte ⁊lang hagan oð cyninges healh . þanon ⁊lang hagan ut on crægean.

⁊lang crægean oð þone hagan . ⁊lang hagan oð pæðfeld . þanon ⁊lang hagan oð æscburnan . of ðam burnan ⁊lang hagan on casincgstræt . east ⁊lang stræte on scofloces sæ̇ . þanon norð ⁊lang stræte oð lytlanlea . þanon east ⁊lang mearce oð enede mere suð-rihte of ðam mere to burnes stede . þanon ⁊lang hagan oþ casingstræt . ⁊lang stræte on þone calewan telgan . þanon ut on crægean . swa eft on fulan riðe. **Hæc** sunt nomina pastuum porcorum . helfreðingdenn . hun-bealding hola . frumesing leah . burnesstedesdenn heanyfre . þaes gemære is on east healfe spachrycg . on suðan plumwearding pearrocas . on westan lindcylne . on norþan auene.

The boundaries given in the charter with which Ethelred granted land at Littlebrook to the bishopric of Rochester in 995 (Sawyer 885, Kemble 688) refer to a *portstraete*. Port here may mean a gate or an entrance as in Milborne Port, Somerset, and not a haven for ships, although there are earthworks at Littlebrook whose possible Saxon or Danish origins are referred to in a later chapter. Wallenberg says the *portstraete* "returns in Portbridge (lost) in Dartford". The statement could be clearer, but it suggests that the *portstraete* was so called, not because of a haven to which it led on the river, but because of some place in Dartford to which the meaning of port as gate or entrance may have applied. Spurrell, who says in the 1889 volume of *Archaeologia Cantiana* that a road could be traced from "the port" at Littlebrook through the fields to Overy Street, Dartford, may have described the course of the road correctly, but also may have erred in his reading of the element *port.* He says nothing about the age of the road; but in view of the possibility that it was Roman his statement is repeated here. It might be possible to identify this road by working out the boundaries on the six inch map with Wallenberg's help. These are the boundaries:

> **Ðis synt ðа landgemǽra tó Lytlanbróce. Ðæt is, ǽrest seó éastmearc of Tæmese súð andlang ðæs bisceopes mearce tó Beorhtflǽde mearce; andlang Beorhtflǽde mearce tó Tryflinges mearce; andlang Tryflinges hagan tó ðǽre portstrǽte; ðonan west andlang weges tó ðám wearhbeorge; norð andlang weges tó bican póle; ðanan andlang Fléotes út on Temese oð midne stréam; éast andlang stréames oð ðæs bisceopes mearce.**

I now come to open speculation. Two roads on the Upchurch marshes now washed away, one from Bayford Point to Burntwick Island, the other from Shoregate near Ham Green to Greenborough Marsh, may have been Roman. There are extensive Roman potteries in the area to which the roads led, and Roman burials have been reported beside the second road.

Study of the 2½-inch map suggests that at least three Roman roads led south from Gravesend High Street, the narrow street which leads down to the former town pier in the centre of Gravesend. These are the roads leading to Wrotham in the south-west, to Singlewell in the centre, and to Strood isolation hospital in the south-east.

Once the Wrotham road is out of the built up area of Gravesend it runs straight, and this straight southern section crosses right over

Watling Street, which I consider significant. The second road, which leads almost due south from the town pier, first as Gravesend High Street and then as Windmill Street, then bears slightly east, and is continued by a path to Watling Street at Singlewell.

The third road, that which leads to Strood isolation hospital (which is not at Strood) has in its northern stretch a course less clear than that of the central road, but once out of the town its course is direct. In two places where it goes out of alignment and returns to it within a short distance the intervening stretch is followed in alignment by a footpath. Its course is continued in alignment south of Watling Street by a path which drives in an outstandingly straight line to Cobham, a known Roman settlement.

I have not examined the paths which at places follow the lines of these roads, but their straightness, the fact that they all converge on Gravesend, and that their line is continued in alignment over Watling Street, these all suggest that the three roads are Roman.

There is another road south-west of Gravesend whose possible Roman origins are even plainer, and that is Coldharbour Road. This road, with a footpath, runs in a straight line from Northumberland Bottom on Watling Street to the edge of a chalk quarry bordering the Thames west of Rosherville. If it continued it would have struck the Thames immediately opposite Tilbury Ness. The 2½-inch map does not show the coldharbour, although there is a reference in the *Gentleman's Magazine Library* to "a coldharbour in Northfleet parish" through which the road passes.

This road, which on the map seems more Roman than them all, completely bypasses Gravesend. If it is Roman its northern terminus must be a matter of guesswork; and while to the south I have examined the footpath which continues its line on both sides of Watling Street, I found no physical evidence of a Roman road there.

What is important about the three roads converging on Gravesend is that no other road leading to the river on the south bank of the Thames between Gravesend and the Medway looks in the least like a Roman road on the map or in the field. It is this which strengthens the possibility that the Gravesend roads are Roman, leading to a Roman town at Gravesend, to a ferry which crossed to the Roman town at Tilbury, and to the Roman road from Tilbury to Brentwood.

According to a note already quoted there are 307 coldharbours in England of which 30, the greatest number in any county, are in Kent.

John Topham

Plate 22. Barges, Orient, P. & O. — the river and docks at Tilbury seen from the Kent bank.

By courtesy of Tony Withers

Plate 23. Barges at Faversham in Kent before the Thames sailing barge race of 1977.

Sunday Express

Plate 24. Neck and neck in the Thames sailing barge race. In the background the World's End inn at Tilbury.

Plate 25. Canvey Island from the air.
For further details see list of plates

By courtesy of Fairey Surveys Limited and the Greater London Council

Plate 26. The royal yacht *Britannia* in Higham Bight in 1893.

Beken of Cowes

United Press International

Plate 27. The *Archibald Russell*, the last square-rigged sailing ship built on the Clyde, coming up the Thames estuary in the 1930's. Sold for £5,000 to Captain Erikson of Mariehamn in 1923, a British prize of war in 1942, she was bought for scrap by the British Steel Corporation in 1949.

Ullstein, West Berlin

Plate 28. Purfleet under air attack on September 7th 1940. A photograph taken from a German aircraft showing

The note does not name them, and at the time of writing the English Place-name Society has published no volume for Kent.

The Victoria County History lists and names fifteen coldharbours, all south of Watling Street save for those at Bobbing and Iwade, which are east of the Medway and south-west of Sheppey. That at Bobbing is about 800 yards west of the village at the point where Rook Lane crosses the railway line. That at Iwade is a mile east of the village, and south of the bridge over the Swale. The County History does not include Coldharbour Road south-west of Gravesend already mentioned; Cold Arbour on the road from Hoo to Stoke at the point where the road makes its first right angle turn after passing over the now defunct railway line north-east of what was Beluncle Halt; and Coldharbour Barn, marked slightly north-west of the central point of Grain Marsh in the first one inch Ordnance Survey, and now called Rosecourt Barn.

CHAPTER 12

The coming of the Saxons

IN this and the following chapter I deal with some of the more important developments in the Thames estuary, and those parts of Kent and Essex which border it, in Saxon and Danish times.

It is not easy, in recalling the history of two areas, each part of a separate Saxon kingdom, to restrict the account to those two areas only — the history of south-east Essex and north Kent can be given meaning only by setting it against the history of England as a whole. I have done what I can to reduce the space given to national events, but have at times still been forced to make sorties into areas far distant from the Thames estuary.

Inaccurate though it may be in detail, it would not be easy to find a more lucid account of the settlement of this country by the Angles and Saxons than that given by Bede (673-735), the Northumbrian monk and chronicler, in his *Ecclesiastical History of the English Nation;* and for those who have taken their history of England from intermediaries it can be refreshing, if frustrating, to turn for a change to such original sources as Bede and the *Anglo-Saxon Chronicle.*

It seems possible that it was at Alfred's suggestion that the *Anglo-Saxon Chronicle* was developed from the older local annals of the church at Winchester. But whatever its origins, this account of the development of the English nation from its earliest days in Britain has no equivalent in any other country of western Europe.

Both Bede's *Ecclesiastical History* and the *Anglo-Saxon Chronicle* are obtainable in the Everyman Library, the first in translation from the Latin by David Knowles, the second in translation from the Anglo-Saxon — or, as it is now fashionable to call it, Old English — by James Ingram. There is a more recent translation of the *Chronicle* by G. M. Garmonsway, also in the Everyman Library, more accurate in translation and better edited; but the two main versions of the *Chronicle* are in this second translation set out separately, and usually on facing pages, with translations of subsidiary versions, where these are used, appearing below them. While valuable to students specialising in the history of the period or in the Anglo-Saxon language, for those who come fresh to the *Chronicle* it does not provide the straight-through reading possible with Ingram; and some loss of accuracy is a small price to pay if interest in the period can be aroused by an uninterrupted reading of the earlier translation.

A third translation of the *Anglo-Saxon Chronicle* by Professor Dorothy Whitelock published by Eyre and Spottiswoode is also set out in a form which makes a straight-through reading difficult. On the other hand the inclusion in footnotes of material from other chroniclers, including those who have drawn material from versions of the *Chronicle* now lost, is invaluable.

The very existence of Bede's *Ecclesiastical History* and the *Anglo-Saxon Chronicle* is in itself an indication of the greatness, where greatness existed, of the Anglo-Saxons and of their culture; and although in this and the following chapter we are strictly concerned with the history of the East Saxons — that is those who lived in the kingdom which later became Essex — and of those who lived in a narrow corridor of north Kent, it is impossible without some wider knowledge of Saxon history to do justice to the highlights of that slightly more restricted history — the settlement of the Saxons as illuminated by a study of large scale maps of Essex and of the results of excavation at Mucking; the conversion of Kent by Augustine, that of Essex by Cedd; finally the long drawn out campaigns of the Danes, which first brought the country to its knees and then conquered it wholly, campaigns which finally centred on the Thames, on the Thames estuary, and on the city and citizens of London.

The Saxons have been compared, and to their disadvantage, with the Danes. But they did not go back on their word quite as often as the Danes. Nor were they so bloody minded or pointlessly destructive. Alfred treated the Danish leaders with consideration even after they had broken faith with him. The Danish leader Hasten, at an early stage in his dealings with Alfred, swore oaths to him and consented to the baptism of his two children, Alfred being godfather to one, Ethelred Alfred's brother to the other. Then, when Hasten had broken faith with Alfred and taken up arms against him, the two boys and their mother were captured by Alfred's forces at Benfleet in Essex; and Alfred returned them to Hasten. Harold Godwinsson, the last of the Saxon kings, let Harald Hardrada's son return to Norway with his men and ships after his father had invaded England in league with Harold's brother Tostig, and been defeated and killed at Stamford Bridge — although the cynical might say this was not a difficult gesture to make: it needed three hundred ships to bring Hardrada's host to England; twenty-four were enough to take the survivors home.

Weakly organised and led, as in the time of Ethelred the Unready, the Saxons were less staunch and less effective than their enemies. Strongly led, as under Alfred, Edward the Elder, Athelstan and Harold, they could stand up to them and prevail; and though final defeat was his portion, there is something epic in Harold's forced marches north and south with his housecarles in the months of September and October 1066, and in the decision of many of his followers, in defeat, to join their erstwhile Viking enemies in the Byzantine Varangian Guard.

It would be unwise to canvass here the effect which conversion to Christianity had on the Saxons, although it seems to have given them greater courage than it gave those who set out to convert them. For Bede tells us that when Augustine's saintly band of monks told him they were frightened of going to a "barbarous, fierce and unbelieving nation to whose very language they were strangers" they sent their leader back to ask Pope Gregory that they should not be compelled to undertake "so dangerous, toilsome, and uncertain a journey". Gregory sent them a letter telling them to get on with it and do as Augustine told them. But Augustine (who is not to be confused with the rather more saintly Augustine who wrote the *Confessions*) does not come too well out of the transaction.

There were no such misgivings on the part of those Saxons who went as missionaries to the lands from which their ancestors had come to Britain. But while the English mission to the Continent was a remarkable achievement, there is something less edifying in the way in which the Saxon church, founded by the Roman Augustine, engaged in controversy with the Welsh, Irish and Scottish churches, which had an unbroken tradition going back to the foundation, by the Romans, of the Christian church in Britain. Matters of contention included the use of the tonsure; the date of Easter, which in Bede, both by repetition and the inflated importance attached to it, becomes a matter of tedium; and the only matter of substance, the unwillingness of the British Christians to proselytise the heathen English.

Augustine behaved with some rigidity in this controversy; and when at a second meeting with the leaders of the Celtic churches they still would not submit, he said in a threatening manner that if they would not join in unity with their brethren they would be warred upon by their enemies; and if they would not preach the way of life to the English, they would at their hands undergo the vengeance of death.

Bede, recounting this, records that on a later occasion near Chester the Saxon leader Ethelfrid, before making "a very great slaughter of that perfidious nation" murdered some 1,200 Welsh monks who were praying for the success of their arms. Bede, without expressing distaste, comments, "Thus was fulfilled the prediction of the holy bishop Augustine, though he himself had been long before taken up into the heavenly kingdom; that those perfidious men should feel the vengeance of temporal death also, because they had despised the offer of eternal salvation".

I cannot help recalling that at certain celebrations at University College, London, in the early 1930's, one of the attractions was a paper given by the English scholar, R. W. Chambers, Quain Professor of English Language and Literature, entitled the Venemous Bede. I did not attend; but it is possible that the lecturer had something to say on these matters.

Fuller, the seventeenth century divine, showed less scepticism. According to him, Bede was known as Venerable because "a dunce-monk, being to make his epitaph, was *non-pluss'd* to make that dactyle, which is onely of the quorum in the hexameter, and therefore at night left the verse gaping

Hic sunt in fossa Bedae *ossa*

till he had consulted with his pillow, to fill up the *hiatus*; but returning in the morning an angel (we have often heard of their singing, see now of their poetry) had filled up the *chasma* with *venerabilis*".

Bede has been given an honourable place in history, for reasons well set out in Knowles' introduction to the *Ecclesiastical History*. Speaking of the age in which Bede lived, he writes, "It was a dark age in the history of Europe, when learning and civilisation were at their lowest ebb on the Continent, when western Christendom was reduced to a narrow belt of lands between the unconverted Germanies and the Mohammedans debouching from the Pyrenees, and when the heritage of early Christian art and thought, as well as that of ancient Rome, might well have seemed to be in danger of disappearing altogether. Yet away in the north, on the shore of that dark sea over which the long ships of the sea rovers were to appear, a monk, unknown save to his brethren and a few of the local magnates, was writing a series of works . . . one in particular which made him, not only the Father of English History, but one of the great historical writers of all time . . . In the annals of letters and learning there is no more impressive instance of the ultimate fame of work accomplished in silence, for the sake of truth, by a good man."

Bede relies for much of his account of the end of Roman rule and the coming of the Saxons on the monk Gildas, the only contemporary British chronicler of the period, who a little before 547, and after he had emigrated to Brittany, wrote an account of the conquest of Britain in Latin. The earlier of the only two manuscripts of his work still in existence, both of which are in the Cambridge University Library, has the title *Liber querulus de excidio Britanniae.* A later title which seems in commoner use is *De Excidio et Conquestu Britanniae.* The title usually given the work in English is *The Groans of the Britons* — the translation of a phrase in an appeal quoted by Gildas to the Roman commander in Gaul, and made by the Britons when under northern attack. It is not equivalent to the Latin titles.

Both Bede and the *Anglo-Saxon Chronicle* draw on Gildas for their accounts of the fifth century; but by repeating one of his errors, which shall be identified later, they have made even more difficult our understanding of what really happened.

Tempting though it might be, therefore, to rely on the clarity of Bede for the Saxon settlement of England, any account of that twilight period between the ending of direct Roman rule and the final victory of the Saxon invaders must be based on more widely chosen material.

The final withdrawal of Roman forces took place in 407 when the usurper, Constantine, crossed over into Gaul to make an unsuccessful bid to become Emperor. Although there is slight evidence that some military forces may have remained, Britain was then for all practical purposes undefended by the forces of the Empire.

It is a complication, but I think a necessary one, to mention at this point the effect which the heresy of Pelagianism had, or may have had, on the course of British history in succeeding years. Pelagius, a Briton, whose name in Greek means *sea born* and may be a translation of its British equivalent of Morgan — *môr* sea, *gan* from — was sent to study law in Rome shortly after 380; and it is not known that he ever returned to this country. But after his arrival in Rome he became prominent as a theological disputant and wrote, among other works, *Expositions of Thirteen Epistles of St Paul*, the earliest surviving literary work from the British Isles. His teachings were based on a rejection of divine grace as a means of salvation, and on the belief that man is capable of working out his own salvation. His teachings caused bitter controversy, led ultimately to his excommunication, and almost split the Christian church.

The ideas of Pelagius took strong hold in Britain and particularly, according to Sheppard Frere in his *Britannia*, among the ruling classes; and it has been suggested that since his emphasis on individual initiative in religious matters had particular appeal to them, that the British leaders were all the more prepared to show initiative in temporal matters also — if necessary against Rome, whose spiritual and temporal powers were opposed to the teachings of Pelagius. Whether that is so or not it seems likely (and Gildas is our only authority here) that there was a period of peace and prosperity after the break with Rome during which the raiding Picts and Scots were defeated. It was also during, or perhaps towards the end of, this period, that Germanus, the bishop of Auxerre, was chosen by a council of Gallic bishops to visit England and combat the heresy of Pelagianism. He came in 429, and addressed a vast multitude of believers whom he converted from heresy to orthodoxy.

Perhaps even more significant, however, was the wealth of the British ruling classes at that time and the strength of their following as described in the life of Germanus by Constantius. This shows that what had been a prosperous society in south-east Britain was not yet in eclipse.

On the other hand raiding was also taking place at the time, for Germanus, formerly a general in the Roman army, himself led a British force which gained the victory, in mountainous terrain, against a mixed force of Picts and Saxons. It is known as the Alleluia Victory because the battle cry of the British forces at the moment of attack was *Alleluia!*

It is now necessary to refer to the leader known as Vortigern who was ruling in south-east Britain at the time of Germanus's visit. Frere states that Vortigern was a Pelagian, and suggests that the success achieved by the mission of Germanus must have done much to weaken his authority. Nennius, the eighth century historian, certainly says in his *Historia Britonum* that Vortigern was afraid of Roman intervention; and for that reason, when menaced by Picts from Scotland and Scots from Ireland, asked for help from Saxon mercenaries whom he settled in Thanet. Frere suggests that there was opposition to Vortigern's policy of relying on Saxon mercenaries; and that it was from this opposition that the appeal for military assistance quoted by

Gildas was sent to Aetius, Roman commander in chief in Gaul, in or soon after 446. Whatever the motives of those who sent this appeal, it is one of the last fairly fixed points in fifth century history.

Aetius defended the frontiers of the Empire for some twenty years before his death, during which time he defeated Attila near Châlons-sur-Marne in 451. The appeal to him began, "To Aetius, thrice consul, the groans of the Britons" and concluded with the well-known passage, "The barbarians drive us to the sea; the sea drives us back to the barbarians: between them we are exposed to two sorts of death; we are either slain or drowned."

The fact that in their appeal the Britons referred to Aetius as "thrice consul" suggests that the appointment may have been a recent honour, one still in mind, and therefore worth mentioning by suppliants. Since his third consulship began in 446 and his fourth in 454, the appeal may therefore have been made in 446.

To recapitulate: after the separation from Rome there was a period of material prosperity during which the Picts and Scots were driven back and their raiding reduced. This period ended with renewed attacks, which were followed by Vortigern's invitation to Saxon mercenaries to help against the Picts, by this time the chief danger.

Vortigern's Saxons came in three ships in about 430 or shortly after — a small defence force indeed — were settled in Thanet, and drove the raiders back. And here we may quote Bede, who says that once their victory was known in their own country, "as also the fertility of the country, and the cowardice of the Britons, a more considerable fleet was quickly sent over, bringing a still greater number of men, which, being added to the former, made up an invincible army. The newcomers received of the Britons a place to inhabit, upon condition that they should wage a war against their enemies for the peace and security of the country, while the Britons agreed to furnish them with pay."

What Bede does not make explicit is that the first Anglo-Saxons invited to Britain to help defend the country against attack were mercenary soldiers who had been trained by, and had experience with, the Roman army. Their friends and dependents followed later, and Bede lists the tribes represented, and where they came from.

"In a short time," he continues, "swarms of the aforesaid nations came over into the island, and they began to increase so much, that they became terrible to the natives themselves who had invited them.

Then, having on a sudden entered into league with the Picts, whom they had by this time repelled by the force of their arms, they began to turn their weapons against their confederates. At first, they obliged them to furnish a greater quantity of provisions; and, seeking an occasion to quarrel, protested that unless more plentiful supplies were brought them, they would break the confederacy, and ravage all the island; nor were they backward in putting their threats into execution . . . they plundered all the neighbouring cities and country, spread the conflagration from the eastern to the western sea, without any opposition, and covered almost every part of the . . . island." Of the original inhabitants, Bede comments, "Some with sorrowful hearts, fled beyond the seas [mainly to Brittany]. Others, continuing in their own country, led a miserable life among the woods, rocks and mountains, with scarcely enough food to support life, and expecting every moment to be their last."

It is now necessary to refer to the error in Gildas which is repeated in Bede and the *Anglo-Saxon Chronicle*: his placing of the appeal to Aetius before the period of prosperity. There is no doubt that it came after it, and that both Bede and the *Anglo-Saxon Chronicle* therefore date the coming of the Saxons some twenty years too late.

We have already seen that the appeal to Aetius, in or soon after 446, is a key date. There are three others, although of varying importance. In 442, according to the *Gallic Chronicle*, "Britain, long troubled by various happenings and disasters, passed under the authority of the Saxons"; and it may be that this is a reference to the rebellion of the Saxon settlers in that year. In 446 or 447 Germanus paid a second visit to Britain with the Bishop of Trier, which seems to show that the Britons in the south of the country were still to some extent their own masters. Then in 454 Aetius was murdered on the orders of the Emperor Valentinian who suspected that he had plans to usurp his authority; and it is suggested by C. F. C. Hawkes in the book *Dark-Age Britain* that the Saxons "burst out" in that year when they no longer feared the possibility of his intervention. There is difficulty in reconciling these dates, and Hawkes' suggestion, although it bears to me the ring of truth, is supposition and the date a late one. But I have recorded all three dates for what they may be worth.

After the period of warfare which followed the Saxon rebellion the British rallied; and in the battle of Mount Badon, or Mons Badonicus as Gildas has it, they defeated the Saxons and there was peace for some two generations.

This second period of peace came to an end in about 550, or even as late as 571, when an area from Buckinghamshire to the upper Thames was overrun, and four British towns — Limbury in Bedfordshire, Aylesbury in Buckinghamshire, and Benson and Eynsham in Oxfordshire — were captured. Six years later Gloucester, Cirencester and Bath were taken, and by 600 most of England was in Saxon hands save Cornwall and parts of the north and north-west.

The most recent and authoritative account of the Saxon settlements is the paper by Sonia Chadwick Hawkes in *Sachsen und Angelsachsen*, which was published in German by the Helms Museum, Hamburg, in 1978. I was referred to it when this chapter was being paged up; and can do no more than insert a paragraph commending it and its extensive bibliography in the certain knowledge that they are likely to prove the foregoing historical account, and my later references to the evidence of pottery, at least, to some extent outdated — and, for that reason, in parts erroneous.

I may, however, be on slightly firmer ground in referring to some of the admittedly uncertain evidence that Saxons may have settled in eastern England before the final break with Rome in 407. This depends partly on a study of large-scale maps of the area, and partly on the findings of archaeological excavation. As to the former, the way in which the field systems in Essex are so consistently Roman, with the villages showing Romano-British influence in their layout, suggests peaceful settlement rather than the destruction of a system following conquest.

The relatively undisturbed Roman field systems at Orsett and Asheldham have already been described. Nothing more is needed to identify these than a large scale map and the knowledge that the Roman unit of land measurement was 116.05 feet. The way in which the layout of Romano-British villages has been preserved in Essex is pointed out by Rupert Coles in volume 24 of the *Essex Naturalist.* He states that a Romano-British hamlet pattern, with unified agricultural holdings, has been maintained in south-east Essex in contrast to what he calls the "linear" and "rose" settlements of the Saxons elsewhere; and that this area, heavily populated during the Occupation, was therefore brought under Saxon rule by peaceful penetration, not violent conquest. If this was so, then it is possible that Saxon mercenaries were invited to settle in eastern England at strategic points near the coast before the breakdown of Roman rule to keep the northern invaders at bay; and that when that rule ended they simply took control of districts too weakly held to oppose them.

Where archaeology is concerned, J. N. L. Myres has suggested in *Dark-Age Britain* that the shores of south-east Britain may have been settled by Saxons for something like a century before the final breakdown of Roman rule. He bases his suggestion on two things: the existence in East Anglia of fourth-century Saxon cemeteries, some on Roman roads or outside Roman settlements; and the discovery in eastern England of pottery made in this country during the Roman Occupation which could be said to be of Saxon type.

Myres states that Romano-British pottery, decorated in a style in conformity with Anglo-Saxon taste, and made between the closing years of the third century and the breakdown of Roman rule in Britain, appears in the Forts of the Saxon Shore at Burgh Castle, Bradwell, Richborough and (possibly) Felixstowe; at ports like Caister near Yarmouth, Felixstowe and London; and in the principal Roman towns of the hinterland such as Caister by Norwich, St Albans, Brundall (Norfolk), Sawbridgeworth, Baldock, Chesterford and Sittingbourne. He points out that the evidence for this concentration of what he calls Romano-Saxon pottery in the coastal centres of the Saxon Shore is the more striking in view of how little deliberate excavation was responsible for the discoveries; and suggests four possible explanations: that the Roman defence of the Saxon Shore was ineffective or too late, and that by the end of the third century it had been partially settled by Saxons in circumstances of which we know nothing; that the Roman garrisons of the Saxon Shore forts were recruited largely from the overseas tribes whose raiding and piracy they were intended to suppress; that the defensive efforts of the regular garrisons were supplemented by the deliberate settlement of Saxons in the coastal areas, in the same way that Alamanni from the middle Rhine under their king Fraomar were settled somewhere in Britain in the third quarter of the fourth century; or that the pottery was simply the outcome of trading contacts between the Empire and the tribes beyond the North Sea frontier.

Excavation of one early Saxon site in south-east Essex — that at Linford near East Tilbury — suggests that settlement there was peaceful and took place before the end of Roman rule. K. J. Barton, writing in volume 5 of the Thurrock Local History Society Journal, states that excavation there suggested that Saxon settlement began in about 400 and that there were two stages of settlement, one in which the site was undefended, a later one in which the defences would have been inadequate against determined attack. This suggested to the writer either local acceptance of the settlers' presence, or lack of authority to object. In a later and definitive report in the Essex Archaeological Society Transactions for 1962 he suggests that the settlers came from the mouth of the Elbe late in the fourth or early in the fifth century.

If the first Saxons did in fact settle at Linford as early as 400 it prompts the observation that this was nearly fifty years before the ineffective appeal to Aetius by the British; that children born here shortly after their parents arrived grew up in reasonably settled conditions, became identified with their new countryside if not country, and were middle-aged before the last appeal was made by the British for Roman help — and yet lived out their days in conditions which we, influenced by Gildas, might regard as of utter darkness and chaos.

Whether or not widespread Saxon settlement did take place in the south-east towards the end of the Roman Occupation, excavation at the Saxon site at Mucking, also near East Tilbury, suggests that it took place shortly after it ended; and this may be confirmed by the fact that the Saxon settlement at Feddersen Wierde between the mouths of Elbe and Weser in northern Germany — whose inhabitants are assumed to have settled in eastern England, and possibly in Essex — was according to one report abandoned before about 425. If this is so, then it is clear that there were settlements elsewhere in the Thames estuary at the same time as, or before, Vortigern enrolled Saxon mercenaries in about 430 and settled them in Thanet — if, of course, that is a reliable date.

One thing we do know is the vital importance to Saxon studies in the Thames estuary, and indeed in England, of the early Saxon site at Mucking (archaeologically speaking the same site as that at Linford) which was excavated between 1965 and 1978. Whenever those who settled at Mucking came to this country, they were the founders of Anglo-Saxon England, if not of England itself. In these pioneer settlements is the beginning of an era which saw the introduction of the English language; the foundation and growth of the English church; the missionary work of the Anglo-Saxons in Germany; the growth of monasticism, when for a century Northumbria was "a sunlit region in a shadowed world". It saw also the two monumental works of the *Anglo-Saxon Chronicle* and Bede's *Ecclesiastical History of the English Nation*; Alfred's valiant resistance against the Danes; the reign of Canute; the end of Saxon England with the coming of the Normans. It may not be fanciful to see these all contained in what is now regarded as one of the most important Saxon sites in England.

On the edge of the ninety-foot gravel terrace north-east of East Tilbury, the site has uninterrupted views across the Lower Hope to the hills of Kent and, most impressive of all, down the Sea Reach of the river to the open sea. It is a place of strategic importance which was in continuous occupation for some 3,000 years, from the Neolithic to the early Saxon period.

Aerial photographs of the site taken in and after 1959 suggested the presence of Iron Age, Roman and Saxon settlements; excavation later showed that most of the features there ranged from the Bronze Age to the early Saxon period. The first dramatic sign of the archaeological value of the site came when gravel working was already advanced in the area, and an iron axe and spearhead were picked up by a gravel worker. They were found among gravel rejects which, with gravel which could be used, had been dug out of the ground by a dragline bucket which lifts one ton at a time, dropped through a hopper, carried a quarter mile by conveyor belt, passed through washing and grading screens, sorted out to the reject pile, and loaded on to a lorry before being spread out on a muddy quarry road. They were seen, picked up, and handed over scarcely damaged. When the quarry foreman soon afterwards saw two pieces of iron sticking out of the quarry face, the first Saxon cemetery came to light. The pieces of iron were Saxon spearheads.

The site at Mucking has no visible boundaries and no strategic earthworks. It covers some forty acres and is the most extensive settlement of the Migration Period in England, including over 200 sunken houses and traces of perhaps fifty Saxon "halls". Of these the best preserved was nearly fifty feet long, double square in plan, with one end partitioned off, and having opposed entrances in the middle of the long sides. The huts with sunken floors — a Saxon innovation which called for less timber than an orthodox above-ground dwelling — were smaller, between twelve and twenty-four feet long. Two cemeteries were discovered in addition to these settlement features, the first (as we have seen) only as it was being destroyed. The second, the first sizeable Saxon cemetery to be entirely excavated in this country, contained 336 inhumations and 468 cremations. These discoveries made it possible for both settlement and cemeteries to be excavated together, the first time this has taken place on a Saxon site in this country.

Many graves contained weapons such as swords, spearheads and the iron bosses of wooden shields. From the graves have also come several hundred remains of Saxon textiles, either actual threads preserved in the corrosion layer of metal objects or as replaced shapes of threads. There is also evidence on the site of the making of bone objects and of metalworking in iron, lead and bronze. Iron buckles with inlaid designs in silver, bronze and brass, and more than a hundred brooches, usually of bronze and sometimes gilded or tinned, have been found, as well as thousands of glass and amber beads from women's graves. Two slag blocks suggest that the Saxons smelted iron ore on the site.

Saxons lived at Mucking for perhaps three and a half centuries. Three silver coins found on the floor of a sunken house were minted in Canterbury in the 690's by King Wihtred of Kent, and it seems likely that the settlement ended not long after.

But the really interesting question is when it all began; and here what is significant is the discovery in both graves and houses of bronze belt fittings of a type worn by mercenary soldiers of the late fourth century, including the five-piece silver inlaid belt-set from a wide leather belt of the type worn by Germanic soldiers in the Roman army. This suggests that the first Saxons settled at Mucking during, or immediately after the end of, the Roman Occupation. It should also be mentioned that one of the earliest graves contained what is called a Luton-type brooch, a type which can be dated to about 400 A.D., and a bronze belt buckle of a kind sometimes dated to the late fourth century.

The pottery found on the site — of the hundreds of thousands of finds most are potsherds — also points to early settlement. Of the pottery found in the first twenty huts excavated, Myres has said that there are "more pieces to which a date in the decades before and after A.D. 400 must be assigned than from any other domestic site in England, more indeed than are known at present from all the other recognised domestic sites of the pagan Anglo-Saxon period in this country put together . . . This emphasis on the earliest period of settlement before 450 is at present unparalleled elsewhere."

Components of German mercenaries' belts, together with pottery found on the site, suggest that the first settlers at Mucking were Saxon mercenaries in Roman pay, possibly posted to the area to give warning of suspicious shipping in the lower reaches of the Thames, then as now the main river entry into Britain from the Continent. It also seems likely that they chose to settle on, or near, an already existing Romano-British settlement at Mucking. Whether in fact they came before the end of Roman rule is a question which archaeology cannot answer. But it does seem possible that the first Saxon settlers here came at the same time, or shortly before, the mercenaries invited by Vortigern, and well before the period of mass immigration, when Mucking may have become a centre into which immigrants poured, and from which further extensive settlement took place.

The excavations at Mucking began on September 5th, 1965 and ended a few weeks more than twelve years later. During that time some 5,000 student excavators came to work on the site from all over the world; and in 1978 some of the Saxon finds were flown with a special courier to an exhibition at the Helms Museum in Hamburg at which only three English sites were shown individually: the Sutton Hoo ship burial, the early Saxon settlements at West Stow in Suffolk, and Mucking.

The end of the operation at Mucking was recorded on television, when according to Mrs M. U. Jones, director of the excavation, the dig's stray mongrel dog, Reject of Mucking, adopter of and adopted by those on the site, stole the show.

Apart from one or two references which came immediately after the first mention of Mucking, I have referred only to Saxon finds. And although strictly speaking this chapter is restricted to the Saxons, it is of convenience to deal here also with earlier and later occupation of the site, from the New Stone Age and through the Bronze and Iron Ages to the end of the Roman Occupation.

Evidence of the New Stone Age came from a few pits containing pottery, and from two graves. Round barrows, traces of a field system and domestic pits indicate Middle Bronze Age settlement. In the late Bronze Age two circular earthworks, the single-ditch North Ring and the double-ditch South Rings, the first some 145 feet in diameter, the second 250, were raised. Although it is clear that people lived in or near them, their purpose is at the moment uncertain. No other site is at present known with two such earthworks.

Evidence of Iron Age Occupation is provided by the discovery of some seventy penannular gullies (gullies shaped almost like a ring) which indicate the sites of round houses, with the break in the ring serving as the entrance. Settlement based on peaceful farming and herding continued during the later Iron Age; and during the course of excavation curved and rectangular ditches were found which may have served as sheepfolds immediately before the Roman Occupation. Bronze and silver coins of Cunobelin, the British king of the first century A.D., more familiar as Shakespeare's Cymbeline, have also been found on the site.

In the middle of the first century A.D. a rectangular double-ditch enclosure with square corners which covered about 1½ acres was built. Present knowledge suggests that this was not a Roman marching camp because such camps have round corners. On the other hand a bronze pendant of the type used to weigh down the sporran-like leather strips which formed part of a first century legionary's armour was found within it, and I find it difficult to believe that the earthwork had no military purpose. No evidence has, however, been uncovered to suggest that the invading Roman army camped here on its way to Colchester — although the suggestion, even so negatively expressed, might imply the possibility of greater precision in evidence than archaeology can provide.

This enclosure was set up where the late Bronze-Age double-ditched "mini-hillfort" — the South Rings — was raised centuries before. It was later incorporated in the field system of a Roman villa, whose existence is shown by the discovery of roof and flue tiles, patterned wall daub, and window glass, all found as rubbish in ditches and wells. The villa lay beyond the excavation area, but the debris suggests that its buildings were timber framed, either post-built or with a jointed frame resting on sleeper walls, probably of flint, chalk blocks and tile. Wall fragments of clay keyed to timber panels and pargeted by being impressed with a diamond stamp, possibly as a key for plaster, have also been found.

Late Roman corn drier flues, one of chalk, one of flint, and one of flint, tile and chalk, have also been found, together with timber-lined wells and many clay walled pottery kilns. There are in all four Romano-British cemeteries on the site, and an isolated burial in a stone coffin. The coffin was made of limestone, probably from the Oxford area. Roman coins found cover the period from Vespasian (69-79) to Arcadius (378-408).

If we may rely on the *Anglo-Saxon Chronicle* — and it is possible that it did not record earlier landings — settlement in Kent was less peaceful than that at Mucking, for in 455 Hengest and Horsa are said to have fought against Vortigern at Aylesford, when Horsa was killed. Two years later Hengest and his son Aesc fought against the Britons at a place called Crecganford (which according to Professor Whitelock cannot be identified with Crayford) and slew four thousand men — or in another version, four "companies". The *Chronicle* adds "the Britons then forsook Kent and fled to London in great terror".

The Saxons who invaded Britain called the areas they settled the lands of the East, Middle, West and South Saxons — that is Essex, Middlesex, Wessex and Sussex — and of the North and South Folk, that is Norfolk and Suffolk. Angles from Schleswig-Holstein overran the east coast farther north, while according to Bede, Kent was settled by Jutes from Jutland.

It is an interesting example of the way in which topography does not always bulk largely in the minds of historians that Stenton, in his magnificent work of scholarship *Anglo-Saxon England*, points out that the early social system of Kent was Frankish in character, while the field systems there had affinity with those in the Rhineland; and adds, "It seems probable that Bede was mistaken in the position which he gave to the pre-migration Jutes, and that it was not from the western fiords of Jutland but from the mouths of the Rhine that they descended upon England". The same doubt had crossed my mind, but for a different reason: if the Angles and Saxons crossed the North Sea in a more or less direct line to the nearest point on the coast of Britain, it seemed curious that Bede's Jutes, in emigrating, should have crossed over the tracks of Angles and Saxons who lived to the south of them on the Continent, but finished up living north of them in what later became England. If, however, the direct crossing was too much for the migrants' boats, or if for other reasons they kept near the coast all the way to the Straits of Dover, crossed there, and repeated the process up the east coast, then my comments lose some point. In that case it may have been first come, first settled — those coming from farther away having to travel farther up the coast to find landfall. But these matters, which must bear on the course of the settlements, are not as far as I know discussed in the authorities.

The next development of importance in our chosen area of Essex and Kent was the coming of Christianity. The story of how the faith was brought to Kent, well told by Bede, is too familiar to need repetition here. But those who visit Canterbury are recommended to seek out the church of St Martin, in which Queen Bertha of Kent, wife of King Ethelbert and herself a Christian, worshipped before the coming of Augustine. It is built of Roman bricks, and it is possible that part of one wall dates from the Roman Occupation when the building, before it went to partial ruin, had been in use as a Christian church. It is, in any case, the oldest church in England. (The poet Flecker cannot have read Bede: he has Augustine and his monks marching from Dover instead of from Thanet; but the poem in which he makes the error, *The Dying Patriot*, is one of the finest in the English language).

After Augustine had successfully completed the first part of his task of converting England, Pope Gregory sent him four more ministers, Mellitus, Justus, Paulinus and Rufinianus. Mellitus was later ordained by Augustine to preach to the East Saxons, that is to those living in what is now Essex. Bede, commenting on this appointment, makes another interesting remark when he adds, "Their metropolis is the city of London, which is situated on the banks of the aforesaid river [Thames] and is the mart of many nations resorting to it by sea and land". Mellitus was appointed in 604 and Bede was writing in about 730, and his description of London applies to the later date. But even more interesting than the fact that London was an international trading centre in the time of Bede is that it was also then the metropolis of Essex. I do not know when the western boundary of the East Saxon kingdom changed, but in the early Saxon period it struck the Thames somewhere near Staines, well to the west of London today. London was therefore in origin an Essex town, and it was natural that King Ethelbert of Kent, the convert of Augustine, who was uncle of Sabert the ruler of the East Saxons, should have paid to have a church built there for Mellitus and his successors for their episcopal see. It was the church of St Paul, forerunner of the building better known today as St Paul's cathedral. At the same time, Mellitus's colleague Justus being ordained Bishop of Kent at Rochester, Ethelbert built him a church there dedicated to St Andrew the Apostle, its successor again being better known as Rochester cathedral.

When Ethelbert of Kent died in 616, his son Eadbald who

succeeded him refused to become a Christian, as did the three sons of Sabert of Essex, who succeeded him at much the same time. They obliged Mellitus and his followers to leave, and Mellitus and Justus went to France to await events. Eadbald, later converted, asked them to return; but while Justus was received at Rochester, the Londoners still rejected Mellitus "choosing rather to be under their idolatrous high priests; for King Eadbald had not so much authority in the kingdom [of the East Saxons] as his father, nor was he able to restore the bishop to his church against the will and consent of the pagans". On the death of Laurentius, who had succeeded Augustine as Archbishop of Canterbury, Mellitus succeeded him, and on his death was in turn succeeded by Justus.

In spite of the fact that Mellitus was not accepted by the people of London, Christianity returned in the form of simony. For Bede records that in 635 Wini, expelled from the see at Winchester in the kingdom of Wessex, took refuge with the king of the midland kingdom of Mercia "of whom he purchased for money the see of the city of London, and remained bishop thereof till his death".

London must have passed out of the control of the East Saxons between Mellitus's attempted return to his see there in 616, and 635 when the see was controlled by Mercia; although the way in which Stenton says that London and Middlesex were "finally" detached from Essex in the first half of the eighth century suggests that there may have been some restoration of East Saxon rule for a period after 635.

It was not until 653 that Christianity came a second time to Essex as a result of the influence of the Christian King of Northumbria, Oswy. Oswy persuaded his friend Sigebert, King of East Anglia, to become a Christian. Sigebert was the overlord of the East Saxons; and when he asked Oswy to send him teachers who might convert them, Oswy sent him two priests, one of whom was Cedd, a follower of Aidan, the (Scottish) Bishop of Lindisfarne, and therefore a Celtic rather than a Roman churchman. "When these two, travelling to all parts of that country [Essex] had gathered a numerous church to our Lord", writes Bede, "it happened that Cedd returned home, and came to the church of Lindisfarne to confer with Bishop Finian [then Bishop of Lindisfarne]; who, finding how successful he had been in the work of the Gospel, made him bishop of the church of the East Saxons, calling to him two other bishops to assist at the ordination. Cedd, having received the episcopal dignity, returned to his province, and pursuing the work he had begun with more ample authority, built churches in several places, ordaining priests and deacons to assist him in the work of faith, and the ministry of baptising, especially in the city which, in the language of the Saxons, is called Ithancestir [Othona, the name of the Fort of the Saxon Shore at Bradwell on Sea] also in that which is named Tilaburg [Tilbury]; the first of which places is on the bank of the Pante, [Pant, then the whole of the Blackwater] the other on the bank of the Thames, where, gathering a flock of servants of Christ, he taught them to observe the discipline of regular life, as far as those rude people were then capable." (The church at Bradwell, St Peter on the Wall, is still standing; the site of the church at Tilbury is not known, although an attempt is made to establish it in chapter 14.)

Cedd was one of four brothers, all priests, the others being Chad (sometimes spelt Ceadda), Caelin, and Cynibill. There are a number of places in Essex said (incorrectly) to be named after Chad, with whom Cedd is sometimes confused. There is no evidence that Chad, Bishop of York and then of Lichfield, ever visited the county, and the element Chad in Chadwell near Tilbury comes from a word meaning *cold*.

Cedd had charge of the bishopric in Essex for many years, but died at the monastery of Lastingham in Northumbria which had been endowed for him by King Ethelwald of that nation. When his brethren in Essex heard that he was dead, thirty men from one of the monasteries he had founded there (Bede does not state which) went to Lastingham, either to live near the body of their father, or die there and be buried. All "save one little boy" died from the same pestilence which had killed Cedd.

By 665 Essex was subject to Mercia and so continued until the reign of Beornwulf who succeeded to the throne of Mercia in 823. Then in 825 Egbert of Wessex defeated Mercia in one of the most decisive internal battles of Anglo-Saxon history at Wroughton near Swindon, and Mercian ascendancy came to an end as Northumbrian ascendancy had come to an end earlier with the rise of Mercia. Essex thereupon became a dependency of Wessex and so remained until it was conquered by the Danes and became part of the Danelaw.

In Kent none of the successors of King Ethelbert, Augustine's patron, achieved a position of equal influence. Eadbald his son, a heathen who ultimately became a Christian, had as his second wife one of the Frankish royal house. Two children of his son and successor Eorcenberht had Frankish names, and one of them, Hlothhere, became King of Kent in 673. In 685 he died of wounds received in battle after an army from Sussex invaded his kingdom. In 686 Kent was divided among a number of obscure contenders for the throne, but in or after 690 was united under King Wihtred who reigned until 725. In the middle of that century three kings, two of them sons of Wihtred, were reigning in Kent, but all seem to have died in 762, and with them the Kentish dynasty "founded by Aesc son of Hengest" came to an end. It was largely as a result of the ending of the dynasty that Offa, King of Mercia, was able to extend his influence over Kent. His series of Kentish charters dating from 785 show that he then treated Kent as a province of Mercia.

In 825 the same defeat at Wroughton which ended Mercian ascendancy forced Kent as well as Essex to submit to Wessex. Immediately after the battle Egbert of Wessex sent an army into Kent; and Kent, with Essex, Surrey and Sussex, submitted to him. Thereafter Kent was never again separated from the West Saxon monarchy.

CHAPTER 13

The Danish wars

Carrington and Jackson, in the very readable history of England which they wrote before the war for schools, said of the Danes, "Never have there been more splendid, more ruthless, or more energetic seafarers". G. K. Chesterton, commenting on these same Danes a little earlier, wrote, "Roughly speaking, from the seventh century to the tenth, a dense tide of darkness, of chaos and brainless cruelty poured on these islands and on the western coasts of the Continent, which wellnigh cut them off from all the white man's culture for ever". *Roughly speaking* is right: the Danes did not land on our shores until the middle of the eighth century at the earliest; but dates apart, Chesterton was nearer the truth.

The Danes were a fiercer, more destructive, more adventurous race than the Saxons. Unlike them they came at first, not as settlers, but as plunderers, bearing away what loot they could, burning and destroying what they could not. Yet when they did finally settle in the country their investment was as great as that of the Saxons; and Canute's transformation from the sea rover to the man who built churches on the field of his victory over Edmund Ironside at Assendune and could be charmed by the monks of Ely singing was a symbol of that change. (He has recently been given the supreme accolade known to Englishmen: a public house on Canvey Island, formerly the Red Cow, has been named after him — The King Canute.)

From long usage the term Dane has been used for all the Scandinavian marauders who attacked these islands from the eighth to the eleventh centuries. Strictly speaking, however, the title Danes should not be applied to the Norwegian invaders who settled in Scotland, Ireland, and the north of England, but only to those who settled mainly in eastern and north-eastern England, who were the true Danes. The term Viking covers them all, but fails where distinction has to be made. In the Thames estuary and south-east England we are concerned almost exclusively with the Danes, but where we are concerned with raiders and settlers from Norway this will be made clear.

Where racial origins are concerned I believe it is still possible to recognise the Dane in the tall and often forthright Norfolkman (who is sometimes called the Yorkshireman of East Anglia) and the Saxon in the more retiring man of Suffolk. The long and bony face of some Lancashiremen and Yorkshiremen is also, I believe, an indication of Norse origins; and when there were such things as music halls in London and the chorus was recruited largely from Lancashire, I can remember thinking, on more than one occasion, that the chorus in Collins' Music Hall was largely made up of female Vikings.

But the Danes — and the Norwegians — were a long time settling, and during that time caused appalling havoc and destruction in a divided country. The first recorded Danish attacks were on Thanet in 753 — *A.D. 753 Prima Danorum rabies in Thaneto* writes Thomas of Elmham, in a phrase expressive even to those who have no Latin — although the *Anglo-Saxon Chronicle* says that the first attack was on the coast of Dorset in 787 (in fact 789).*

At first the Danes came in the summer and went back home in winter. Later they over-wintered with their boats, and as time went on their invasion, which began with a few dozen men in a handful of boats, became organised on a national scale, whole areas of the country becoming Danish settlements and bases for national expansion.

Whether or not treachery had a part in the defeat of the Saxons in the last and decisive battle of the campaign, that at Assendune in Essex in 1016, one thing is abundantly clear: throughout the whole of the final years of the Danish wars, when it was no longer groups of Danish adventurers but the states of Denmark and Norway which were attacking this country, the Thames and Thames estuary were a disadvantage to the Saxons who had little or no sea power, and an advantage to the invaders, who had.

To understand how the Danes were so successful it is necessary, not only to know something of the divided state of England, but something about the Danish and Norwegian ships and, what is more important, how they were used.

A Viking ship preserved in waterlogged alluvial soil was found at

*The events in the *Anglo-Saxon Chronicle* are set out in chronological order in years, but many of the entries are for various reasons a year or two out. The matter is discussed in detail in the introduction to Garmonsway's translation. It is an indication of the difficulties involved that both the *Anglo-Saxon Chronicle* and *Whitaker's Almanack*, to say nothing of other works of reference, have Alfred dying in 901. Apparently he died in 899.

Gokstad in Norway in 1880 and is now in an Oslo museum. It is seventy-eight feet long, clinker built with sixteen-inch-wide oak planks, the lower ones lashed to the ribs rather than fixed by bolts or pegs, which helped to give the boat stability in a heavy sea. If, as is assumed, the Gokstad ship was typical of those used by Norwegian and Danish raiders on these shores, then they were more or less flat-bottomed for easy landing on beaches, and bow and stern reared up to high stem and sternpost. The long and massive rudder had its pivot on the starboard quarter, and was swung by a short tiller at right angles to it. There were keyhole-shaped openings for sixteen oars along each side which could be closed by shutters when under sail. Outboard of the gunwale was a rack in which the crew's round shields were placed when in harbour — they would have interfered with rowing had they been so placed at sea. The ships were open and undecked, and propelled mainly by the oars, although each boat had a simple sail.

According to H. R. Loyn, writing in *The Vikings in Britain*, the Gokstad ship had a keel made of a single timber nearly sixty feet in length, so substantial that when a replica was built in 1892, Canadian oak had to be used for want of suitable straight, solid oak timber in Scandinavia. The replica then crossed the Atlantic in less than a month in April 1893. A detailed description of the Gokstad ship, with an analysis of the Vikings' skill in navigation and the author's observations on the reasons why they risked their lives in exploring, plundering, trading and settling all over the known world, are given in *The Vikings in Britain.*

Why the Vikings took to their ships in the way they did certainly takes some understanding. One explanation — not offered by Loyn, who thinks rather deeper than this — is that the "hunting economy" of Scandinavia became strained in the middle of the eighth century, and as a result raiding followed by emigration took place on a large scale. The explanation is partial. It may be far fetched to make a comparison between the Danes and the Hare Indians in John Buchan's book *Sick Heart River*; but that tribe also suffered from strains in its hunting economy, and instead of seeking new hunting fields was like to die. The fact must be that where the Hares suffered from lack of morale, the Danes had too much of it; and Kipling gets nearer the heart of the matter in his haunting *Harp song of the Dane women* when he poses the question,

What is a woman that you forsake her,

And the hearth-fire and the home-acre
To go with the old grey Widow-maker?

Stenton suggests (I think rightly) that the possibility of plunder and the prospect of exciting adventure were the main motives for raiding. He also outlines the political conditions in Scandinavia and the borders of the North Sea which encouraged it.

But whatever drove them, and whatever the restraints which might otherwise have held them, the Norsemen in particular went to both ends of the known, and even the unknown, world. Reaching Iceland at the end of the ninth century, they travelled from there to Greenland and, in the eleventh century, to north America. In 862 they founded Novgarod and what ultimately became the kingdom of Russia. Known to the Slavs and Greeks as Varangians, some of their number were recruited as a bodyguard by the Eastern Roman Emperor Basil II in 988; and the Varangian Guard, which was joined by a number of Saxons after their defeat in 1066, served his successors until the fall of Constantinople in 1453. *Count Robert of Paris* by Sir Walter Scott and *The Wanderer's Necklace* by Sir Rider Haggard deal in part with their activities.

In their assaults on this country, from their first raids to the successful full-scale invasion of Canute over two centuries later, the whole of the invaders' strategy was centred on their ships. These comfortless vessels, small open boats of shallow draught much the same size as fishing smacks, were their homes, their camps, their castles, their transport, their campaign headquarters, their all. Where the Saxons had to move against them by land, the Danes — the reign of Alfred, in particular, apart — could move unmolested by sea or river; and if in their marauding things became too hot for them, they could retire to their ships and be off before the Saxons could touch them.

But all this would have been as nothing unless the Danes had secure bases for their ships in this country. The *Anglo-Saxon Chronicle*, which names the sites of a number of these bases, which were designed to defend the boats on summer raids or while overwintering, refers to them by the Saxon word *geweorc*, which means a *work*; and in the sense of an earthwork the word, while partial, is correct. They were usually roughly square-shaped basins dug out of alluvial soil near a navigable river, tidal creek or estuary, and it was in these basins that the Danes docked their ships. The spoil was used to make a defence bank round each basin, and possibly on each side of the short channel leading out of it. Less common (I know of one case only) were earthworks defending from inland attack a piece of sea shore on which the ships were drawn up.

While a number of Danish and Norwegian basins on or near tidal creeks, estuaries and rivers are known in England, they must be a small number compared with those still in existence elsewhere in the British Isles, in Ireland, on the Loire and in northern France, and farther afield. Such *geweorcs* as I have visited in Essex and Kent are described in this chapter. Others are listed in Appendix V.

A sketch map of Danish basins on the Ouse at Willington some three miles east of Bedford appears in *Earthwork of England* by A. Hadrian Allcroft. According to Allcroft, the largest of the three basins here measured up to 105 feet in width and 170 in length, and may at one time have been longer. Allcroft thought it might have taken between twenty and thirty Danish ships. At the southern end of this basin a passage twenty-five feet wide opened into a second basin sixty feet wide by 110 in length. This feature of a small inner basin giving on to the main basin was also seen in the docks — in this case Norwegian — at Dockacres near Carnforth in Lancashire before their destruction; and may be characteristic. I suspect it may have been done to provide a primitive sort of lock which would allow boats to float in and out on a head of retained water.

The only other fact which need be mentioned to explain the Vikings' raiding tactics is that once set on plundering they stole what horses they could to give them greater speed and mobility and carry their plunder back to the ships.

One of the first great raids was in 793 when the Norwegians sacked the monastery at Lindisfarne and, in 794, that at Jarrow. But the main body of Norwegian, as opposed to Danish, adventurers passed round the north of Scotland to Ireland, establishing intermediate colonies in the Shetlands, Orkneys and Hebrides as well as in Caithness and Sutherland. They seized and fortified two ports in Ireland, one of them Dublin, in 838; took Waterford in 914, and Limerick in 920; but were defeated by Brian Boru at the battle of Clontarf in 1014. They also made considerable territorial settlements in the north of England in the tenth century by migration from Ireland, and for a time founded a Norse kingdom and dynasty based on York.

The first Danish — as opposed to Norse — raiders of whom reliable record remains arrived in Sheppey in 835. During the next thirty years, which ended with the arrival in East Anglia of a great Danish army which had no intention of returning, there were more than twelve separate raids on England. During the course of these raids the Danes ran riot and plundered, burnt, and murdered throughout the length of the southern and eastern coastal areas of England. Kent suffered more heavily than other regions, and in 839 there was great slaughter in Rochester and London. In 850 a Danish army wintered in England for the first time, in the Isle of Thanet. In 851 (the date is Stenton's and that of the *Anglo-Saxon Chronicle*, although Garmonsway gives it as 850) 350 ships, each carrying some thirty-six fighting men, came into the Thames estuary. Their crews stormed Canterbury and London, put to flight the King of Mercia and his army, and then crossed over the Thames into Surrey. Here King Ethelwulf with an army drawn from all Wessex fought with them and had the victory, and according to one version of the *Chronicle* "made the greatest slaughter of a heathen host that we have heard tell of up to this present day". It had little lasting effect, for in 854 the Danes overwintered in England again, this time in Sheppey. Then, in 865, there arrived what might be loosely called the first Danish army of occupation, which set up its headquarters in East Anglia.

It was the habit of this Danish host to move quarters each autumn. In 866 it occupied York; in 867, Nottingham; in 868, York once more; in 869, Thetford. From Thetford the Danes went to Reading, and made their base behind an earthwork dug from Kennet to Thames shortly before the point of meeting. After taking London and wintering there in 871-872, they moved to Torksey, and late in 873 to Repton. Then, after a campaign of which no record remains, the King of Mercia left England and the Danes appointed Coelwulf, one of his thanes, as king on condition that the kingdom should be at their disposal whenever they might wish to occupy it. Three years later they took half of it for division among themselves and gave the other half to Coelwulf. It was in this way that the Danes began to settle in England.

In 874 the Danish army divided into two groups. One went to the mouth of the Tyne and made settlement in Yorkshire. The other went to Cambridge, and by 877 had divided their half of Mercia among those in the army who wanted a share in it. Those who did not want to settle descended on Chippenham under their leader Guthrum; and Alfred withdrew into the Isle of Athelney in Somerset, with every prospect that before the end of the year Wessex also would be divided out among the members of the Danish army. But after seven weeks of engaging Danish raiding parties, Alfred began operations against their main army; and at the battle of Ethandune, with the men of Somerset, Wiltshire and part of Hampshire, fought the Danes and defeated them. Three weeks later their leader Guthrum and some thirty of the most honourable men in his army were baptised. This encounter led to the treaty of Wedmore, by which Wessex was held by Alfred and the country north and east of Watling Street was ceded to the Danes.

Ethandune is not mentioned in this form in the *Anglo-Saxon Chronicle*, but is the common denominator of slight variants appearing in other, and later, chronicles. The *Chronicle* says the battle took place at Edington, which is some three miles east of Westbury in Wiltshire; so that Chesterton stretches it a bit in the Penguin edition of his essays and poems when he says, "Over a vast dim region of England this dark name of Ethandune floats like an eagle doubtful where to swoop and strike", before saying in a later paragraph that the battle took place near Chippenham, which it did not. Nonetheless his essay on Ethandune, from which the quotation is made, is a powerful piece of writing and one worth quoting because it does so clearly sum up the drama and the savagery of the Danish wars. "But the other day," he writes, "under a wild sunset and moonrise, I passed the place which is best reputed as Ethandune, a high, grim upland, partly bare and partly shaggy; like the savage and sacred spot in those great imaginative lines about the demon lover and the waning moon. The darkness, the red wrack of sunset, the yellow and lurid moon, the long fantastic shadows, actually created that sense of monstrous incident which is the dramatic side of landscape. The bare grey slopes seemed to rush downhill like routed hosts: the dark clouds drove across like riven banners: and the moon was like a golden dragon, like the Golden Dragon of Wessex."

This is Chesterton at his best, capable if read in youth of casting a spell which in later years still hangs in wisps about the name of Ethandune; and perhaps, by association, about that of the later decisive battle — and, for the English, defeat — of Assendune.

In 884 a group of Danes who had been raiding on the Continent landed in Kent and besieged Rochester. The town, the first known to have held the Danes at bay, resisted all attacks until Alfred relieved it. Part of the Danish army took to the sea; the remainder went raiding and were supported by the Danes of East Anglia. As a reprisal Alfred sent a fleet into their waters which captured sixteen ships off the mouth of the Stour, but was defeated by a larger Danish force while returning.

Alfred had already sent an armed fleet to fight the Danes at sea on two occasions, and the account in the *Anglo-Saxon Chronicle* of how he built new and longer ships to tackle the Danish marauders makes fascinating reading. They were almost twice as long as "the others". Some had sixty oars, some more (the Gokstad ship had thirty-two). They were swifter and steadier, and with more freeboard than "the others", and not built according to the Frisian or the Danish designs, but as Alfred thought would be most serviceable. But in general they fought well outside our area where we cannot follow them.

In 886 Alfred occupied London, which may have been in Danish hands since the Danes wintered there in 872. He repaired the walls and stationed an English garrison there; and London thereafter became a centre of national resistance to enemies from any quarter.

It is clear that Essex was by now in Danish occupation, because a settlement made between Alfred and the Danes after the fighting in 886 had the boundary of the Danelaw running up the Thames, up the Lea to its source, in a straight line to Bedford, and then along the Ouse as far as Watling Street. This makes more understandable the fact that in succeeding campaigns the Danes took refuge in Essex on a number of occasions.

The Danes did not restrict their attacks to this country. They also raided northern France, and raided this country from northern France as well as from Denmark. Thus in 892 an army of Danes from France crossed from Boulogne to the mouth of the river Lympne in 250 ships, horses and all, rowed (or towed) their ships up the river, and made a fortified dock at Appledore. At the same time Hasten, of whom we hear for the first time, also left Boulogne with his forces in eighty ships, entered the Thames estuary, and made a *geweorc* at Milton near Sittingbourne.

The river Lympne up which the Danes took their ships was an artificial distributary of the Rother, which rises near Rotherfield in the High Weald of Sussex some twenty-four miles west of Rye. It is sometimes referred to as the eastern Rother to differentiate it from the western Rother, a different stream which also flows through Sussex, but to the Arun. Today the eastern Rother falls into the Channel near Rye, and while I regard both the present course to Rye, and the earlier course of the Lympne, as artificial below their point of separation, it is difficult to suggest where the two streams did in fact divide — possibly at The Lock east of Iden. Whatever the point, the Lympne then flowed north and east along the northern edge of Romney Marsh past Appledore, Kenardington, Ruckinge and Lympne, and so to Hythe; the Rother flowed south to Rye.

The Danes are said to have pulled their ships up the Lympne to a point four miles from the entrance to the estuary, destroyed a Saxon fort within the marsh, and then wrought a *geweorc* at Appledore.

The Lympne was mentioned as *Liminaea* in a charter of 697 given in Birch's *Cartularium Saxonicum.* It took its name from Portus Lemanis, the Roman Fort of the Saxon Shore at Lympne, of which the remains are now known as Stutfall Castle. I have no doubt its course from Rother to Hythe was dug by the Romans. It was at odds with the natural drainage of the area and dried up in the Middle Ages, possibly in the reign of Edward I, although Hasted, the late eighteenth century historian, says its course could still be seen in his time. What is now known as the Royal Military Canal was dug along its bed as part of our coastal defences when it seemed possible that Napoleon might invade England.

I have not been to Appledore, but the Victoria County History says the Danes' work there is now buried under silt. Hasten's work at Milton was probably off Milton Creek near Sittingbourne. This narrow sheltered tidal creek is some three miles long and runs roughly north-east from the centre of Sittingbourne to the Swale, which runs round the back of Sheppey and connects the Medway estuary to the west with the Thames estuary to the east. It is probable that the Danish docks were at Bayford Court at the head of a short creek which leaves Milton Creek not far from Sittingbourne itself. According to a sketch map with a paper on the subject by Spurrell in the 1885 *Archaeological Journal*, it was a large square area enclosed with banks partly protected by a moat on the creek side, and having an entrance, presumably for boats, on the same side. Spurrell said nothing of it remained. Such was Hasten's stronghold at Milton. On a hurried visit to the area I failed to identify it.

Returning to the Danes on the Lympne at Appledore: according to the account in the *Anglo-Saxon Chronicle*, Alfred gathered his army and camped between Appledore and Milton, where Hasten had set up his headquarters. Then, when the Danes from Appledore decided to cross the Thames into Essex with their booty, they were caught by Alfred and defeated at Farnham in Surrey, and their booty taken. The defeated Danes then crossed the Thames at a point where there was no ford, and established themselves on an island in the Colne, which falls into the Thames just above Staines. During this period the Danes from Milton crossed the Thames estuary and set up defences for men and ships at Benfleet in Essex — the point to which the Danes from Appledore were making when they proposed to cross into Essex.

I have purposely given the account as it appears in admittedly confused form in the *Anglo-Saxon Chronicle* in order to make the point that there are disadvantages as well as advantages in going to original sources. For the account is obviously wrong in two ways, and confusing in a third. And there is no way in which these matters can be resolved from a study of the *Chronicle* alone.

The source of confusion is that the entry for 894 begins with the statement that whenever "the other hosts" (marauding Danes from overseas) went plundering in full force, the Danes who had already settled in Northumbria and East Anglia went out with them, or on their own. One might therefore suppose that the sentences which follow immediately in the *Chronicle* refer to the Northumbrian and East Anglian Danes; but in fact there is no further reference to this group until later, when they are reported to be attacking Devon in 140 ships. What intervenes concerns the Danes who had camped at Milton and Appledore only. That is the confusion.

The first error in the account is that when the Danes left their camp at Appledore for Milton in order to carry their plunder northwards across the Thames into Essex, and were intercepted by Alfred, they were defeated at Farnham in Surrey; and Farnham is some eighty miles west of Milton as the crow flies.

If we rely on the *Chronicle* alone we are therefore caught two ways. Farnham is too far west for Danes going from Appledore to Essex to be defeated there in battle: a point nearer the Appledore-Milton axis would be an impossible one from which the defeated army could have taken refuge on an island in the Colne near Staines.

The *Chronicle* does not say clearly what happened to the Colne Danes, but it does say later that the Danes from Milton crossed the Thames to Benfleet where they were joined by "the great host . . . which had been encamped at Appledore"; and this is (or appears to be) the second error, for it has already been stated that the defeated

Danes from Appledore were sweating it out on an island in the Colne.

What in fact took place was that within a few weeks of his taking up a position between the armies at Appledore and Milton, Alfred imposed an agreement on Hasten whereby he and his men left Kent for Essex — since 886 regarded as part of the Danelaw — and his two sons were baptised. Then in the late spring of 893 the Danes from Appledore set out on a raid which took them as far as Hampshire and Berkshire; and it was while returning that they were caught, and defeated, by Alfred's son Edward; driven in confusion across the Thames; and forced to take refuge on the island of Thorney, which is formed by two branches of the Colne near Iver in Buckinghamshire. The Danes from Northumbria and East Anglia, who were not concerned in these movements, were attacking Exeter, where Alfred went to resist them.

In the meantime the Danes on Thorney Island were offered terms which stipulated that they should leave English territory, but would be allowed to join Hasten's group in Essex. They therefore went to Benfleet, with the ships from Milton and Appledore.

This account, as given by Stenton, is based on the *Chronicle* of Ethelward, an ealdorman of Wessex, who translated the *Anglo-Saxon Chronicle* into Latin between 975 and 998. He used a text different from all surviving versions and so included passages whose omission from the remaining versions makes nonsense of their account of this particular part of the Danish campaigns.

While Alfred was in the west of England dealing with the Danish attack there, another part of his forces, with reinforcements from London, went east to Benfleet where Hasten and the men from Milton and Appledore were established.

The site of Hasten's *geweorc*, which can be seen by anyone travelling by train between Fenchurch Street and Southend, is on the edge of the low-lying ground on the north side of the track just west of Benfleet station. South Benfleet church stands on it. The outstanding feature of the site is an artificial excavation, or possibly a natural cleft which has been artificially widened, which runs beside the churchyard. (It is similar to those which I also believe to be artificial beside the churches at Mucking a few miles higher up the Thames and at Bluntisham on the Ouse in Huntingdonshire).

The only question is whether the little valley beside the churchyard formed part of the *geweorc*, and if so what part. If it was dug or enlarged by the Danes to dock their boats in, then the landward defence must have been a long one, running from the flood plain on the west round the head of the basin to the flood plain on the east. If, however, the cleft was part of a moat which encircled what is now the churchyard on three sides, while the boats were drawn up in the creek on the fourth side, then the defence line would be shorter and easier to hold. There is some reason to suppose that this may be how things were arranged, because Matthew of Westminster says the work at South Benfleet was fortified "fossatis altis et spatiosis", that is with wide and deep fosses, or moats either dry or wet. This suggests that there was more of the foss than the one section remaining.

Alfred's forces attacked the Danes at Benfleet while their leader Hasten, breaking his agreement with Alfred, was out plundering. According to the *Chronicle* they put the enemy to flight, stormed the fort, and seized everything inside it, booty, women and children; and took the lot to London. It was on this occasion that Alfred restored Hasten's wife and family to him. The Danes' ships they either broke in pieces, burnt, or took to London or Rochester. The accuracy of this account was confirmed when the railway bridge on the London to Southend line was built slightly lower down the creek in about 1855. The workmen excavating for the piers came on the remains of a number of burnt ships and "in and about them" great quantities of human skeletons.

When they were driven out of Benfleet the Danes made their way down river to Shoeburyness and made a camp on low lying land by the seashore. It was in the form of a semi-circular earthwork — an inner bank and an outer ditch — whose two ends ran down to the shore, providing between them a section of defended coast on which the boats could be beached.

There has been a good deal of erosion on this coast since the camp was built. Even so recently as 1908, according to Allcroft, the greatest width of the camp between the shore and its inland face was 750 feet, and the side open to the sea was 1,900 feet in length. Today the area enclosed in the earthwork has a width at its greatest of 700 feet, and the ends of the earthwork are some 1,600 feet apart. I still believe, however, that the ends of the ditch-and-bank continued in present alignment to provide a stretch of defended shore for the ships, and do not (as others have suggested) represent what is left of a circular defence work of which part has been eaten away by the sea. I cannot believe that the Danes would have left their ships outside the defences, and duplicated with trench and bank the stretch of defence line offered by the sea itself. And in any case the name Shoebury comes from the Old English word *burh* meaning fortified place and *sceo* meaning shoe, in this case horse-shoe; which last refers to the shape of the earthwork. The area, which is in army occupation, is known as Horseshoe Barracks today.

Reports of the depth and height of ditch and bank vary. Spurrell, writing in the *Archaeological Journal* for 1885, said the ditch was over forty feet wide and about five feet six inches deep, while the bank was between seven and eight feet higher than the average level of the ground inside and outside the camp. Laver, writing in the Transactions of the Essex Archaeological Society for 1898, said that the ditch was between eight and nine feet deep, and the bank twelve feet higher than average ground level. In 1908, according to Allcroft, the ditch was twenty-five feet wide at the floor; but whatever the correct dimensions, we can take it that it was a considerable earthwork.

Spurrell, in an earlier paper than that already quoted, said the bottom of the ditch was then six feet above high water mark, and there was no evidence in the bottom of it of sea mud or shells. It was clearly not intended for use as a moat filled with sea water.

The ditch would be left dry for a number of reasons. The first is that it is easier to dig a nine feet deep trench dry than wet. Even if they intended flooding it later, the Danes would dig it in one or more sections, leaving a dam at each end to keep out the sea until excavation was complete. But I do not think they intended it to be flooded. A deep wide trench filled with pointed stakes is a better defence than the same trench filled with water. Further, to have filled the ditch with water might have encouraged its sides to collapse; and had the ends of the ditch been open, wave action would have eaten the sides away more swiftly.

Once they had built their fortified camp at Shoeburyness, some of the Danes from there, joined by others from East Anglia and Northumbria, went up the Thames and then to Buttington on the Severn where they built a *geweorc* and stayed many weeks. Defeated there by the English, they escaped back to Shoeburyness and the ships.

A second time they went out marauding, this time as far as Chester and North Wales, but then returned through Northumbria and East

Anglia to a new camp on the island of Mersea, farther up the Essex coast. Laver suggests that the camp there was a large moated area which included the sites of what are now East Mersea church, the churchyard, the Hall, the Hall garden, and a neighbouring small pasture, but that the defence works had been levelled by farming. The Report of the Royal Commission on Historical Monuments says no recognisable trace of Danish works remains there today.

Within a few weeks of arriving at Mersea the Danes set off again. This time they made their way up the Thames and so into the Lea. Why they decided to leave Mersea is not stated; but how they were forced to leave their *geweorc* on the Lea is told in the *Anglo-Saxon Chronicle*, and in slightly different versions by John of Brompton and Henry of Huntingdon.

The *Chronicle*, presumably referring to the point where the Lea falls into the Thames, says the Danes laid up their ships in a defended position twenty miles "above the city of London" — some twenty-two miles by today's reckoning. One day (according to the *Chronicle*) Alfred rode along to see where the stream could be blocked and the ships' route closed. When he found such a spot he began to build fortifications each side of the stream, and camped nearby. The Danes, seeing this, and realising that their ships were now valueless, abandoned them without even firing them and went across country to the Severn. Their fleet was thereupon seized by the English.

If parts of the *Chronicle* were inspired by Alfred, this account may be more reliable than that of Henry of Huntingdon, who in his *Historia Anglorum* says Alfred "divided the river Lea into three branches so that their ships could not be brought out". It has been assumed that this division, if it did take place, lowered the level of the Lea, and so grounded the ships.

The fact that the Danes did not wait to fire their ships before leaving might be taken to suggest that an inexplicable lowering of water level caused them to panic. But it is not easy to make a swift and significant change in the level of a river flowing with little fall into a larger river only slightly below its level, unless its flow is enclosed within floodbanks and is several feet above the surrounding land — and I cannot believe this to have been the case with the lower Lea in Saxon times. On the other hand, the addition of two or three outlets to that already existing in the Lea itself might do the trick — as it did with the Great Ouse over a longer period, when its waters flowed into a Roman canal and as a result some time during the Middle Ages forsook its course through Wisbech for that at Kings Lynn.

The Lea has five separate channels crossing the river's flood plain south-west of Stratford station today. Tradition has it that one of the outlets Alfred created was the most easterly of these, the Channelsea River, which leaves the main course of the Lea in Hackney Marshes some four miles above the Thames outfall, and rejoins it at Bromley about a mile and a half above. A second channel said to have been created by Alfred is near Waltham Abbey, some twelve miles above the river's outlet into the Thames.

If this version of the story is correct, what Alfred probably did was to re-open channels already in existence which had become silted up over the years.

Eliot Howard, writing in the Transactions of the Essex Archaeological Society for 1909, suggests that the Danes put their ships immediately above the junction of the Lea and Stort, some on the east bank of the Lea, some on the west bank of the Stort (which joins the Lea on the east) — both "inner" banks, so to speak. They then cut off the land fork, and the two stretches of bank where the ships were moored, by a moat. If they did this, and if the water level of both streams was lowered, then the moat, probably shallower than the two rivers, might be drained dry; and this would leave the camp itself more open to attack. Howard suggested that the Danes failed to fire their ships, not only because they realised their river escape route was cut off, but because they also feared imminent attack while in a weak position, and avoided doing anything which might attract attention to their plight.

Alfred was succeeded by his son Edward the Elder. At the time of his accession, eastern England from Thames to Tees was divided between a number of Danish armies established on the land by successive partitions of southern Northumbria, eastern Mercia, and East Anglia. Before the end of his reign every Danish colony south of the Humber had been annexed to Wessex.

The first major engagement of Edward's reign was the battle of Holmesdale (the gault valley immediately south of the North Downs) between the Danes and men from Kent, which gave rise to the saying

This is Holmesdale
Never conquered, never shall

In 909 Edward sent an army against the Danes of Northumbria and made them accept his terms. Next year the Danes invaded Northumbria, but were finally defeated at Tettenhall in Staffordshire. Weakened by this defeat, they were unable to resist Norse invaders from Ireland, who by 919 had established a Norwegian kingdom based on York.

The story of Edward's reign is that of the gradual reconquest of Danish England, shire by shire, as far north as Humber, much of the fighting being led by Alfred's daughter Ethelfleda, Edward's sister. Their policy was continued by Athelstan, who succeeded his father Edward in 924. He took possession of Northumbria, and the Norse kingdom of York came to an end. Olaf Guthfrithson, Norse claimant to the leadership of the Northumbrian Vikings, went back to Ireland and became ruler of the Norsemen in Dublin in 934. Hoping to regain his dominion of York, he returned to England in 937; but with his allies, of whom the most important was Constantine King of Scots, was defeated by Athelstan at the battle of Brunanburh, probably somewhere in Northumbria, or possibly at Brunswark in Dumfriesshire. This was so signal a victory that the author of the Parker version of the *Anglo-Saxon Chronicle* bursts into verse when he describes the hasty flight north of Constantine and the escape to Dublin of the remnant of the Norsemen led by Olaf (in the *Chronicle*, Anlaf).

> They left behind them
> raw to devour,
> the sallow kite,
> the swarthy raven
> with horny nib,
> and the hoarse vultur
> with the eagle swift
> to consume his prey;
> the greedy gos-hawk,
> and that grey beast
> the wolf of the weald.

Admittedly far away from the Thames estuary, but I think worth quoting. Garmonsway's translation may be more accurate and Tennyson's more poetic, but in Ingram's, possibly because of the short lines and the slightly archaic phraseology, there does seem to be more of the sword-bite.

Athelstan was succeeded in 939 by his brother Edmund, who reconquered Danish-held territory as far as the border of Northumbria, and Edmund by his brother Eadred. The reign of Eadwig, who succeeded in 955, then began a period of a quarter century when for the first time since the reign of Egbert this country was free from the imminent threat of invasion. Then, on Ethelred's accession as a boy of about ten in 978, the roof fell in.

Ethelred succeeded by an act of treachery, his half brother and predecessor King Edward having been murdered at Corfe in Dorset by Ethelred's retainers. In a moving passage the *Anglo-Saxon Chronicle* comments, "No worse deed than this was ever done by the English nation since they first sought the land of Britain". Ethelred therefore began to rule in an atmosphere of suspicion which ultimately destroyed the prestige of the crown, and his reign of thirty-seven years, the longest of any Saxon king, was a series of disasters.

In 980 the Danish raiders returned, plundered Southampton and killed most of its citizens or took them prisoner; they overran Thanet; plundered Cheshire. In 981 Padstow was laid waste and much destruction caused along the coasts of Devon and Cornwall. In 982 Portland was plundered; in 987, Watchet; in 988, Devon. Then in 991 a larger body of raiders led by Olaf Tryggvasson (who became King of Norway in 995) appeared off the east coast, sacked Ipswich, and in the battle of Maldon killed Brithnoth, ealdorman of Essex, and defeated his forces. The battle is described in a famous poem. In the same year the Danes "because of the great terror they inspired along the sea coast" were bought off for the first time by the payment of Danegeld, a tax on every town and village in England, which on this occasion amounted to 22,000 pounds of gold and silver. The Danes came back for more, and it was not until the reign of Edward the Confessor that the tax was abolished.

In 994 the Danes commanded by Sweyn the King of Denmark, and Olaf Tryggvasson, came up the Thames in ninety-four ships and attacked London, but according to the *Chronicle* suffered greater loss and injury than they ever thought could be inflicted on them. Unable to capture the city they went off, burning, plundering and slaughtering along the coast and inland in Essex, Kent, Sussex and Hampshire. Ethelred and his council bought them off with 16,000 pounds of silver.

In 997 more Danes appeared, plundered Devon, Cornwall, Somerset and South Wales, and burnt the abbey church at Tavistock to the ground, carrying back with them to the ships "an indescribable amount of plunder". In 998 they ravaged Dorset, and in 999 came up the Thames estuary and into the Medway as far as Rochester, defeating those local levies which engaged them. In 1000 they sailed to Normandy to sell their booty; and in 1001 returned to ravage widely over the south of England; but were bought off in the next year by a further payment of 24,000 pounds of silver.

In the same year Ethelred seems to have had a brainstorm. He gave orders that all the Danes in England were to be killed on St Brice's Day, November 13th. Secret instructions were sent in letters from the King to every town so that the massacre should take place everywhere on the same day. As there was peace at this time between Saxon and Dane, the foreign settlers were taken by surprise. Women as well as men were killed, the victims including Gunhild, sister of King Sweyn of Denmark, then living as a hostage in England, who was put to death after having seen her husband and son slain before her eyes.

The massacre brought no military advantage, but simply inflamed Ethelred's enemies against him. They renewed their invasions with greater organisation and determination. In 1003 Sweyn came with a fleet and went on the rampage in Wiltshire; and from that date until the deposition and flight of Ethelred, when for a short time Sweyn came to complete power in England, its history is one long catalogue of carnage and terror.

In 1007 the name of Edric Streona, of whom more will be heard later, appears for the first time in the *Anglo-Saxon Chronicle* when he was appointed ealdorman of Mercia. He was a man of ignoble birth, guilty according to the chroniclers of an unequalled series of treacheries and other crimes. A favourite of Ethelred, he married one of his daughters, and was raised by him to a position of wealth and power which made him almost an independent prince in midland England. He seems to have been that king's evil genius as well as that of his eldest son and successor, Edmund Ironside. His nickname was Streona, or The Grasper.

In 1009 a Danish army, said by Stenton to be the most formidable in fighting quality and probably in numbers to have invaded England since Ethelred became king, descended on England. It came in two groups, one led by Thurkill the Tall, the other by his brother. They were bought off by the men of Canterbury and East Kent; tried to take London; and failed. Early in 1010 they burnt Oxford, then left in their ships for East Anglia, and stormed Ipswich. They defeated a force drawn from Cambridgeshire and East Anglia near Thetford, and raided Mercia and Wiltshire before returning to the ships. They had raided the whole or part of fifteen counties apart from East Anglia in the sixteen months since landing.

In September 1011 the Danes raided Kent, and were paid 48,000 pounds of silver in April 1012 to go away. They demanded a separate ransom for the Archbishop of Canterbury whom they had taken prisoner. He refused to allow it to be paid, and after having been in captivity for some months was murdered by the Danes at Greenwich. Thurkill vainly offered his men all he had save his ship to save the Archbishop's life, but they were drunk; and when the greater part of the army left England later in the year, he remained with forty-five ships at his command and took service with Ethelred. He was given an estate in East Anglia in return for his oath to defend the country against all invaders.

In 1013 Sweyn returned with a great fleet set on conquering the whole of England. Ethelred took refuge in Thurkill's ships, which lay in the Thames. His wife went to Normandy and he sent his two sons by her to join her there. In January 1014 he followed them.

Sweyn died in the following month and the Danes chose his younger son Canute as king; but the English sent for Ethelred, who was brought back by Olaf, later King Olaf II of Norway and the patron saint of that country, whose ships were lying in Normandy at the time. Ethelred, showing a new side to his character, collected a large army and forced Canute and the Danish invaders to take to their ships. They sailed round the coast to Sandwich, where Canute cut off the hands, ears and noses of the hostages his father had taken, put them ashore, and left England with his fleet. He was then nineteen years old.

Canute was joined in Denmark by Thurkill, who brought nine ships from England. It is not known why he left Ethelred's service. Canute returned to England in August 1015 and began ravaging Wessex. Ethelred's eldest son Edmund and Edric Streona began raising an army, but Streona went over to the Danes and seduced from their allegiance to Ethelred the crews of forty ships which had once been Thurkill's. Edmund joined his father in London and Canute prepared to move his fleet to the Thames. Before his arrival Ethelred died, and Edmund was chosen king.

In May of that year Canute sailed up the Thames — according to the chronicles of Thietmar, with 340 ships each containing some eighty men — and anchored off Bermondsey. After a short interval they set off to lay siege to London. London Bridge was defended against them and the fleet could not pass. Canute therefore had his men dig a ditch, later known as Canute's Trench, on the south side of the river and drag their ships along it to the west side of the bridge in the hope they might thereby get inside the city. (Details of the possible course of the Trench are given in an appendix.)

After describing how the Danes dug the ditch and dragged their ships along it to the west side of London Bridge, Ingram's translation of the *Chronicle* adds, "Afterwards they trenched the city without, so that no man could go in or out, and often fought against it; but the citizens bravely withstood them".

The entry is puzzling. It would have been harder for the Danes to dig a trench through the hard and rising ground of the gravel terrace immediately north of London than it would have been to dig it through the alluvium south of the river; and as far as I know no one has claimed to identify a Danish trench north of the city. But there can be no doubt, from the account of how the siege was conducted, that the city was invested to north as well as to south.

Garmonsway's translation, with its suggestion of banks and earthworks rather than a ring trench, makes the entry clearer. It reads, "They . . . built earthworks outside the borough so that no one could get in or out, and attacked the borough repeatedly, but they withstood them valiantly".(The reader should be warned that his reference, here and elsewhere, to *the borough* is not to London's only "borough" of Southwark* or the south-work, once a fortified place somewhere near the south end of London Bridge, but to the city of London itself.)

Canute left London for Wessex before the end of June and fought against Edmund there at Penselwood in Dorset and Sherston in

*London Sessions, Newington, some time in 1944. Defendant being questioned by pompous barrister.

Barrister: And where were you on the morning of April 5th?

Defendant: I wuz inver buwwa.

Barrister: Ah. You were with your brother.

Defendant: Nah! I wuz inver *buwwa.*

Barrister: Ah. You were with your *barrow.*

Defendant: Nah! Nah! I wuz *inver buwwa!*

Judge (with an edge to his voice): He means, Mr So-and-So, that he was in the *Borough* of *Southwark.*

Wiltshire. Both encounters were indecisive. Canute returned to London and Edmund followed him, keeping north of the Thames and avoiding main roads, coming on the Danish positions north of London by unguarded tracks through the woods at Tottenham. The Danes took to their ships and crossed to the south bank. Edmund had to go higher upstream to ford the river at Brentford; and two days after driving them out of their positions north of the city he defeated the Danes in a battle on the south bank. But his losses were such that he had to return to Wessex to raise another army, and the Danes returned to their positions north of London and began besieging the city again. Shortage of supplies then forced Canute to bring things to a speedy decision; but in an attack on the city by land and water with the whole of his force he failed. He abandoned London, sailed to the mouth of the Orwell, and obtained supplies by raiding East Anglia and Mercia. With the food and livestock taken in the raid the Danes sailed down the coast of Essex and across the estuary to the Medway, and so into Kent. Edmund caught up with them at Otford and drove them into Sheppey with great loss. The total failure of Canute's venture now seemed certain.

Edric Streona (according to Florence of Worcester impressed by his gallant resistance) then went to meet Edmund at Aylesford. The *Chronicle* comments, "No greater error of judgment was ever made than this". Florence says that at this moment, when Edmund's success seemed assured, Edric persuaded him not to attack the Danes in their place of refuge. Doubtless Edric was an evil counsellor, but even so the story does not quite ring true. What is clear, however, from the details given later in the *Chronicle*, is that Edmund stood his army down, and that the Danes left Sheppey and crossed the Thames into Essex, and raided there and in the neighbouring parts of Mercia.

Then for the fifth time Edmund called up "all the people of England" and overtook the Danes at the hill of Ashingdon near Rochford in Essex, on the high ground south of the Crouch. According to one story Edmund took Streona into his confidence before what was clearly going to be the decisive battle of the campaign, and Streona betrayed him. According to another account, Streona fled with all his men by previous arrangement with Canute, and at a time when the Danes were beginning to get the worst of it. The *Chronicle*, probably the most reliable of all accounts, simply says that ealdorman Edric did as he had so often done before — he and the men of Hereford and south

Shropshire were the first to set the example of flight; and thus betrayed their royal lord and the whole nation.

Henry of Huntingdon has a more colourful account in which he says that Edmund's army was getting the better of the Danes when Edric cut off the head of a man who looked like Edmund, and holding it aloft cried out *Flet Engle! Flet Engle! Ded is Edmund!* And the English began to flee. A similar story is told by Florence of Worcester of Edric at the earlier battle of Sherston, but without the traitor's dramatic cry. There may be some truth in the story somewhere. But whatever devilment took place on the hill of Assendune, Canute was victorious and ultimately won all England by his victory; but all the flower of the English nation was slain in a battle which lasted even until moonlight.

Canute and Edmund met near Gloucester after the battle and made a compact of mutual friendship with pledge and with oath, agreeing that Edmund should hold Wessex. The Danes returned to their ships; and the people of London having made peace with them, they brought their ships to London and wintered there.

Edmund died in London six weeks after the battle, having been king for seven months. Scandinavian chroniclers and William of Malmesbury say that he was murdered by Streona. Henry of Huntingdon's story is that Edric's son was the murderer, and that Edric came before Canute and hailed him as sole king — and Canute had him killed for treachery. An unlikely story, since Edmund died on November 30th 1016, and in the following year Edric was confirmed as ealdorman of Mercia. It was not until Christmas 1017, according to the *Encomium Emmae*, that he was killed in the king's palace in London on Canute's orders, because the king feared he might act as treacherously towards him as he had to his former lords Ethelred and Edmund. This seems to be the truth of it, although there is little in the *Chronicle* to support it. After his death, according to Florence of Worcester, Streona's body was flung over the wall of the city and allowed to lie there unburied.

At the same time as Edric Streona had been confirmed as ealdorman of Mercia, Thurkill was made ealdorman of East Anglia; and thus became the most powerful layman in England. In that same year Canute also took over the whole government of England; and in 1020, four years after he had defeated Edmund, had a stone church built at Ashingdon and gave it to his own priest, whose name was Stigand. It was consecrated in the presence of Canute, Thurkill,

Archbishop Wulfstan and other bishops, as well as abbots and many monks.

The church still stands, and is worth visiting. One takes the road which leads north from under the railway bridge by Hockley station, turning off to the right by the footpath which leaves the road by the thatched cottage on the crest of the hill. The path then follows the crown of the hog's back, which here runs parallel with, and to the south of, the Crouch, first through fields, then along one of those unmade roads through thin woodland with a scatter of incredibly varied houses which is characteristic of parts of south Essex. Here, in a garden breast high with weeds, is a broken-down gothic summerhouse, inhabited but in the last stages of dissolution; there is a semi-castellated house with velvet lawns; here a two-up and two-down house with a cast iron balcony such as one saw in photographs of Chicago in the 1880's; here a wooden house which seems to have come straight out of the eastern provinces of Canada. Such hotch-potch growth, here less poverty stricken than can still be seen in Laindon or Pitsea, has variety and charm. I find it preferable to the conformity seen in neighbouring and more modern housing estates.

The Chase, as it is known, finally gives on to another main road; after crossing it, and making a short climb to the end of the same long hill, one arrives at the churchyard of Assendune.

The church is small, and although it is doubtful if anything more than its foundations and part of the lower walls of the tower can be as old as Canute, gives an impression of great age. It has been much restored, and that not long after its first building. I saw in its walls Roman bricks, septaria, flints, Kentish rag, sandstone I could not further identify, and limestone of two kinds.

The leaflet at the church, written by a former grave-digger, is to be commended because it deals with the fabric of the church itself, its walls, foundations, and the soil on which it is built, as well as matters more strictly ecclesiastical. It states that there was a Saxon church on the site in about 970 — concerning which the *Anglo-Saxon Chronicle* says nothing. The writer of the leaflet suggests that Canute's church was longer than the present building, because some years before he had excavated about eight feet from the east window at two different places, and found stone and lime mortar in line with the north and south walls. He took these to be continuations of the foundations, and provides other evidence from inside the church to support his theory.

According to the leaflet a large part of the church was rebuilt in the fourteenth century, presumably because it was weakened by the movement of clay on the hill which (the writer adds) "is once again causing us trouble". He suggested that the old east end might have collapsed as a result of this movement centuries ago, and that to save money the church was then made shorter.

The same problems caused by clay subsoil brought the church to the point of collapse in 1950. The vestry, built on behind the north door to the church in 1906, had settled away from the church, and was pulling the north wall with it. The wall was already seven inches out of true when the church was repaired, and re-dedicated in 1951.

Its appearance and known history make Ashingdon church interesting; it is the site which makes it impressive. The church stands at the end of the ridge, with the ground falling away to north and east, giving long views down and across the Crouch. If the area was not wooded at the time of Canute, and it was he who chose the site where today this church stands a lonely sentinel against the sky, then he chose well.

I came to the church for the first time at evensong, and even as I passed through the gate of the churchyard could hear the congregation singing Valiant's song *To be a pilgrim*. A simple notice in the porch listed the incumbents of the church since its foundation. They began with that Stigand who was appointed by Canute in 1020, and became Archbishop of Canterbury in 1052. He was kept in office by William until 1070, when he was imprisoned at the charge of the papal legates and replaced by Lanfranc. Stigand died in 1072, and must by then have been an old man. If he was twenty when he was appointed to Ashingdon, which I would think unlikely, he would have been 72 at his death.

Another notice in the porch records that the church was built on the site of the battle of Assendune and quotes the *Anglo-Saxon Chronicle* in support.

Canute died in 1053 and was succeeded by his sons Harold and Hardicanute. Hardicanute made an agreement with Magnus King of Norway that if either died without a son, the survivor was to succeed to both kingdoms. Hardicanute died without a son in 1042 and was succeeded, not by Magnus, but by Edward the Confessor. The agreement with Magnus was thereby broken; but Magnus, who had intended invading England in 1046 to claim his right, was prevented by trouble with Denmark. But his son Harald Hardrada inherited

Magnus's claim to the English throne; and in 1066 invaded England in an attempt to enforce it.

Hardrada came into the Tyne in September with 300 ships or more, the north-east wind which brought him keeping William and his invading army weather-bound at St Valéry. He was joined by Tostig, the exiled earl of Northumbria and the brother of the English king, Harold Godwinsson. With their combined fleet they went up the Ouse towards York. When the news was brought to Harold he collected his army and "went up by night and day". Before he could get there Edwin and Morcar had attacked the invaders, and been defeated.

Hardrada (the name means ruthless, or hard counsel) fought his first battle at the age of fifteen; found refuge after defeat at Novgarod; later commanded the Byzantine Varangian Guard; later still gained victories in Italy and North Africa. He was one of the greatest fighting men of the age; and one might have thought his victory over the Saxons a foregone conclusion. But he and Tostig were both killed and their army routed. Harold let Hardrada's son Edmund return with the ships to Norway and himself returned south, again by forced marches, to Hastings, where only nineteen days after he had defeated Hardrada, this last of the Saxon kings, who had succeeded Edward the Confessor only forty weeks before, himself met defeat and death.

If one thinks of history in romantic terms — perhaps, even, if one thinks of it in realistic terms — Harold's victory at Stamford Bridge by almost a fluke was something not far removed from disaster. Certainly it is a bitter thing, if one thinks of the Danish invasions against the background of English history, that the greatest defeat inflicted on the Northmen (they were in this case Norwegians rather than Danes) was the most unlucky victory ever gained by the English. For in gaining the victory over Hardrada, fate simply ensured that England, victorious after periods of alternating vacillation and weakness, decision and strength, should be defeated by a yet more alien foe. Had Hardrada been victorious at Stamford Bridge it is possible that he might also have been able to defeat the Normans; and it is possible that our history as a Scandinavian state might have taken a different and perhaps a better course after 1066.

This was the last attempt by Danes or Norsemen to conquer England. Hereward doubtless hoped that he could establish a bridgehead for them in the Isle of Ely; but if so he was disappointed. Thereafter (as has been quoted more than once from one of the

Icelandic sagas)

Cold heart and bloody hand
Now rule English land

CHAPTER 14

Stones, churches, buildings

In an earlier chapter I referred to the use of boulders to mark tracks and crossroads. Such boulders were also used to mark meeting places, boundaries, and the centres of settlements, although it is now less easy to identify those used for boundaries than those which marked roads or the centres of settlements. Watkins, whose comments on waystones have already been given, has in his book a photograph of the mark stone by the market house in Pembridge, Herefordshire, which is in almost exactly the same position relative to village and building as the boulder under the market hall at Thaxted in Essex. There are also mark stones in the centre of March in the Isle of Ely and at Geddington in Northamptonshire — and, indeed, widely elsewhere.

In recent years boulders of this type have been used to protect walls, gate posts, and the corners of buildings from being scored by cart wheels. Stones so used can be seen at the corner of the wall leading out of the station yard at Audley End in Essex, and at the corner of a barn in Bures in the same county. They have been used as mounting blocks, and it is probably in this sense that the fourteen or more boulders at Cliffe in Kent are called "saddling" stones.

When people went to church on horseback there was nearly always a horse block near the church. In some cases these still remain near the porch; in others they have been removed, sometimes being built into the wall of the churchyard. According to Palin the old horse block which used to stand at the south-east corner of Stifford churchyard had by his time been built "into the present south wall" — presumably of the churchyard, but he does not say. It is possible that sarsens or erratics found in or near churchyard walls — for example the sandstone boulders in the churchyard wall at Upchurch in Kent and the block of mountain limestone by the churchyard wall at Manuden in Essex — were at one time used as mounting blocks.

I thought for years that the large rectangular block of limestone by the door of the World's End inn at Tilbury must have been a mounting block although it seemed too ambitious a piece of quarried and worked stone to be used for this purpose. Then one day I passed in fog; and my field of vision concentrated, noticed a depression in the centre of the upper surface of the stone which I found to be partly filled with lead.

Presumably a metal post had been fixed in the stone, probably in connection with the nearby Fort, or with the ferry and landing stage for cattle once in use here.

It is now necessary to consider certain types of stone which are used for building in the lower Thames basin, but are quarried outside the district. These are the Kent, Surrey and Wealden building stones, of which the best known is Kentish rag. Kentish rag has been widely used for building in Kent and Essex, and was used more than any other building stone in Roman and medieval London. Since it is harder and more expensive to work than softer freestone (that is sandstone or gritstone) it is generally found in the form of undressed stone walling. In the Roman Wall of London, however, and in one or two London churches, it was squared and laid in regular courses.

The Roman Wall was made of newly quarried rag with some flints at the core. It had an external plinth of red ferruginous sandstone, also from Kent; and had facing courses of brick. It was built in sections, as was the wall of the Fort of the Saxon Shore at Pevensey in Sussex. Kentish rag, probably from near Lympne, was also used in the Forts of the Saxon Shore at Richborough and Reculver.

Throughout the Middle Ages Kentish rag was almost universally used for the walls of churches and other important buildings in and near London, such as the White Tower in the Tower of London, the Guildhall, the halls of the City Companies, Westminster Hall, and Henry VII's chapel at Windsor. Some of the oldest parts of Westminster Abbey and the Temple Church contain Kentish rag. The foundations of Old St Paul's were said by Wren to be of "Kentish rubble stone, artfully work'd and consolidated with exceeding hard mortar in the Roman manner". Wren believed these to have been also the foundations of an earlier church on the site built during the Roman Occupation, and presumably taken over by the builders of Old St Paul's.

Kentish rag was used in building most of the old churches and castles of Kent, and its use in Essex is almost as widespread. One well known building in Essex made of it is Hadleigh Castle, whose walls are cemented with mortar of an extraordinary hardness and durability. It contains cockle shells thought to have come from the eastern point of Canvey Island where there is still a bed of them today.

Kentish rag at its best is a hard, impervious, compact, blue-grey stone, quite as heavy as many granites. It tends to split irregularly when broken, and to produce rough and irregular surfaces. It also varies in consistency according to its quality. To some extent this depends on how far east it is quarried. As we have seen, the stone comes from the eastern section of the sandstone ridge which runs parallel with, and to the south of, the chalk ridge of the North Downs. The limestone content of stone from this ridge rises the farther east one goes, so that the first Kentish rag to be recognised as such is a sandstone held together with chalky or limy material. Farther east it becomes a shelly limestone with scattered sand grains, and at its best it may contain over ninety per cent calcium carbonate.

The best rag comes from the Maidstone district, where it was quarried by the Romans, probably at Allington, the nearest point to a waterway where it could be obtained, as well as at Boughton Monchelsea, Lympne and Loose. It has been quarried also at Hythe, Sevenoaks, and elsewhere. The Roman ship found in the Thames at Blackfriars and excavated in 1962 had a cargo of Kentish rag.

Less durable than Kentish rag is the fine-grained Reigate sandstone which comes from the same ridge farther west, where it is quarried near the town of Reigate in Surrey. It varies in colour from light whitish grey to pale greenish grey, contains more sand than Kentish rag, and is softer. It is a lightweight stone. In a list of 119 building stones arranged according to their weight to the cubic foot in Hull's *Building and Ornamental Stones*, Reigate stone from Gatton is, at 103 pounds, the lightest, lighter even than Totternhoe stone from Dunstable (116) and Beer chalk from Devon (131). Kentish rag in the same list weighs 166 pounds a cubic foot, almost as much as Tiree marble (172), the heaviest stone listed.

Reigate stone lasts better outside large towns, as I suppose all stones do. Even in the time of Wren it had decayed badly where it was used in Westminster Abbey, having in his words "mouldered away" four inches from the original surface. In Essex, Reigate stone is used for dressings in churches at Basildon, Bowers Gifford, Chadwell, Corringham, Danbury, East Tilbury, Fobbing, Great Stambridge, Horndon on the Hill, Laindon, North and South Ockendon, Orsett, Rettendon, Rochford, West Thurrock, and many others. Orsett church is particularly interesting because its walls contain Barnack, puddingstone, and Reigate stone.

We saw in an earlier chapter that when the layers of greensand, gault and chalk were forced up to form the Wealden dome some thirty million years ago, the lower layers, which were mostly of soft sandstone and limestone, reached their greatest height in the centre of the Weald. Since then, with the denudation of the Weald dome, these layers have come to the surface at a point half way between the Thames and English Channel known as the High Weald. West Hoathly, an attractive village in this area, has a church and manor house made of local stone, and there are quarries still in production nearby.

Some of the Wealden limestones are made of freshwater shells. One, which is known as Bethersden marble, is used in Rochester cathedral, in the church towers of Headcorn, Smarden and elsewhere, and in the polished altar steps of Canterbury cathedral.

Tufa, a kind of limestone formed by the precipitation of calcium carbonate held in solution in streams flowing from limestone or chalk — in the case of the tufa now or formerly quarried at East Malling in Kent, from beds of Kentish rag — is an unusual stone found at places in Kent. I do not know that it is used in Essex, but it appears in the Forts of the Saxon Shore at Richborough and Reculver and, in our area of Kent, in Swanscombe church and the church at Stone. In this last it is laid with string courses of Roman tiles.

Worthy of a final note are the buildings in Kent which contain stone from the first London Bridge. These include Ingress Abbey and Warden church Sheppey, which was demolished in 1877 because of erosion and "almost rebuilt" with the stone of old London Bridge.

In Essex the absence of normal building stone has led to the use of a great variety of materials. There are, or were, cottages at Tiptree with clay walls, while lumps of brown boulder clay with a few flints and courses of Roman brick are found in the walls of Broomfield church north of Chelmsford. Other materials vary from wood, as in Greensted church near Ongar, to bricks, tiles and masonry from Roman buildings. Septaria, puddingstone, flint and clunch have also been used and, from the twelfth century onwards, locally made bricks.

Puddingstone is to be found in the remains of Beeleigh Abbey, Maldon, now a private house, and in the walls of churches at Stifford, Ingatestone, Fryerning, Great Braxted, Little Baddow, and Boreham. Cut into blocks, it is used in the thirteenth-century-style church at Little Burstead, which stands at the end of a ridge and commands fine views to south and south-west. The blocks in this church are much weathered, with the sand wearing away from the pebbles. They do not present such clear cut sections as one sees in the Iron Age and Romano-British querns made of puddingstone in Colchester museum. In any case the walls of Little Burstead church are now largely rendered.

Flint is common in the chalk areas of south and north-west Essex and, of course, in those of north Kent. It has been used in Grays, where there are still knapped flint cottages near the railway line, and at Purfleet, where before the station was improved there was an attractive knapped flint building on the south platform. In some cases flint has been used outside the chalk areas: the south porch of Little Burstead church is all flint.

The use of flint in building deserves, and has doubtless received, a book on its own. All I will say here is that it is difficult to work with flints, whether knapped or unknapped, because they do not key together like bricks, and flint walls must be supported by shuttering each side until the mortar has dried. Otherwise the weight of the flints set in still-fluid mortar, coupled with the fact that they do not key, may cause new work to collapse.

The best building flints are, or were, quarried; those picked from the surface of the ground are hard and durable, but they cannot be dressed so easily. Such surface flints were formerly used for road mending in Essex, and before the Education Act of 1870 were often picked off the fields by children. Gun flints were made in Purfleet as recently as 1845.

Prehistoric flint tools are to be found in abundance in and near the chalk areas of north Kent and south Essex, but since many thousands of faked flint tools have been put on the market from Kent alone, the only guarantee of authenticity is that they should be found on or in the earth itself. Flint fakers boiled their products to give them a patina, and could not always tell their own fakes from Stone Age tools.

Flint is found in the upper chalk only. Clunch, which is strong and compacted chalk, comes from the lower levels where flints are not found. Subject to this, however, one might say that the two of them are quarried together.

Septaria have been used widely for building and other purposes in Essex, even for paving the streets of Harwich in years gone by. The Roman walls of Colchester, based largely on sand, have massive foundations eleven feet thick made of septaria and flints bonded together by mortar which is also made of pounded septaria. The wall has a core of septaria, and is faced with courses of Roman bricks and septaria. The walls of the Roman fort at Bradwell on Sea were made of two or three courses of Roman bricks alternating with two or three feet of septaria and other materials.

Septaria were used in Stanesgate Priory on the Blackwater. The same kind of stones can be seen today breaking down under the effect of salt-laden sea winds in the wall of the old churchyard at Frinton. Churches at Asheldham, Broomfield, and Rainham are also among a great number in which septaria have been used.

Septaria, powdered bricks, shells and other materials were used by the Romans for making cement and mortar in Kent and Essex. The practice was resumed as far as septaria were concerned in 1796, when James Parker of Northfleet patented what he called Roman cement. This cement set hard even under water, and was intended for use in "aquatic or other buildings, or in stucco work".

Harwich, where septaria were found on a large scale, became one centre of the industry; but when in 1845 it was reported that the harbour was threatened with destruction following widespread quarrying in the cliffs, those seeking septaria turned to dredging. By 1851 between 300 and 400 fishing smacks, each carrying three or four men, were engaged in the trade. Most of the boats came from Kent, and most dredging was done at West Rocks off Walton, which is apparently a vast heap of septaria. The production of cement from septaria died out after the invention of Portland cement.

In later years, when Harwich harbour was being deepened, the contractors came across masses of calcareous sandstone so hard that it had to be blasted away — probably the only occasion when a layer of stone has had to be blasted through in Essex. The stone was not in continuous layers. It was assumed that it was hardened patches of Thanet sand or Reading beds, which when appearing on the surface break down to produce sarsens. This Harwich stone, quite different from the septaria which had been dredged earlier from the bed of the harbour, was used for rockeries in various parts of Essex.

The Romans made brick and tile from gault as well as from brickearth and other types of clay. Tiles and bricks were also made in Essex, very much later, by that capable journalist Daniel Defoe, who became secretary, and ultimately owner, of a brick and pantile works at Tilbury in or about 1695. The business came to an end in 1703 when he was imprisoned for writing *The Shortest Way with the*

Dissenters, a "scandalous and seditious pamphlet" which was said to libel the established church by misrepresenting its principles.

Defoe's brick works were just to the west of what is now Tilbury Riverside station. William Lee, author of *Daniel Defoe*, visited the site in 1860 shortly after the completion of the London, Tilbury and Southend railway line, and found evidence of the works there. "Immediately on the west side of the Tilbury station," he writes in the first of his three-volume work, "a large plot was being dug over to form potato-ground for the railway servants; and a deep trench had been previously cut through the same to the river to drain the Company's estate. In this way the whole of Defoe's brick and pantile works had been laid open, including the claypits, drying-floors, foundations of kilns, and other buildings."

Defoe is known to have had a house in the neighbourhood during the whole or part of the time during which the works were in existence, and to have kept a pleasure boat on the river. He lost heavily over the collapse of the business, and lamented the fact that a hundred poor labourers were thrown out of work, they and their families being "reduced to beg elsewhere for employment".

* * *

As we have already seen in an earlier chapter, Cedd founded a number of churches in Essex of which we know only the two mentioned by Bede, those at Bradwell and Tilbury. That at Bradwell, St Peter on the Wall, is still standing. The site of the church at Tilbury is unknown, although I am inclined to think that it was at East Tilbury rather than at either the present town of Tilbury or (as Tout has it in the *Dictionary of National Biography*) the village of West Tilbury.

The matter might be decided at once if it were possible to know which of the three Tilbury's (the town by the river or the two villages to north-east and east) was first known under that name, and how long it was before the name was applied to one of the other two settlements. I have been unable to establish this. We must therefore consider other less definite pieces of evidence.

The first is that Cedd, in considering sites for the monasteries he founded — and Bradwell and Tilbury were both primitive monasteries rather than individual chapels — seems to have had a preference for wild and isolated places. When Ethelwald, son of King Oswald of

Deira, offered him land to found a monastery in the area, Cedd chose a place at Lastingham "among craggy and distant mountains, which looked more like lurking-places for robbers and retreats for wild beasts, than habitations for men". It may be that in founding monasteries in Essex he also chose places similarly isolated.

The second piece of evidence is that Cedd was familiar with Essex. He had already been at the invitation of King Sigebert of the East Saxons to re-convert his people to Christianity, and with another priest had travelled to all parts of "that country" — the kingdom of the East Saxons, or Essex — and "gained a numerous church to our Lord". It was on his second visit, after having returned to Lindisfarne and been created a bishop, that he went south again "pursuing the work he had begun with more ample authority", and building churches in several places including Bradwell and Tilbury. It is therefore likely that the sites were chosen with prior knowledge.

The site at Bradwell was at the end of a Roman road and therefore accessible from inland Essex. There were also Roman ruins there which provided building materials. (The advantages of such a site were well put by Dr Johnson, speaking through the mouth of the Arab chief in *Rasselas*: "Buildings are always best preserved in places little frequented and difficult of access; for when once a country declines from its primitive splendour, the more inhabitants are left, the quicker ruin will be made. Walls supply stones more easily than quarries; and palaces and temples will be demolished to make stables of granite and cottages of porphyry.")

To what extent the availability of building material in an isolated place at the end of a Roman road influenced Cedd in his choice of Bradwell — or of "Tilbury" — we do not know. But if he was so influenced, then all three factors were present at East Tilbury; two (availability of building materials and a site at the end of a Roman road) were present at Tilbury; and as far as I know, none at West Tilbury.

It is known that there were Roman buildings near the river at East Tilbury, and according to the Victoria County History a manuscript in the Bodleian, which I have not seen, states that in the eighteenth century gravel digging at East Tilbury often uncovered tessellated pavement. I also find it difficult to believe that the straight road which leads to East Tilbury can be anything but Roman.

There is even stronger evidence that a Roman road led to Tilbury and that there was a great deal of Roman building material there; but the site could not be regarded as isolated.

No road comparable with those which I believe led to Tilbury and East Tilbury led to West Tilbury, nor do I know of Roman remains there, or regard the site as isolated as those at Bradwell and East Tilbury. Some have, however, attached importance to a site south-west of the church which shows signs of having supported a building, although at the time of writing nothing is known of its age or purpose. And while A. Saunders, in volume 13 of the Thurrock Local History Society Journal favours East Tilbury, he also gives reasons for supposing that there may have been a hitherto unknown medieval hospital there. This fact, together with other evidence set out in the Addenda and Corrigenda, confirms me in my belief that Cedd's monastery must have been at East Tilbury.

It is accepted that St Catherine's, the present church at East Tilbury (which was formerly dedicated to St Margaret) is the second on or near the site. It has also been suggested that the first was possibly below present high tide level, and therefore nearer the river and not on the site of the present building — partly because Roman remains have been found between it and the river, partly because a map of 1735 in the Essex Record Office shows the offshore ruins of the blockhouse built in the reign of Henry VIII as well as "lost land" and "old sea wall". Further, erosion here, considerable enough since 1735, would have been greater since Roman times. I. G. Sparkes, writing in volume 7 of the Thurrock Local History Society Journal, says the blockhouse ruins were visible at low tide at least up to 1775.

I have no doubt that in Roman times the whole area as far as the Ovens buoy was dry land and carried Romano-British buildings. If the first chapel at East Tilbury was built by Cedd and, like that at Bradwell, made of Roman materials, then it is possible that Roman bricks which have been found between the present church and the river, and in the foundations of the present church, came from the same ruined Roman buildings which provided bricks and tiles for his church.

East Tilbury has another and more recent place in history. It has always been accepted locally that the tower and south aisle of the church were destroyed by Dutch gunfire when De Ruyter's fleet attacked British ships in the Hope in July 1667, and that the blocks of masonry which now lie on the grass nearby are the result. But

Port of London Authority and Handford

Plate 29. Gravesend Reach showing, in rising order, the Tilbury landing stage, Tilbury Fort and power station, and in the distance Coalhouse Fort at the turn into the Lower Hope. Higham Bight is at the top of the photograph, Gravesend to the right.

A.F. Kersting

Plate 30. The church of St Peter on the Wall at Bradwell in Essex, built for St Cedd in the seventh century. It is made of brick and stone taken from the Roman fort of Othona on whose site it stands; and is the oldest church in Essex.

A.F. Kersting

Plate 31. The interior of the church of St Peter on the Wall — save for the furniture, looking much as it did in the seventh century.

Plate 32. This photograph of the north bank of the Thar
above

Port of London Authority and Handford

urrock in Essex shows the pilgrim church of St Clements
on jetty.

Plate 33. The World's End inn at Tilbury. The wooden sheds to the right were used to store soldiers' kitbags during the Napoleonic Wars, and the walls are still partly papered with early nineteenth century newspapers. One, the *Sunday Times* for September 19th 1830, has an item headed The Atrocious Poor Laws, which tells of the suicide of a Dorset farm labourer refused parish relief. The modern building to the right is across the river in Gravesend.

Jackson's Photo Service, Canvey

Plate 34. This cottage on Canvey Island, now a local museum, was built in the seventeenth century by the Dutch who drained and reclaimed the island.

By courtesy of the Essex Record Office

Plate 35. The stepping stones which formerly connected Canvey Island with mainland Essex at South Benfleet. A Southend train is seen passing in the background.

Oppenheim, the naval historian who wrote the maritime history of Essex for the Victoria County History, pointed out many years ago that no contemporary record of the event existed; and the truth of the story has been doubted on this score.

The earliest known statement which describes the destruction of the tower is that of the Reverend William Holman. In an unpublished manuscript history of Essex which he wrote little more than forty years after the event, and which was drawn on by Salmon for his history of Essex, Holman says of East Tilbury church, "The steeple was of stone and tower'd and stood on the south side near the west ende. 'Tis now down, and the Inhabitants say 'twas beat down in the Dutch Wars by the Ships Guns." His statement has been copied by Salmon, Morant, Muilman and other Essex historians.

The parish register of March 1675, referring to the institution of the Reverend William Wray nearly eight years after the raid, states that the vicarage and its fences were then in ruins and there was no money to rebuild them; but it is significant that nothing is said as to the cause of their destruction, or of damage to the church.

There are, however, vague reports quoted by Miller Christy in the *Essex Review* for 1905 of a cannon ball being seen embedded in the wall of the church at East Tilbury, and another of cannon balls being found in or about the wall. At a meeting of the Essex Archaeological Society a ball "found in the vicinity" was shown; while some years later Sherwin A. Chase, writing in volume 11 of the Thurrock Local History Society Journal, stated that cannon balls had been found from a point on the river at East Tilbury as far down as Fobbing church.

One small cannon ball was found in 1965 when the site of a new parish hall was being excavated opposite Fobbing church. All these, as well as two cannon balls in the Thurrock Local History Museum, one found under the floorboards of Old Garlands Farm, Corringham, are thought to date from the incursion of 1667.

According to Mr Chase, the English ships in the Hope had cannon called sakers, which fired a six pound shot. These have been found only at the water's edge at low tide. The Dutch ships had as their standard armament cannon which fired twelve pound shots. These cannon balls, which are those found round East Tilbury and Fobbing churches, had an effective range of between three and four miles; and it would have been physically possible for the Dutch ships to knock down the tower of East Tilbury church with them.

Another contributor to the same journal points out that no contemporary, official or private, noted an event which is now part of the district's history; and adds that the story of the damage having resulted from the bombardment was "first mentioned by the inhabitants in 1707, and that there was no contemporary comment, either by Pepys, or Sir Edward Spragge in his report to the Commons".

It is perhaps risky to say that there was no private mention of the event at the time, nor would it be easy to prove that mention was not made by the inhabitants before 1707. Further, Christy points out in the *Essex Review* that it is practically certain that many of the official letters and reports relating to the action, especially to the battle in the Thames, have disappeared. He says that so few of the documents among the State papers refer to this engagement, and so surprisingly meagre is the account they give, that there must be more to it than "damp, rats, and the neglect of custodians". "If we remember," he says, "that this national humiliation was due primarily to the political rottenness of the time, that a Parliamentary inquiry was started, and there must have been, in consequence, many highly placed people who had a direct interest in the suppression of evidence, we shall probably find an adequate explanation of the disappearance of many documents which must once have existed."

I suppose it is possible that some of the cannon balls found at Fobbing and East Tilbury may have been collected from the river bank immediately after the action by children and others, and taken farther inland. On the other hand the church and vicarage at East Tilbury stand on a tongue of hard ground going down to the flood plain of the river, and thus command the whole great bend in the Thames where the action took place. If there was firing from anywhere in the area which was returned by the Dutch there is no need to seek further for the cause of the partial destruction of the church and the complete destruction of the nearby vicarage, which took place at or about the same time.

These are speculative comments. More realistic is the suggestion of my friend Mr Hayston that the tower just fell down, as they sometimes did; and that the parishioners, seeking a government grant towards rebuilding, blamed the Dutch. Subject to these possibilities, and to the chance that time will yet turn up some literary evidence bearing on the matter, I think I would be inclined to take Holman's word for it.

Whatever caused the destruction of the tower of East Tilbury church, the matter had an interesting sequel. A company of the London Electrical Engineers stationed at nearby Coalhouse Fort during the First World War built the base of a new tower for the church to take the place of that supposedly destroyed by the Dutch, and at the same time built a memorial inside the church. A plaque on the south wall of the tower recording the fact that the work had been done in memory of men killed on the Western Front was then unveiled before a gathering of local dignitaries. The War Office, on hearing of the episode, sent down a senior officer who ordered work on the tower to cease, the memorial inside the church to be cast down, and the plaque to be removed. The soldiers pasted a piece of brown paper over the plaque and plastered or cemented it over for his later inspection and, when he had gone for the second time, tore away the paper and left the plaque as it now appears. The memorial, however, was cast down, and the stones of which it was made are now among those on the grass near the church.

I am not certain that in combining two separate reports of the incident I may not have sacrificed some accuracy of detail. I wonder in particular where the memorial was placed in the church, what form it took, and whether the War Office had power to order its removal. The story about the plaque being covered over for higher deception is, however, correct. I had it from a former vicar. Even so, how the story can be squared with the plaque now on the church I do not know. It reads:

> This tower was erected by No. 2 Company London Electrical Engineers in 1917 to the memory of the Officers, N.C.O.'s and Men of Coalhouse Fort who gave their lives for their country in the Great War of 1914-1918, also to commemorate Gordon of Khartoum who as O.C.R.E. Gravesend, built Coalhouse Fort in 1869.
>
> The original tower — on this site — the South Aisle and Vicarage were destroyed in a naval battle against the Dutch in Tilbury Hope on July 23rd 1667.

At the bottom of the plaque are the names of Capt. C. W. C. Kaye, commanding officer of No. 2 Company, and the Rev. R. H. J. Cook, Vicar of East Tilbury.

The plaque itself calls for some explanation — how, for instance, a tower could be erected in 1917 to the memory of men who died in the war of 1914 to 1918. This suggests it may have replaced an earlier plaque.

Another interesting church in this corner of Essex is St Clement's at West Thurrock. At one time it stood alone on the low-lying land between railway and river, and could be seen to advantage just as the train from London began drawing into Grays. Hemmed in now by industry, it no longer stands in impressive isolation; it is still well worth a visit.

The present building (now declared redundant) is the second on the site. The first, which was built in the twelfth century, was round. It had an internal diameter of twenty-five feet, and was the smallest round church in this country of which record remains. It was presumably built to satisfy the spiritual needs of those going to Canterbury, which became a place of pilgrimage after Becket's murder in 1170 and his later canonisation. Certainly this and the succeeding church were on the main pilgrim route from the eastern counties.

The evidence that there had been a round church on the site was discovered by accident in 1906 by Christopher Shiner, the architect to the church. He came across a fragment of foundation wall which formed a small segment of a circle on the south side of the present church tower; and when this was excavated in 1912 the complete plan of the earlier circular church was discovered. The walls, as excavated, were of flints with footings of Roman bricks. They were found north, south and west of the present tower, and within the tower on the east side.

It was proposed, shortly before the First World War, that the outline of these foundations should be marked on the surface of the ground by a ring of stones embedded in the soil. This proposal was not put into effect, but part of the circular foundations can be seen today under an iron plate to the south of the building.

Although two round churches in this country were Saxon — that which St Athelwold began building at Abingdon Abbey in 960, and that found under the abbey church of St Augustine at Canterbury, and dated to before 1059 — most were modelled on the round church of the Holy Sepulchre at Jerusalem, which became more widely known following the conquest of the city in the first Crusade. This church was built by Constantine in the fourth century, ruined and rebuilt at least twice, and rebuilt "on old lines" in 1047. The Crusaders entered Jerusalem in 1099; the first church at West Thurrock, built in or after

1170, was therefore presumably among those modelled on the church of the Holy Sepulchre.

Mention of the round church at West Thurrock reminds me of the three round, or rather octagonal, cottages built by the Dutch who reclaimed Canvey and turned its three separate islands into one in the seventeenth century. The workmen were not paid, but received one acre of land out of every three they reclaimed. Three of the cottages they built for their own occupation are still standing, one at Rayleigh and two on Canvey, and the better preserved of the two on Canvey has been put to excellent use as a pleasant little local museum.

The museum is of course minute — I could well believe it is the smallest in the country. It has two rooms, one on the ground floor, one above, connected by a staircase. When built, the cottage had a floor of beaten earth, and one stepped down into it. Now there are five separate layers of floor, the uppermost of brick, which is why the ceiling on the lower floor is so low.

There is an interesting reference to a fourth circular Dutch cottage in volume 21 of the Transactions of the Essex Archaeological Society, where the excavation of an "enigmatic" mound at Butlers Farm, Shopland, previously thought Romano-British, is reported. It was found that the main constituent of the mound was salt water clay, which the author says was not procurable at a time when tumuli were built (I presume because waterways in the area were not then tidal). The mound had a ditch round it, presumably as a drain. The clay was mixed with chalk; and since a well-rammed mixture of chalk and clay provides a floor which will stand any ordinary wear, the author decided that the mound was the site of a Dutch cottage such as those at Canvey and Rayleigh.

I have said little enough about buildings in Kent in this chapter, my choice being arbitrary and based on personal interest alone. But Mr Cattermole of Cliffe once told me that his grandfather told him that the Higham and East Tilbury crossing, or the roads connecting that crossing, ran from "Merston church to Merston church", it being his understanding that there was a Merston on each side of the river. That on the Essex side has so far eluded me; the position of that in Kent is given in chapter 7.

Merston means marsh village. The church at the Kentish Merston, fifty-three feet nine inches by twenty feet to the outside edge of the foundations, was already in ruins in the 1640's. The church was dedicated to St Giles, the patron saint of lepers, beggars and cripples. It is perhaps worth adding that the church at Cliffe not far away is dedicated to St Helen, the wife of the Emperor Constantius Chlorus and mother of Constantine the Great, the first Christian Emperor of Rome; and that on the Essex bank of the Thames the two saints are found together in the church of St Helen and St Giles in Rainham.

One church in Essex which was destroyed by fire in 1878, and whose site has now been ploughed down, is that which formerly stood at West Horndon. Its site, unlike that of Merston church in Kent, is still marked on the map — probably because, according to an obscure passage in Worley, its east wing, saved from the fire and then restored, "now forming the residence, with the Roman Catholic chapel of Our Lady and St Lawrence attached to it". Worley wrote in and before 1915; the buildings must have been destroyed since.

Another chapel, also now pulled down, was West Lee Chapel, dedicated to St Mary Magdalen, and built on the site later used for Tilbury Fort. According to Salmon it was founded "in the time of St Thomas the Martyr". In common with the church at West Thurrock it was built for the use of pilgrims crossing the river to go to the shrine at Canterbury. When this chapel was pulled down for the construction of Tilbury Fort a new chapel, still standing inside the fort, was built in its place.

One *Ecclesia destructa* of which I would like to know more is that which was washed away by the sea off Southend. According to Salmon the remains of this chapel had been seen "within memory" at low water mark where the sea encroached on the land at Milton Hall, Prittlewell, between Leigh and Southchurch.

I have referred to the chapel inside Tilbury Fort which replaced the chantry of St Mary Magdalen, and will end this chapter by saying a word or two about the Fort itself. I knew the Fort as a boy, but from the outside. Those great portals were always closed against me, and against all members of the public. It was, in a way, a place apart. I assumed it to be full of buildings: line on line of heavily armoured fortifications, cellars, walls, pits, and so on. The reality, when long years after I went inside, was refreshingly different. There was nothing there but a Wimperis sky; space in the form of a parade ground floored with curiously uneven limestone; a few plane trees; a line of cottages; two ancient pumps — the whole giving an impression of something at once simple and unsophisticated; a civilised, pleasant, peaceful sanctuary. There is, of course, more to it than that, and it is set out in a booklet on sale inside. But I am purposely not describing anything save walking through those great doors for the first time and seeing the open space in front of me, wide enough to give a sense of freedom, limited by walls which gave it some sense of seclusion. The views of the river from the top of the walls are good; one could not choose a better place for watching the ships go by. And that is all I think I need say of Tilbury Fort.

CHAPTER 15

Chalk and deneholes

The London clay which covers much of Essex tends to be mildly acid. This is a disadvantage because food crops do not grow well in acid soil. It is also dense and sticky when wet, dense and iron hard when dry, and at all times one of the least easily worked of soils. This means that the farmer's task in cultivating the soil is harder on Essex clay than in most other growing areas. It also means that the soil is less open and aerated, has fewer of the beneficial soil bacteria which encourage plant growth, and in its natural state has a lower organic content than other soils elsewhere. All these factors, unless overcome, tend to discourage the vigorous growth and profitable yield of food crops on London clay.

Both acidity and density in London clay can however be countered by adding chalk, which is alkaline. Chalk reduces, and could in time remove, the acid content of the clay; because of its physical and chemical nature it can also help to break the clay down into particles and let in the air — or, in the agriculturist's word, flocculate it.

Chalk has a third advantage when added to London clay and some other soils: it contains essential plant food in the form of calcium. It also helps to produce nitrogen, another essential plant food, and possibly other nutrients. These are among the reasons why chalk has been quarried from time immemorial in south Essex and north Kent for "marling" Essex clay land; and why a large traffic in chalk carried by wagon and barge developed between these chalk areas and central and northern Essex.

It is not only in the heavy clay lands of Essex that chalk and chalk products have been used to neutralise acidity, but also in the chalk areas themselves. Where the chalk is covered with other deposits such as sand or clay, those sand or clay soils can become acid through leaching, that is by the draining away of alkaline content in solution; and this can take place even if the chalk is only a foot or two beneath the surface, as it is in parts of the higher ground round Stifford, West Thurrock and Grays, and elsewhere in the chalk areas of south Essex.

In some of these areas the surface soil is what is known as clay-with-flints, which is formed when chalk hills are broken down by frost, surface water, and slightly acid rain. Throughout the body of the chalk there are traces of clay, and as the chalk is eroded, these insoluble particles settle out, and with any flints present form a capping on the chalk. Where beech trees grow on the chalk downs, as at Chanctonbury Ring in Sussex, it is in this clay capping, rather than in the chalk, that the trees are rooted. But although the clay which forms a layer on top of the chalk came out of alkaline chalk, it can still be acid; and that is one reason why, even in a wholly chalk area, it may still be worth while to dig chalk to marl the land above it.

Of the size of the traffic in chalk in times past there can be no question. An early reference to it was by Defoe, who in *A Tour through the Whole Island of Great Britain* said of the chalk quarries on the Kent bank of the Thames, "... from thence the city of London, the adjacent countries, and even Holland and Flanders, are supply'd with lime, for their building, or chalk to make lime, and for other uses. From these chalky cliffs on the river side, the rubbish of the chalk, which crumbles away when they dig the larger chalk for lime, or (as we might call it) the chips of the chalk, and which they must be at the charge of removing to be out of their way, is bought and fetch'd away by lighters and hoys, and carry'd to all the ports and creeks in the opposite county of Essex, and even to Suffolk and Norfolk, and sold there to the country farmers to lay upon their land, and that in prodigious quantities; and so it is valued by the farmers of those countries, that they not only give from two shillings and sixpence, to four shillings a load for it, according to the distance the place is from the said chalk-cliff, but they fetch it by land-carriage ten miles, nay fifteen miles, up into the country.

"This is the practice in all the creeks and rivers in Essex, even to Malden, Colchester, the Nase, and into Harwich Harbour up to Maningtree, and to Ipswich; as also in Suffolk, to Albro, Orford, Dunwich, Swold, and as high as Yarmouth in Norfolk.

"Thus the barren soil of Kent, for such the chalky grounds are esteem'd, make the Essex lands rich and fruitful, and the mixture of earth forms a composition, which out of two barren extreams, makes one prolifick medium; the strong clay of Essex and Suffolk is made fruitful by the soft meliorating melting chalk of Kent, which fattens and enriches it."

Defoe is referring here to quarries at Erith, Greenwich, and Northfleet "in which places the chalk hills come close to the river". He uses the word "countries" to refer to rural areas. The spelling, including that of names, is that of the original; Albro is Aldeburgh, and Swold, Southwold.

Hasted, in his history of Kent, which was published between 1778 and 1799, repeats most of the above passage from Defoe word for word without acknowledgment.

Even though Defoe records that the Essex farmers bought the "rubbish" of the chalk for putting on their land, they still felt that surface chalk was not as good as deep-mined chalk for farm use. Surface chalk was friable because of the superficial action of frost, and impure because surface water carried down particles of clay through fractures in the chalk. They preferred chalk which had never been "near the day" — that is exposed to the atmosphere — and maintained that it was stronger or fatter than surface chalk, and powdered more easily under the action of winter frosts.

Muilman recorded in 1771 that chalk from Stifford was carried by farmers as much as thirty miles inland for use as manure. Arthur Young, who in 1767 wrote, "Of all the cursed roads that ever disgraced this Kingdom in the very ages of barbarism, none ever equalled that from Billericay to the King's Head at [West] Tilbury", also commented, "to add to the infamous circumstances that continually occur to plague a traveller, I must not forget the eternal meeting with chalk-waggons".

In later years Essex chalk went even farther afield. Elizabeth Linklater, mother of Eric, whose father was captain of a sailing ship, records in her book *A Child under Sail* which was published in 1938 by Jonathan Cape, that chalk used to be shipped from Grays to Boston in the United States.

A second use for chalk was in building. Chalk footings have been found in one of the Roman buildings at Springhead in Kent, while one wattle and daub building there had a floor of rammed chalk measuring twenty by twenty-five feet. Chalk was also used in Roman roads — one at Springhead had an agger of clay topped with rammed chalk blocks fourteen inches thick, above which were at least three levels of packed gravel. Chalk blocks were used in the Roman villa at Darenth, while squared chalk blocks with a herringbone pattern on the face were used in a Roman building, possibly a mithraeum, at Burham south-west of Rochester. A chalk wall was found in the Roman building at Chalk, while chalk bricks about six inches by four inches in size were used in Romano-British buildings near Greenhithe. Chalk blocks a foot thick were also used in a lime kiln in which chalk was burnt at Northfleet, although the interior of the kiln had been lined with brick earth two or three inches thick, which was hardened and burnt to a red brick colour as a result of fire.

Chalk was also used for building dwelling houses in more recent times — Chalk Row, Grays, where the tenants used to scrub the outside walls to make them white, was a case in point. These cottages, formerly near Duval's Quarry, have now been demolished.

Chalk was used in foundations for one specialised purpose — to reduce the adverse effects of building on London clay, which is always an unsatisfactory foundation. London clay, by drying and contracting in dry weather, and taking up moisture and expanding in wet, so "works" on walls with ordinary foundations that they can be seriously weakened. It was to avoid the effect of this working that chalk blocks were used in the foundations of Great Mollands Farm, South Ockendon. It was for the same reason that when the church of All Saints at Eastchurch in the Isle of Sheppey (where the soil is all London clay) went to ruin some time before 1432 "by reason of the sudden weakness of the foundation", deep and solid foundations of chalk were provided for the new church by digging wide trenches some feet deep which were filled with blocks of chalk brought from mainland Kent.

In some cases chalk has been used for load-bearing construction work, as in the crypt of the Guildhall in London, where the pillars are of chalk. At West Thurrock, hard blocks of chalk cut for building purposes at the end of the fifteenth or the beginning of the sixteenth century were put round the interior wall of the church instead of stone or brick. Chalk blocks were also used in the central arch of the tower, where they have been under considerable pressure for five centuries or more without apparent effect.

Clunch, as deep mined chalk is known, is used for dressings in the churches at Abbess Roding, Aythorpe Roding, Beauchamp Roding, Berners Roding, Blackmore, Boreham, High Laver, Fryerning, and elsewhere in Essex. Clunch is also used in the church font at High Easter.

The fact that a demand for chalk has existed in Essex for centuries has been established. It is now necessary to consider the chalk quarries known as deneholes in connection with that demand.

Although found in all chalk areas, deneholes are a particular feature of the chalk areas of south Essex and north Kent. They are circular vertical shafts three or four feet in diameter, driven through the surface soil and into the chalk. They then open out into one or more large chambers to the side of the base of the shaft — or, in rare cases, into a single bell shaped chamber forming an extension of the shaft itself. Deneholes with two or more side chambers are commonest; and these, with the shaft, are often like a clover leaf in plan.

The narrowness of denehole shafts, as well as the foot holes which were cut in the sides, made it possible for miners to straddle the shaft and so descend and ascend more easily. Shafts go down for distances of up to eighty feet, although one 140 feet deep has been reported from Eltham — in which district, and neighbouring Blackheath, deneholes are deeper than average. For purposes of comparison I may say that the Nelson Column in Trafalgar Square — the column alone — is almost 185 feet high.

Deneholes are known in Hertfordshire, Bedfordshire, Oxfordshire, Buckinghamshire, Norfolk, Suffolk, Berkshire, Gloucestershire, Hampshire, Wiltshire and Surrey, and on the Somme in France. The best known are in Hangmans Wood near Grays, where at least seventy-two have been identified in one small area. Others have been found elsewhere near Grays, Purfleet, West Thurrock and Stifford. A group of forty was found at Stifford in 1956 on the south side of the Mardyke some 300 yards south-west of where the railway crosses the river.

As for Kent, one author has said that deneholes are found "almost anywhere in the northern half of the county". The six-inch Ordnance Survey map for 1910 showed twenty-five in an area of about five acres in Stankey Wood near Bexley. They are common in Thanet, and are to be found all round Sittingbourne and Rochester.

The deneholes near Crayford were mentioned, although not under that name, by the Kentish historian Lambarde in 1570. In the second edition of this work, which appeared in 1596, he says:

> There are to be séene, as well in the open Heath neare to this Towne, as also in the closed grounds about it, sundry artificiall Caues, or holes, in the earth, whereof some haue ten, some fiftéene, and some twenty fathoms in depth: at the mouth (and

thence downeward) narrow, like to the Tonnell of a chimney, or passage of a well: but in the bottome large, and of great receipt: insomuch as some of them haue sundry roomes (or partitions) one within another, strongly vaulted, and supported with pillers of chalke.

And, in the opinion of the inhabitants, these were in former times digged, as well for the vse of the chalke towardes building, as for to marle (or amend) their arable lands therewith. But I suppose, that they were made to another ende also, by the Saxons our auncestors, who (after the manner of their elders) vsed them as receptacles, and places of secret retraict, for their wiues, children, and portable goodes, in the times both of ciuil dissention, & foreine inuasion. For, Cornelius Tacitus, treating of the maners of the olde Germanes (the verie Syres of these Saxons) writeth thus: *Solent & subterraneos specus aperire, & si quando hostis aduenit, aperta populatur, abdita autem & defossa aut ignorantur, aut eo ipso fallunt quod quaerenda sunt.* They vse to dig (saith he) certeine Caues vnder the grounde: and if the enimie come he spoileth all that is abroade: but such things as bee thus hidden, either they lie vnknowne, or otherwise they deceiue him in that he is driuen to seeke after them. If these be not founde in other places, it is to be imputed to the soile, which in chalke onely will afforde this workmanship. Besides that many beasts haue tumbled into some of these: it happened a late Noble person in following his Hauke, not without great perill of his life, to fall into one of them, that was at the least twelue fathoms deepe.

In spite of Lambarde's comments I should make it clear that deneholes were dug for chalk, and for no other purpose. Their shape, depth, and distribution were decided by the need to win chalk, usually of a certain purity and hardness, and to transport it by the most economical method below and above ground.

The rare single-chamber deneholes were the earliest type. They were abandoned when those who dug them found more chalk could be won by making two or more openings at the bottom of the shaft each leading to its own chamber, and that the safety of the shaft and chambers could be ensured by leaving chalk walls between entrances and chambers, and perhaps pillars of chalk within the chambers themselves.

The logical and ultimate development of the multi-chambered denehole, in which as a result of replacing skips with barrows the chambers became galleries, is seen in the Chislehurst caves in Kent, which are made safe by columns at suitable intervals. The Chislehurst caves — they, like deneholes, are simply chalk mines — cover almost twenty acres. They are outside our area, but it is worth recording that they were probably dug about 1700, and that the middle series of workings bear so strong a resemblance to some of the old High Main coal workings near Newcastle that they may have been worked under the direction of a pitman from that district.

In *Archaeologia Cantiana* for 1972 two shallow deneholes with three chambers each are described, in which the third chamber from each shaft was deliberately made into a tunnel or gallery linking the two. The chambers were also so much longer than is usual with such shallow deneholes that it would have been necessary to use a barrow below ground to bring the chalk from the farther working faces to the base of the shafts. The longest heading was forty-one feet from working face to shaft; but according to J. E. L. Caiger, who reported the discovery of these linked deneholes at Northfleet in Kent, nothing was found which could date them. It is, however, reasonable to wonder whether they represent a half-way stage between single-shaft deneholes and the Chislehurst mines.

Before discussing deneholes in greater detail I should make clear that the term includes what are known as chalk wells, which were also dug with shaft and chambers for the winning of chalk, but may be of later construction, and do penetrate to lesser depths. Those at Northfleet were so denominated.

Another development of the traditional trefoil arrangement of denehole chambers was that of the pillared denehole, of which examples found in Stankey Wood, Bexley, are described by R. F. Le Gear in the 1976 issue of *Archaeologia Cantiana*. Here double trefoil deneholes with two sets of three chambers had the baulks separating the chambers cut away. This produced from forty to fifty per cent more chalk from the mine without increasing the critical distance from working face to shaft, while at the same time leaving up to six pillars to support the roof.

Having said what deneholes are, I should also say what they are not. They were not dug for the storage of grain or other food, nor were they dug as shelter for man or beast. Underground silos for the storage of grain and root crops have been identified in this country and on the Continent, and have also been described by classical writers, but they are quite different from deneholes.

In this country such underground silos have been found on the ridge between the Avon and Nadder valleys in Wiltshire. They are circular pits seven to fifteen feet deep, with a diameter below ground of six to twelve feet. When in use they had covers of clay on a wattle framework, and could on occasion be used as pit dwellings. In the Toulouse area of France similar holes about six feet deep and four feet wide, having a small opening which could admit a man, were in times past dug for the same purpose. When these pits had been filled with grain they were stopped up with earth.

Tacitus and other classical authors described similar silos in Gaul which were on occasion used as shelters. Antiquarians in this country, Lambarde included, have suggested that what Tacitus was referring to were deneholes; and the fact that the name, although not in use before the sixteenth century, is pronounced as if it were written Daneholes confirmed them in the belief that the shafts and chambers were dug as shelters (or, once dug for another purpose, were then used as shelters) against the marauding Danes. This theory, which will be examined in detail later, does not hold water. Not only was Tacitus not referring to deneholes, but the element *dene* has no connection with *Dane*, and deneholes in this country have never been used as shelters from the Danes or anyone else.

The meaning of *dene* in deneholes is obscure. According to the Oxford English Dictionary it probably means *a wooded vale*; and vale — according to Ruskin's excellent explanation of the six terms vale, valley, dale, dell, glen and dingle in his *Deucalion* — means a large extent of level land surrounded by hills. But while deneholes may now be found in woods, they are not usually found in vales, let alone valleys.

Dene can also mean a low sand hill or dune; and many of the deneholes, at least for the first few feet, are driven through sand. My own guess is that *dene* comes from *den* — but since we know the purpose of deneholes and when they were first dug, which was long before any form of English was spoken in this country, the matter is of minor importance.

It is now necessary to describe deneholes and where they may be found.

Single deneholes, which were dug to provide chalk for individual farms, were dug wherever chalk could be obtained; they are found throughout the chalk areas of south Essex and north Kent, and indeed in all chalk areas.

Groups of deneholes were sited in clearly defined areas such as Hangmans Wood, where chalk of better quality could be obtained. This chalk was mined less for local use than for sale at home and abroad.

Individual deneholes therefore answered the needs of individual farmers, groups of deneholes wider agricultural and commercial purposes.

The depth of the shaft and the height of the chambers in deneholes vary according to the nature and depth of the top soil. Some deneholes — according to Spurrell, the earliest — go down into the chalk through little top soil. These are not the commonest (possibly, of course, because they fell in and were lost centuries ago) and should not be regarded as typical. Such deneholes are found in the Rochester area, where their shafts enter the chalk at once, and pass through it for up to twenty feet before the chambers spread out. The Hangmans Wood deneholes, on the other hand, go down through some twelve feet of sand and gravel and then about forty-six feet of Thanet sand before striking chalk. The depth from the surface of the ground to the floor of the shaft and chambers here can be up to eighty feet. The chambers are something like seventeen or eighteen feet high, and the chalk roof above them three or four feet thick.

Deneholes in Kent, says Spurrell, have chambers varying in height from fifteen to thirty feet, and in diameter from fifteen to fifty feet.

Some of the chambers are round, some square; some have supporting pillars, some not. The shafts vary in diameter from two feet to three feet six inches. Spurrell, who gives these details in volume 38 of the *Archaeological Journal*, says he has been down all the deneholes "in the neighbourhood" to which a rope ladder could conveniently be carried; and the details with which I have credited him are based on the observations he made in the course of these descents.

Four special aspects of deneholes must now be considered: the nature of the tools used in their excavation; the width of the shafts; the way in which access was offered to shaft and chambers; and the factors which affected the size and shape of the chambers. As to the first, no denehole has been found not worked with metal tools, probably of iron. The Reverend J. W. Hayes, who was Vicar of West Thurrock from 1902 to 1921, and in those years devoted much painstaking research to the investigation of deneholes, described the crowns of two denehole chambers which he examined in 1918. He said that metal pick marks in the form of squared holes were to be seen all round the walls, and added, "and this is always the case when these chambers are opened up".

The second aspect, the width of shaft, to some extent depends on its depth; and this, as we have seen, is decided by the amount of overburden. If the shaft is eighty feet deep, then it means that at the beginning of the lift the weight of eighty feet of rope must be added to that of chalk and container. Since deep mined chalk, bulk for bulk, is between fifty and a hundred per cent heavier than ordinary coal, this imposes a fairly low limit to the weight which could be lifted with primitive equipment. If for these reasons the amount of chalk which could be raised at one lift was contained in a basket little bigger than a bucket, there would then be no need to sink a shaft more than a couple of feet in diameter, which would also save the time and labour of digging a wider shaft.

Where the shaft passes through material which is not liable to fall in — Thanet sand for example, which in spite of its name bears the wear and tear of use well — there are usually foot holes on either side of the shaft, either part of the way, or the whole of the way to the bottom. They are usually eighteen inches apart up and down, and go from six to twenty inches into the side of the shaft. Shafts which passed through crumbly surface soil such as London clay or Woolwich pebble beds had to be lined with stones to prevent their collapsing. Footholes have not been observed in these steined shafts, so access was presumably by rope, and perhaps also winch.

The size and shape of denehole chambers were decided by two things: the way in which the chalk was cut away, and the need for the miner not to go more than a certain distance from the bottom of the shaft. To take the second point first, no chamber was extended beyond a point from which excavated material, placed in some sort of skip, could be hoisted directly up the shaft by pulling on a rope from the surface. I take it that a wicker basket with a flat bottom, having some sort of runners and connected by rope with a winch at the top of the shaft, would be filled by the miner at the working surface. When filled, the container would be dragged to the surface by the rope, the distance it could be dragged along the floor of the chamber, with a change in the direction of pull at the bottom of the shaft, depending on friction between container and floor, and between the rope and the chalk roof where it turned the corner into the shaft; and so on.

Friction therefore meant that for a given depth of shaft, and height of chamber entrance, there was a certain distance from the entrance beyond which a pull on the rope from above would not be enough to drag a laden skip along the floor to the base of the shaft. If the man at the face dragged the loaded skip to the base of the shaft himself it would be possible to work beyond this distance. But this was economically unprofitable compared with sinking a new shaft, which involved less time and labour, and therefore expense, than one might think.

The second factor which limited the size of the chambers was safety. It was safe to work as far as the limit of effective operation only if the roof was supported in some way, usually by continuous partitions between segments of the working; and this meant having two, three or four chambers in clover leaf form. The design of deneholes as far as chambers were concerned was therefore a compromise between efficient operation and safety.

These, then, were the factors which dictated the distance from the bottom of the shaft to the working face. In other respects the shape of the chambers resulted from the way in which the chalk was won. Miners did not work forward with newly excavated roof and wall at a right angle, but in a curve, and when they came to the farthest extent of working the curve remained, because it would not be economical to dig more material from it at the roof cove.

The chalk was dug in this way. The upper part of the face — in the miner's phrase, the upper canch — was cut out first so that a wide step, the bottom canch, was left to a height of perhaps two feet between floor and wall. Some writers have called these benches, but I think the word step may be a little clearer. The miner stood on this step and worked at the highest point of the face, which would otherwise be out of reach from the floor. As he worked forward he would at intervals cut away the chalk which formed the step, but would always leave it high enough to continue working at the upper part of the face. Sometimes these steps were not cut away, and where they remain they have been described as (for example) Druids' Altars — at least in the Chislehurst caves, where the same upper and lower canch method of working was used.

Those who dug groups of deneholes in such areas as Hangmans Wood, where chalk of good quality could be obtained, obeyed the miner's dictum of "When in ore, stick to it" by keeping as close as possible to deposits already proved. Then when it became difficult to move chalk from the working face to the bottom of the shaft, the miner, already knowing that more good quality chalk was available on the site, would decide in which direction to continue working. He would make a rough measurement of the distance he had already worked underground in the chosen direction, and site his next shaft so that when he had reached the farthest extent of economic working in the chamber nearest to the previous denehole, the minimum thickness of unworked chalk consistent with safety would be left between the two. It was this need to keep as close as possible to what had already been proved which caused concentration of deneholes.

We have already seen that two shallow deneholes connected by a gallery have been found at Northfleet in Kent — as far as I know the first so identified. This proves that in one case at least deneholes communicated with each other by tunnel. It does not, however, solve the question which exercised the minds of earlier researchers, that of whether the chambers of one denehole when first dug communicated *immediately* with those of another. This was a matter concerning which those who first explored deneholes in modern times are in conflict.

There are, however, theoretical reasons for supposing that miners in areas of concentrated chalk working stopped short before breaking through into the chamber of a neighbouring denehole. The deneholes in Hangmans Wood are at least four centuries old, and for reasons later advanced are probably much older. They therefore date from a time when accurate underground surveying was probably not practised. The miner in one chamber working towards the chambers of the previous denehole therefore could not tell with any accuracy at what point he would break through if he continued. If he did so in line with one of the chambers it might be safe enough, but if he worked into a pillar or buttress separating adjoining chambers, then the roof might fall on him. For these reasons, as the sound of his blows showed he was close to the next pit, he would stop working because of this danger.

Apart from considerations of safety, there was also no point in working into air. For this reason the matter of whether deneholes connected with each other immediately, as with so much which touched deneholes, may have been a simple matter of work study. There was a distance beyond which it was difficult or uneconomic to move chalk to the base of the shaft, and to dig another shaft where there was a possibility of chambers communicating would simply reduce the effective working area.

Another theoretical reason why deneholes did not connect immediately (if they did not connect) was put forward by Hayes. He suggested that deneholes in a concentrated group were probably self-contained because there would be no point, and might be danger, in working into the debris which had fallen into a worked out and abandoned denehole, or into the spoil from newly dug shafts which was usually dumped at the bottom of the old. He also suggested that deneholes in a concentrated group were self-contained because each was worked by a separate interest. My own feeling is that safety and economic effectiveness were the real reasons why deneholes were self-contained.

Hayes' suggestion that debris which had collected in the chambers of a worked-out denehole would run through into the new one if workmen broke through the party wall allows me to describe this one final feature of all deneholes save such as are individually isolated: the cones of debris found at the bottom of many of their shafts. In most cases these cones of debris result from the dumping of material dug from a newly opened shaft nearby. This has been proved in the case of the Hangmans Wood deneholes by J. G. N. Clift, who in two papers published in the *British Archaeological Association Journal* for 1908 has shown that only sixteen per cent of the material at the bottom of these deneholes resulted from denudation of the shaft. The remainder was spoil from newly opened shafts. His findings were confirmed by Hayes in the case of a denehole at Purfleet, where the heap of sand at the bottom of the shaft contained 250 cubic feet of material, while the contents of the shaft above the chalk would have amounted to 128 cubic feet only. This was a case where the sand came from more than one denehole, and could not have been formed by attrition of the sides of the shaft. The existence in worked-out deneholes of more debris than could have come from the shafts of those same deneholes proves that once a denehole was worked out its useful life was at an end — which also proves that they were dug for chalk only.

Examination of deneholes opened up during the last seventy years or so has proved that they were not dug or used as stores or shelters. Attempts to prove that they were so used led to a fascinating byway in antiquarianism, and to complete the case against it it is necessary to see how it became accepted.

The theory was built up on the vague, and misinterpreted, comments of the classical historian Tacitus whom I have already mentioned. Tacitus, who lived from A.D. 55 to 120, referred in his *Germania* to the German habit of digging holes in which to store food. Of the *Germania*, described by Quiller-Couch as "an old political skit", G. T. Griffith, writing on the historiography of the Greek and Roman world in *Chambers's Encyclopaedia*, says "The *Germania* was itself original in conception and in execution admirable, though it could have been better if it had carried conviction, for example, that its author had troubled to set foot in Germany or set eyes on a German".

The particular passage, which is in Book 16, reads as follows in the translation by Sir William Peterson. "They [the German tribes] are in the habit also of opening pits in the earth and piling dung in quantities on the roof, as a refuge from the winter or a root house, because such places mitigate the rigour of frost, and if an enemy come, he lays waste the open; but the hidden and buried houses are either missed outright or escape detection just because they require a search." It will be noticed that the translator refers to pits; three other standard translations refer to caverns, caves, or cellars — which must show lack of precision in the original. It will also be noticed that the translated passage makes no mention of the storage of grain, but refers to these pits, when not in use as human shelters, as root houses. It is on such foundations that some antiquarians have suggested that Tacitus was referring to deneholes.

The fact is that he was referring to the German equivalent of what are known in Scotland as weems or earth-houses. Weems are underground shelters and storehouses contemporary with, and earlier than, those described by Tacitus. They are found in Caithness, Sutherland, and the Orkneys and Hebrides, as well as farther south in Aberdeenshire and Angus. They are usually in the form of a curved gallery from forty to ninety feet long, dug out of the earth and roofed with stone or timber, and having a stone-walled beehive-shaped chamber at the far end. While differing from the German pits in having galleries, they were also used for storage and as hide-outs and winter shelters. The remains of shelters of similar construction are found in Cornwall and Ireland.

Camden was the first to connect deneholes with the storage of farm produce as mentioned by Tacitus. After six editions of his *Britannia* in which he referred to deneholes in the Faversham area of Kent as chalk pits, in the seventh he referred to pits near Tilbury for the first time and commented, "For my part I have nothing to offer as my conjecture, unless they were those pits out of which the Britons dug white chalk to manure their land as mentioned by Pliny. For they used to sink pits a hundred feet deep, narrow at the mouth but of great size below, and just such are those very pits we describe, nor are they met with any where but in chalky grounds." Camden continues, "Unless some imagine that the English Saxons dug such holes for the same purpose as the Germans, from whom they were descended, did. They were wont (says Tacitus) to dig holes underground, and to overlay them with great quantities of dung; thus they provided a refuge against the winter and a garner for their produce; for the bitterness of the cold is thus allayed in such places." It will be seen that the suggestion on Camden's part concerning Tacitus is half-hearted, credited to others, and perhaps even derisory.

Lambarde, as we have seen, took up Tacitus with enthusiasm and suggested that deneholes served, not only as grain pits, but as places of refuge for people and goods. Lambarde was apparently not satisfied with the sound comments of the locals who said the deneholes at Crayford were dug for chalk. Seeking to justify a more exciting reason for their existence he therefore assumed they were similar to the pits described by Tacitus.

Later writers, with or without reference to Tacitus, have carried on the tradition of seeing deneholes as refuges for people or stock, possibly during the Danish invasions, or as storehouses for grain and other farm produce. Thus Salmon, referring to "the Caverns of East Tilbury" suggested that they might have been hiding places to take refuge on the approach of an enemy.

But even if we discounted entirely the fact that a denehole, once dug, was of no further use to its makers, it is impossible to believe it was ever general practice for deneholes to be used as human refuges. It would be necessary for someone to remain above and camouflage the opening in some way so that it was not obvious to those passing by, and then to return when the danger was passed to give the all-clear to those below. If in spite of these precautions the refuge was discovered, those inside would be trapped. Deneholes did not lead to a series of galleries or tunnels which might be more easily defended, or to any sort of outlet which did not require climbing up or being hauled up a vertical shaft. If in addition they did not communicate with each other — and even if they did — the shelter theory is punctured entirely.

One writer who accepted that deneholes were dug first as chalk pits, but still wanted to introduce an element of drama into his speculations, suggested that those taking refuge could escape "through the thin division of chalk between them and safety". One wonders what their pursuers would be doing while women and children were knocking through the wall of chalk; and whether, once in the neighbouring denehole, they could climb up the shaft any quicker than the men after them; or what hope they would have, once having climbed the neighbouring shaft, of escaping through an entrance only a few feet away from that discovered and entered by their pursuers. The writer also suggested, in support of his theory, that deneholes were set in the heart of dense woods for the sake of cover, overlooking the difficulty of sinking a shaft through tree roots. He also overlooked the fact that the presence of trees in Hangmans Wood and Joydens Wood now is no evidence that there were trees there in Saxon times; and that the trees probably grew there in later centuries because such pitted and dangerous land could not be used for raising stock or crops; he also overlooked the fact that if concealment was of importance, the pits would have been scattered rather than concentrated. It is into such difficulties that the supporters of the denehole refuge-theory are led.

These theoretical objections are confirmed by the fact that no one has ever found human remains in a denehole which would suggest even the shortest period of occupation. Hayes, describing a denehole at Purfleet, said that human beings could not have used this "or other deneholes" as refuges or dwelling places because the edges of the walls would show signs of rubbing, and the flecks thrown by the force of the blows from the square dies of the pick marks would have been knocked off — and they still remained in position.

While few modern authorities would now accept the suggestion that deneholes were ever used as refuges, even so sensible a researcher as Spurrell believed they were used as secret hiding places for grain. He said their depth gave secrecy, while the chambers, each about as large as a haystack, were used for storing grain, forage, straw and hay.

The simplest objection to this theory comes from Hayes, who points out that if grain had been stored in deneholes the floor and walls would show traces of debris; the pick holes, in particular, would have been filled with its remains. No sign of this debris, or indeed of any organic material, has been found in any denehole. It is also true to say that deneholes are unlike any known storage pits in size or construction; while I must say that in all my reading I have come across no references to traces of wooden barriers which would have been necessary to hold back the heaped grain from overflowing into the shaft, or of vertical grooves into which those barriers might fall.

Perhaps this section on the refuge-granary-storepit theory of deneholes may be concluded with a quotation from the paper on deneholes by Clift already referred to: "Not one fragment of pottery, not one single object of any kind, has ever been recorded as having been found in any pits in Hangmans Wood which can remotely be associated with the period during which they are supposed to have been mostly used as refuges and stores".

The suggestions that deneholes were dug as shelters or for the storage of food are far fetched enough, but the wildest of all reasons put forward for their construction was produced in 1705 when Plot referred in *The Natural History of Oxfordshire* to deneholes in Hangmans Wood as "the Gold-mine of Cunobeline, in Essex". He did so in the following words, after describing his descent elsewhere of what he supposed may have been a silver mine.

"From all which it may be concluded, that 'tis probable at leaft that here may have been formerly fuch a *Mine*, ftopt up as I firft thought by the *Ab-original Britains*, who not being able to recover their *Country* within the Memory of Man, it might be loft like the *Gold-mine* of

Glafs-Hitten in *Hungary*, when *Bethlem Gabor* over-ran that *Country*; or the Gold-mine of *Cunobeline* in *Effex*, difcover'd again *temp. Hen.* 4. as appears by the King's Letters of *Mandamus*, bearing Date 11 *May, An.* 2. *Rot.* 34. directed to *Walter Fitz-Walter* concerning it; and fince that loft again."

Cunobeline, or Cymbeline, was the British king whose headquarters were at Colchester in the same county. Plot we have already noticed in chapter 8. It is recorded that for many years it was a boast among the Staffordshire squires how readily they had humbugged him in his researches. It seems, from his reference to gold mines, that there were some squires in Essex who humbugged him too. Within fifteen years, at the height of the South Sea Bubble in 1720, a proposal was made "For improving a Royalty in Essex" — to mine gold from Cunobeline's Gold Mines. Even in 1818 the myth persisted: the *Cambrian Register* of that year describes how one adventurer descended one of the Hangmans Wood deneholes in pursuit of gold. He had a surgeon in attendance in case of accident, and explained his lack of success by saying that the cunning British had a second mine leading off that which he had descended, and had sealed and hidden the entrance.

A last dying flick of the gold mine myth was in 1905, when the manager of the Queen's Hotel in Grays obtained a lease of Hangmans Wood, intending to turn it into a pleasure resort, with the deneholes as its main tourist attraction. A *History and Guide to the Hangmans Wood Deneholes* was published which represented the pits as Roman or pre-Roman, and dug as secret hiding places, probably for grain, possibly for men. Arrangements were made for the safe descent of the shafts; and light refreshments were available at the Cunobeline Retreat in the middle of the wood.

The gold mine theory of deneholes is so absurd that no very detailed answer is necessary. The way in which the whole thing developed, quite falsely, from a mandamus of Henry IV is exposed in a careful analysis of literary sources by Clift in his paper. It is a capable, but in one sense an unnecessary piece of scholarship — unnecessary because all one need say is this: you don't get gold from chalk.

So far the reader may not have quarrelled with my reasoning. But I suspect one objection will not have been far from his mind: that deneholes cannot have been dug for chalk because those who needed it could have won it more easily by digging from surface chalk, chalk outcrops, or cliffs.

It certainly seems a roundabout way of quarrying chalk to sink a shaft and then hollow out chambers in the bowels of the earth; and the difficulty in answering this objection convincingly, coupled with the human tendency to introduce violence and drama into the unknown past, is probably the main reason why the theories of origin earlier outlined have been so slow in dying. It can, however, be proved that where chalk was mined by small groups of individuals without power machinery, deneholes were the most efficient method. This can be done in two ways: by reference to deneholes which have been dug in recorded time; and by considering the digging of a denehole as a work-study exercise.

As to the former, the Deneholes Exploration Committee of the Essex Field Club reported in 1887 that chalk was won during the 1880's in mines at Beaconsfield in Buckinghamshire and Hampstead Norris in Berkshire from mines similar to deneholes. The committee added that although bare chalk was to be found about one sixth of a mile away from one of these chalk mines, it was cheaper to sink the shaft at the spot where it was required than to cart the chalk uphill that distance. This report proves that in the 1880's chalk was being mined from what were in effect deneholes although opencast chalk was available nearby.

These facts are confirmed in a general way by Hayes, who said that he had seen chalk being mined "on the denehole pattern" at Hemel Hempstead in Hertfordshire, Wickham (presumably) in Kent and Plumstead in south-east London — and that in the early nineteenth century, before the introduction of chemical fertiliser, farm deneholes dug by farmworkers in winter to obtain chalk for marling were common.

The digging of deneholes for chalk is described by John Bannister of Horton Kirby in Kent in his book *A Synopsis of Husbandry* (1799) and in the Board of Trade's *Report on the Agriculture of Hertfordshire* (1804). Bannister describes two ways of obtaining chalk, the first by uncovering a piece of ground and making a pit or small quarry, the second by sinking several shafts according to the extent of the field. In the author's opinion the second was to be preferred. "These pits are to be made in the form and circumference of a well," he says, "with an apparatus at the top, and a bucket to draw up the chalk. The people who undertake this business, having been brought up to it from their

Plate 36. The bank shown in these two photographs, with the hollow way and field boundary to the right, are on the line of the Brentwood to Tilbury Roman road just east of Tilbury Riverside station.

Plate 37. Gravesend Reach, the Lower Hope, and th

Port of London Authority and Handford

·f the Thames seen from above Northfleet in Kent.

By courtesy of the Thurrock Gazette

Plate 38. This photograph, taken at the bottom of a denehole shaft near Grays, shows lampblack stains, and grooves in the roof made by the ropes used to haul up loads of chalk.

cradle, perform it with great facility, and without timidity, though attended with much danger. When the labourer has dug some little time in the chalk in the perpendicular form wherein he began the pit, he proceeds to form apertures in different horizontal positions."

The Board of Trade report describes how a spot was fixed in the middle of the area to be fertilised with chalk, and a shaft from four to five feet in diameter dug through to it. At the base of the shaft, which might be twenty feet deep, three separate headings were driven until enough chalk had been cut for about six acres. Men would distribute the chalk up to a distance of 330 feet from the shaft, but would dig another shaft if a larger area needed treating. One man dug the chalk while the other two wound it up the shaft by windlass and then distributed it by cart. It was estimated, since sixty tons of chalk were used to the acre, that each of the deneholes described in the report produced about 360 tons of chalk. The report added that in the 1790's high cartage costs and poor farm roads made it uneconomic to excavate chalk for farm use far from the field which needed treatment.

These examples prove that deneholes were dug in modern times where chalk was needed for the land and where farm labour only was available. It is now a matter of deciding why it was won in this way rather than in any other. One general answer is given by Hayes, who pointed out that two men could dig a denehole shaft in under a week, and that it was more convenient to sink another shaft than to extend the underground workings, which would give the miner too great a distance to walk from the working face to the base of the shaft. But this was not the only consideration. Another reason why farmers, even in the nineteenth century, preferred to sink a shaft for chalk by the field they wanted to marl rather than send for it to the nearest outcrop, was that cartage costs, where wheeled vehicles were uncommon and roads bad, were higher than the costs of sinking a shaft. To sink an eighty-feet shaft was less laborious than carting every load of chalk an extra mile over undrained and unmetalled country roads. These comparisons depend as much on the cheapness and simplicity of sinking a shaft as on the expense of cartage; this cheapness and simplicity, which will be analysed later, must for the moment be accepted.

Much less overburden had to be dug away when sinking a denehole shaft then when opening up a quarry, or digging chalk from trenches. Deneholes, with their small entrances, also took less land from cultivation than open cast quarrying, which threw valuable land out of cultivation for some time, and might damage it permanently. A series of trenches on fairly level land, or a quarry in the side of sloping ground, involved first the removal of the overburden; the site, once worked out, then had to be filled in completely, and the soil put back if the land were to be restored to effective cultivation; and this would be a difficult operation. In the case of a denehole, however, only the shaft needed to be filled — the chambers from which most of the chalk came could be left unfilled without subsidence necessarily resulting. A farm denehole would also damage only some ten square feet at the top of the shaft; and where more than one was dug, waste material from the second and succeeding shafts could be dumped down that previously abandoned, as was done in the Hangmans Wood deneholes.

The work involved in digging the shaft downwards was also justified because once the shaft was sunk the miner could work at a vertical face, or even a face above his head, where the position of work was easier, and the amount of chalk to be won considerable. The position of work relative to the face of the chalk is a factor whose importance can be assessed by those with no experience of quarrying chalk. One has only to compare the ease of working along the natural horizontal layers of chalk from the side, as in chambers, with the difficulty of working from the top, as in surface quarrying. Wet weather, too, would make dealing with surface deposits a messy business, while most of the work on a denehole could be done in reasonable comfort in all seasons, and in all weathers. Deneholes were mostly dug in autumn at a time when other farm tasks were few so that the chalk could be used for winter spreading; but even if deneholes were dug in winter, the temperature below would always be equable, however fierce the frost above. Artificial light was of course necessary and lampblack stains can often be seen on the roofs of denehole chambers.

The fact that chalk from deneholes has to be hoisted to the surface in containers held at the end of a rope rather than lifted out of a trench is an argument in favour of deneholes. If lumps of chalk have to be lifted from the bottom of a trench to ground level or above by spade or shovel, and then collected together for loading on to a cart, each spadeful will have to be given individual treatment. This is more laborious than dropping lumps of chalk into a skip at the working face, or even dragging the loaded skip to the bottom of the shaft to be hoisted to the surface.

The last word on what I have called the work-study aspect of deneholes was said by Clift in one of the papers to which I have already referred. Clift is rather too much for those who supported the refuge-granary-storepit theories of deneholes. His paper, which ranges widely over the subject, is an amusing exercise in academic slaughtering of a polite kind. As far as work study is concerned, Clift considers the job of digging a denehole under the four headings of time, space, labour and cost. The smallest number of men who could dig a denehole would be two, one to dig, and one to take the material away. Mechanical aids would be a skip or bucket, perhaps a winch and rope. Clift points out that it has never been denied that metal tools were used with which an excavator (he means a labourer used to digging) could in his time extract from five to ten cubic yards of material in an eight-hour day.

Clift takes the case of one of the Hangmans Wood deneholes whose shaft passes through eight feet of gravel and forty-seven feet of Thanet sand before striking the chalk. He assumes that these materials, which are much more easily worked than chalk, could be excavated at the rate of 7.5 cubic yards in eight hours. On the basis of these figures, and by calculations which are given in full in the paper, Clift worked out that to dig the shaft of these deneholes from surface to chalk would take two men two eight-hour days at a cost in 1908, when farm labourers' wages were 17s. 6d. a week, of £1 0s. 6d. (87½p. and 102½p. in modern currency). He comments, "It will be seen that one of these shafts could be sunk with a comparatively slight expenditure of labour and at a trifling cost. If done by agricultural labour the cost would be less than £1 0s. 6d., because excavation would be intermittent, and done when other work was at a standstill."

The quality of chalk mined had no great bearing on the digging of individual farm deneholes, but it had a good deal of bearing on the digging of groups of deneholes whose product was commercially exploited. This factor must now be considered. Chalk needed for cutting into building blocks is better quarried from a depth. It is purer and more compact than surface chalk, which is friable and impure because of the superficial action of frost, and because surface water has carried down particles of clay through fractures in the chalk. While purity and density were less essential in chalk used as fertiliser, the better quality chalk was still preferred by farmers for lime burning and even for spreading on the land. Hayes, who had no doubt that quality was an important factor, went so far as to say, "We now know that deneholes were purely holes to obtain chalk of a certain density suitable for lime burning and for the land as marl or manure."

There were therefore commercial reasons why chalk miners sought the best deposits. But deep mined chalk of better quality could be obtained only in certain areas, particularly by those using primitive mining methods; and it was in these areas, which have recognisable geological characteristics, that concentrations of deneholes are found. According to Hayes the dense, pure chalk which was best for lime burning or for use as building blocks was invariably found where the Thanet sand above the chalk was thickest, as at Chislehurst, in Hangmans Wood, and at Purfleet. He said that those who dug the deneholes at Purfleet knew exactly where to seek for chalk of this quality; for while chalk of a certain kind could be obtained within two feet of the surface only a hundred yards away, this friable and impure surface chalk was rejected for that under the greater depth of Thanet sand. This latter was not vitiated by clay as was that at the surface, and since it retained its natural block form was easier to mine and use.

Hayes called this formation "the two-foot slittings", the slittings being cleavage surfaces usually covered with iron oxide from iron-bearing water which washed down the faces of the fractures. These slittings made it possible to remove the chalk in two-foot blocks; and he pointed out that it was impossible, except by digging a shaft through the sand, or by the wholesale removal of top soil and upper layers, to get at chalk of this nature. And wholesale removal of top soil and top layers of chalk would be too great an undertaking for two men, particularly when by sinking a shaft they could get at block chalk after removing only a small part of the overburden.

The first mention of deneholes is in the Latin author Pliny, already referred to in the quotation from Camden. Pliny was a writer on agriculture and natural history who lived from A.D. 23 to 79, and whose zeal for research led to his death by suffocation in the eruption of Vesuvius which destroyed Pompeii. In book 17 chapter 4 of his *Natural History* he refers to the use of chalk as fertiliser and soil conditioner. According to him this "method of feeding the earth by means of itself" was discovered in Britain and Gaul. After dealing with other kinds of marl (in its widest sense, a soil which fertilises and conditions agricultural soils) he continues, "Another variety of white marl is the chalk used for cleaning silver; this is obtained from a considerable depth in the ground, usually from pits made one hundred feet deep, with a narrower mouth but with the shaft expanding in the interior, as is the practice in mines. This chalk is chiefly used in Britain. Its effect lasts for eighty years, and there is no case of anybody having scattered it on the same land twice in his lifetime."

It is therefore clear that in Roman times the fine white chalk used for cleaning silver was also used as fertiliser on the land, chiefly in Britain. It is also clear that the pits from which it was dug were deneholes, and that some of the deneholes found in Essex and Kent must have been dug in and before the Roman Occupation.

Pliny's statement finds dramatic confirmation in Johann Georg Keysler's *Antiquitates selectae Septentrionales et Celticae*, which was published in Hanover in 1720, and his *Exercitatio historico-philologica de Dea Nehalennia* (Celle 1717), in which he describes a score of Roman altars found on the coast of Zealand in south-west Holland dedicated by dealers in British chalk to Nehalennia, a vegetation goddess concerned with fertility and the abundance of crops. Among these altars, according to Keysler, was one dedicated by Silvanus Negotiator Cretarius Britannicus — Silvanus, a dealer in British chalk. It is therefore clear that chalk from British deneholes was exported during, and possibly before, the Roman Occupation of Britain.

I end these comments on marling with a speculation. I do wonder whether some of the groups of deneholes in Hangmans Wood, at Crayford and elsewhere in the chalk areas north and south of the Thames, were not the source of the chalk exported to Holland and other parts of the Roman Empire.

There is some evidence of Roman remains having been found in deneholes. A. R. Goddard, although not the most reliable of commentators, said that Roman remains had been found in Kentish deneholes. Spurrell said that abundant Roman remains had been found in old deneholes near Perry Street, Crayford, adding, "The majority belong to the age of iron, but they extend through the Roman period, and were largely used by that people as rubbish tips, which have hereabouts furnished many a Roman relic". Richard Meeson, who lived at Duvals in Meesons Lane, Grays, said that he had opened up one denehole "full of Roman burial vases crushed by the fall of the roof, but from which I extracted one nearly perfect, containing the bones of a female and child, with bronze armlets, and a spindle whorl of lead." George Payne, writing in volume 21 of *Archaeologia*

Cantiana, records the fact that fragments of seven or eight Roman vessels, oyster shells and broken Roman flange tile, as well as part of an iron knife and an iron bell with handle and clapper of Roman date, were found near the base of a denehole at Plumstead.

There is evidence that some deneholes were worked in the later Middle Ages. According to Spurrell, excavations carried out in Joydens Wood, Bexley, established that six-chamber deneholes were dug there before 1280, while excavations in a six-chamber denehole in Darenth Wood dated it to between 1200 and 1250. A denehole on the other side of the river, at South Stifford, was in 1956 dated to much the same period.

CHAPTER 16

Literary references

There are references to the lower Thames in the works of Dickens, Conrad, Belloc, Butler and Bram Stoker; and of all these writers Belloc, as with so many subjects, comes nearest to the heart of the matter.

Belloc's interpretive ability is seen at its best in *The River of London*, where he explains how it is that London grew up where it did, and in the opening pages of *The Historic Thames*, where he analyses the place of rivers in history and in the history of London in particular — although references in the latter book to Aveney, Mordyke, Wellington and Suffolk are to Aveley, the Mardyke, Wennington and Southwark.

Belloc writes of the river with the best of first hand knowledge. As he says in *The River of London*, to know it one must make the journey from the sea upwards in something not larger than a barge, taken on one tide with an easterly wind "as all the men of the past took it. In this way," he continues, "with little freeboard between one's feet and the changing level of the broad water, and with not too rapid a passage of the stations upon either bank, and with some true measure wherewith to gauge in detail what one sees, one can understand the river."

Those who understand the river in this way are, I fear, a dwindling company. The knowledge and skill of the men who took sailing barges up and down the Thames will in a few years' time be gone for ever. The feel of sail, and how one fabric is better than another, and why it is better; how sail behaves in rain or frost or drought or storm; how one can judge position on the river by the sound of the water under the hull; why one barge is friendly, and another isn't; what ropes feel like, and why some ropes are good, and some bad; what the voice of the wind in the sails tells the man at the wheel — I am imagining these things, because I cannot speak with first-hand knowledge; but these are the practical things of days in sail which only the often incommunicative, and now the ageing, can know as far as the commercial operation of barges is concerned. In a few years, unless someone does a good deal of digging and interpreting, such knowledge will be lost for ever in all fields where the machine is taking over.

I have wandered away from Belloc, one man who understood these things and in his own way did something to record the spirit, and the actuality, of physical things. He, too, understood the menace of machinery, then in the first stage of its final attack on humanity, for he wrote of the lower Thames, "Here and there an odd survival left remaining of deliberate purpose serves but to emphasise the capture of the lower Thames by that crazy mechanical giant so recently born and already so blind and old".

Belloc had an eye for the essential. It is interesting to see how he noticed from the river, as at one time one so quickly noticed from the land, the church by the river wall at West Thurrock. "Of all that life of the Middle Ages which the English countrysides preserve in so many visible relics — and specially in a host of parish churches surpassing all of the kind in Europe" he writes in *The River of London*, "the lower Thames has but one clear instance remaining to the eye: and that is the little isolated church of St Clements."

The church at West Thurrock is certainly the most obvious of all beside the river. The stone triangle which marks the church of St Catherine at East Tilbury is farther away from the river bank, has a background of trees, might hardly be seen by those taking a sailing boat upstream, and could easily be missed by those taking one down. There is, however, on the Kent bank one church which might be held to complement the church at West Thurrock — that at Chalk. It is on high ground some way from the river, although clearly visible from it. And as the church of St Clement once did, it stands alone.

Conrad is the only writer who stands comparison with Belloc where the Thames is concerned. Certainly nothing better has been written about the Thames estuary and river than chapters 30 to 32 of his book *The Mirror of the Sea*. In one particular sense, too, Conrad was closer to the river than Belloc. For while Belloc lived south of Horsham in the Weald of Sussex, Conrad lived from 1896 to 1898 at Stanford le Hope in Essex, in the heart of the lower Thames area.

Before I had by chance come across the site of Conrad's second and more permanent home in Stanford, the town seemed to me the most unlikely place for this strange but admirable man to have settled; and stranger still, having settled in the Essex Stanford, that he should have moved to the Kent Stanford south of Canterbury.

To regard the Polish sailor's choice of Stanford le Hope as strange resulted from my own earlier associations with the place, and is perhaps too personal a judgment. The reason for Conrad's choice was simple enough. He left the sea to dedicate himself to writing in his adopted tongue, and had to find somewhere to live in England. He therefore chose to stay near his friends Captain G. F. W. Hope and his family, who lived in Stanford. At Stanford Conrad was not only within reach of London, but also within easy reach of the Thames, then the world's greatest shipping highway. His choice was sensible enough.

Yet to one who in pre-war days got off the bus or train from Grays, itself no metropolis, the centre of Stanford dozing in the sun seemed something of a backwater, reminiscent of such Northamptonshire boot and shoe manufacturing village-towns as Wollaston or Finedon. Its torpidity might assume more pleasing light in an older town which had throughout the centuries garnered atmosphere and personality; in a town to an extent artificial, something little better than a nineteenth-century cutting of East Ham planted half way between London and Southend in the hope that it might strike root, this atmosphere of quiet produced contrasting reactions. I went there once or twice at most, and felt a certain tedium on arriving, and a certain lightening of the spirit on returning to Grays.

I have described my early memories of Stanford to give emphasis to my reaction when by chance I came across the site of Conrad's home there. On all pre-war visits I had been dropped by bus or train in the centre of the town. Long years later I came to the southern outskirts of the town after walking across the marshes from the river and climbing up through ploughland. The road on which I found myself ran along the edge of the bluff on which Stanford stands. On the side from which I came the fields fell away to the river, south to the Lower Hope Reach, east to the Sea Reach. Miles of sea and estuary approaches to the Thames were spread out below me. On the inland side of the road were neat houses. I fancy there was a small park or recreation ground nearby. It was spring, and the trees were in flower. I thought what a pleasant road it was, how attractive the view across the river to the hills of Kent, how unlike my previous ideas of Stanford. And then, crossing the road to look at the only house on the river side of the road, I saw its name was Ivy Walls — the name of the fifteenth-century farmhouse in which Conrad lived, and that of the modern house which since his time has replaced it.

Ivy Walls was not Conrad's first home in Stanford. That was more in the town itself, in Victoria Road — a "damned rabbit hutch of a place", as he called it, and in an area more in tune with Stanford as I earlier described it. But once having come across Ivy Walls on a spring day, seen the splendid view enjoyed by those who lived there, it did not seem a strange place for the novelist to choose, but the most natural place in the world.

The original Ivy Walls was set back from the road and screened in front by elm trees, now felled. Some dwarf hedges which Conrad is said to have planted during his eighteen months' stay are still there. The house was burnt down after Conrad moved, and the present house built on the site.

Conrad wrote *Youth*, *The Return* and *Karain* at Ivy Walls, began *Lord Jim* and *Heart of Darkness* and "went through his worst struggle with *The Rescue*".

One of a number of references he makes in his writing to this part of the world appears in *Heart of Darkness*. This powerful tale is set in the Congo Free State and in Brussels during the administration of Leopold II, although these places are not mentioned by name. Conrad had visited the Congo in 1890 to become second in command of a river boat *Roi des Belges*. He made the journey overland from Matadi to Nselemba, where he joined his ship for the up river journey; and it was the breakdown in his health after this trip which caused him to give up the sea and settle in England.

The activities of the concessionaires of the Association Internationale Africaine, which was founded by Leopold to exploit the then almost unexplored regions of the Congo, were described by Conrad in his essay *Geography and Some Explorers* as "the vilest scramble for loot that ever disfigured the history of human conscience and geographical exploration". Certainly *Heart of Darkness*, which describes the experiences in the Congo of Marlow the narrator, is shot through with evil.

What is more to our purpose is that the tale is told on the deck of a cruising yawl anchored at a point where, in Marlow's words, "the sea-reach of the Thames stretched before us like the beginning of an interminable waterway". He continues, "The air was dark above Gravesend, and farther back still seemed condensed into a mournful gloom, brooding motionless over the biggest, and the greatest, town on earth".

The yawl was presumably anchored in Mucking Haven, in the Lower Hope Reach where the Thames flows north between Gravesend Reach and Sea Reach. Mucking Haven, the northern part of the reach, is so called because in days of sail it offered protection against storms from both east and west. Its most northerly point, where Mucking Creek enters the Thames in the angle formed by the northward flowing Lower Hope Reach and the eastward flowing Sea Reach, is probably where the yawl was anchored. It is the nearest part of the river to Ivy Walls.

I first read *Heart of Darkness* when I thought there was a ford at the south end of the Lower Hope Reach in Roman times, and found Conrad's introduction to the story interesting because he drew a parallel between the civilised Englishman visiting the barbaric Congo, and the civilised Roman visiting the barbaric Thames. Conrad pictured the feelings of a Roman ship's captain ordered north to "the very end of the world, a sea the colour of lead, a sky the colour of smoke . . . and banks, marshes, forests, savages — precious little to eat fit for a civilised man, nothing but Thames water to drink . . . cold, fog, tempests, disease, exile and death — death skulking in the air, in the water, in the bush . . . Land in a swamp, march through the woods, and in some inland post feel the savagery, the utter savagery . . . the fascination of the abomination . . . the growing regrets, the longing to escape, the powerless disgust, the surrender, the hate . . . " Conrad, perhaps taken in by Caesar, seems to have pitched it rather high as far as Britain was concerned, but his comparison has point for the purposes of his story.

A similar technique is used in *Falk: A Reminiscence*, although here it creaks slightly. This story is told in a "small river-hostelry not more than thirty miles from London, and less than twenty from that shallow and dangerous puddle to which our coasting men give the grandiose name of German Ocean. And through the wide windows we had a view of the Thames; an enfilading view down the Lower Hope Reach." Conrad said the wooden dining room stuck out over the mud of the shore; and referred to the light of the crimson sunset, "all ablaze behind the London smoke fading away from the Hope Reach".

Conrad would have taken care that no riverside hostelry could be identified with that in the story because he said the dinner served was "execrable". In any case, for the windows to give an enfilading view down, rather than up, the Lower Hope Reach would mean it was on the south side of the river, somewhere near Higham Bight. Further, for him to see the crimson sunset behind London smoke fading away from Hope Reach must mean (if the reference is to the Lower Hope Reach) that the hostelry was on the east or south-east bank; and there have never been hostelries in these places. On the other hand for there to be a Lower Hope Reach I suppose there must have been a Higher Hope Reach; and this suggests that Conrad might have been referring to that stretch west of Gravesend where Gravesend Reach turns into Northfleet Hope — which would fit in better with his reference to the sunset. For the dining room to stick out over the mud of the shore some concentration of nearby building must be assumed, and for a wooden barque towed by a paddle tug to appear "in front of the window" suggests the room was as close to the fairway as the buildings near the former landing stage at Gravesend. Gravesend is certainly the only place in the area where there were, at least in the past, wooden dining rooms over the mud of the river. But from such a point a view down the Lower Hope Reach, enfilading or otherwise, is impossible. It is clear that in this case Conrad has laid a false trail.

Conrad must have had a number of literary visitors to his house in Stanford during his stay there. Stephen Crane, the American author whose work is highly praised by Thomas Burke in *Son of London*, and who was a friend of Conrad from about October 1897, certainly visited Conrad there, as did Hugh Walpole, Galsworthy, Henry James, and Ford Madox Hueffer (this last, according to Captain Hope's daughter "a calamity"). It is curious that the Conrad industry, which has contributed one or two pearls to the lunatic fringe of transatlantic literary criticism, hasn't gotten on to these things yet.

A passing reference to the river below Gravesend appears in *The Way of All Flesh* by Samuel Butler. Ernest Pontifex, the main character in the novel, boarded out his children with a couple who lived on the waterside a few miles below Gravesend, "just where the sea was beginning". A visit to their home is described by the narrator of the book, who took the train to Gravesend with Ernest, and walked for a few miles along the riverside wall until they came to the "solitary house".

Between the last riverside building in Gravesend, which in Samuel Butler's time would have been the Ship and Lobster Inn at Milton, and the small settlement on the river at Cliffe Creek, there is no house, solitary or otherwise, anywhere near the river. But Cliffe Creek would have been useful for barge owners such as the foster parents were. If Butler's solitary house had been built there — and it is about the only place below Gravesend where the hard ground comes down to the river — to walk there and back from Gravesend station would mean a ten mile walk along none too easy a river wall, while the easier journey to and from Higham station would involve a walk of four miles at the most. No wonder the narrator fell asleep in the train on the journey back to London.

Concerning Purfleet, where Bram Stoker placed the headquarters in England of his character Dracula, speculation is less soundly based. Stoker wrote much of his novel on the Scottish coast at Cruden Bay south of Peterhead, and took his details concerning Transylvania from a guide book; but for the fact that Purfleet is not the sort of place mentioned in guide books he could have done the same for Purfleet. On the other hand he did at one point refer to "... the wonderful smoky beauty of a sunset over London, with its lurid lights and inky shadows and all the marvellous tints that come on foul clouds even as on foul water ..." This suggests that, like Conrad, he really had seen a sunset over London from the lower Thames.

Jonathan Harker, the estate agent who is given the task of finding a house for Dracula, states in his journal, "At Purfleet, on a by-road, I came across just such a place as seemed to be required . . . It is surrounded by a high wall, of ancient structure, built of heavy stones, and has not been repaired for a large number of years. The closed gates were of heavy old oak and iron, all eaten with rust.

"The estate is called Carfax, no doubt a corruption of the old Quatre Face, as the house is four-sided, agreeing with the cardinal points of the compass. It contains in all some twenty acres, quite surrounded by the solid stone wall above mentioned. There are many trees on it, which makes it in places gloomy, and there is a deep, dark-looking pond or small lake, evidently fed by some springs, as the water is clear and flows away in a fair-sized stream. The house is very large and of all periods back, I should say, to medieval times, for one part is of stone immensely thick, with only a few windows high up and heavily barred with iron. It looks like part of a keep, and is close to an old chapel or church . . . The house has been added to, but in a very straggling way, and I can only guess at the amount of ground it covers, which must be very great. There are but few houses close at hand, one being a very large house only recently added to and formed into a private lunatic asylum. It is not, however, visible from the grounds."

The reference to the old chapel or church is interesting. There is no parish church in Purfleet in the accepted sense. A private chapel was attached to the manor house known at various times as La Vineyard, West Hall, and now High House, but while High House remains, the chapel has long since disappeared, and certainly before Stoker's time. When Samuel Whitbread the brewer built Purfleet House in about 1790 he had a chapel of ease built for his family and staff in The Dipping, the worked-out chalk quarry in which the house stood, and it was here that the inhabitants of Purfleet worshipped until the estate was sold in 1920. The chapel was later converted into a private house, and was pulled down in 1951.

A church intended for temporary use, which has now become permanent, was built after the sale of the Whitbread estate with materials from part of Purfleet House. Two relics of the chapel of ease, the bell and pulpit, are incorporated in it; the communion plate, a gift of the Whitbread family, bears the name Poorfleet as that of the village. The church contains, among other memorials, one to Timon Walter Lockyer, of whom more later.

There is no house at Purfleet now, and there was no house at Purfleet then, which could be regarded as faintly like the large house with its walled twenty acre estate and stone keep which Harker describes. The only large house at Purfleet in the 1890's when Stoker wrote *Dracula* was that built by Samuel Whitbread. Stoker, who was Henry Irving's secretary and manager and a friend of Hall Caine (to whom he dedicated *Dracula* under the name of Hommy Beg or Little Tommy, the nickname given Caine by his Manx grandmother) might have visited the Whitbreads' house; but he would hardly have associated it with such goings-on as are described so frighteningly, or so amusingly, or so interestingly, according to one's taste, in *Dracula*.

Stoker shows little familiarity with the natural features of the area, or with Essex building practice. For anyone in a county completely free from building stone save flint or clunch to surround a twenty acre estate with high walls of heavy stone would not be impossible, but it would be unusual. Perhaps Purfleet might have been a good choice for anyone wanting to build a castle to control river traffic on the approaches to London in the same way that Upnor Castle was built on the Medway; and this might be held to justify the stone building like a medieval tower. But this would hardly explain why the "very large house only recently added to and formed into a private lunatic asylum" should also be made of stone.

Springs, too, are not impossible at the edge of the chalk which outcrops at Purfleet; but the only fair sized stream which flows near Purfleet is the Mardyke, which has its rising some miles to the north. We must, I think, assume that Stoker chose, and described, Purfleet quite arbitrarily.

It was to this spot, now a highly industrialised area, that Dracula came with the boxes of soil and his fellow vampires; and it was from here, following the intervention of Jonathan Harker and Van Hesling, that Dracula made his escape when he found refuge denied him. He did not make directly for London, but first crossed the river, a thing he could do only at slack of tide. There was, in those days, a ferry at Purfleet, and the steps down which Dracula went to it, now destroyed, could be seen until recently near the Royal Hotel. They were of stone, and looked to me like stone sleepers. (I assume they came from the iron railway with tipping trucks which was installed by Whitbread before 1807 to take chalk from the quarries for burning, and then to take the burnt lime to the waterside for tipping directly into ships' holds. There are other stone sleepers, showing the marks of the square metal plates formerly fitted on them, by the approach to the church.)

I have certain personal associations with the name Carfax. One man who while almost a stranger to me did me a signal kindness was Timon Lockyer, who in 1933 gave me my first job at the Thames Board Mills in Purfleet. It was a kindness for which I was never able to thank him adequately, or even at all.

I mention this episode because Lockyer lived at Purfleet in a house called Carfax. When I worked there the house name was associated so commonly with his own that it was accepted without thought; and although I had read *Dracula* at the time, I do not know that I connected the two.

After I left the Thames Board Mills I re-read Stoker's masterpiece; and began to wonder why Lockyer lived in a house so named. Thirty years later I met his son by chance, and learnt from him that the name was probably given to the house by the previous owner, a Canadian; and that while there was some question of changing the name when the film *Dracula* came to Grays, and errand boys knocked at the back door and asked to see the bodies in the cellar, the name had in fact remained the same throughout the Lockyers' tenancy. I was told that the family had left the house many years before, and without doubt its name had since been changed.

A year or two after this conversation I visited the old village of Purfleet down by the river. Even though I had worked nearby for two years, it was the first time I had been there. Having seen all there was to see of the square in front of the Royal Hotel, the steps which then led down to the Thames, and the place where the Whitbreads' house once stood, I made my way back to the main road to catch a bus to Grays. On my way I noticed a modest house on the other side of the road, and as I went by glanced at the gate hanging none too securely on its hinges. It had not been painted for some time, probably because like everything else in the area it had a generous coating of cement dust; but I had no difficulty, even from the other side of the road, in reading on it the familiar, even the well loved, name of Carfax.

APPENDIX I

Centuriation at Asheldham and Orsett

Reference to the 2½-inch map of the Asheldham area suggests that the northern limit of centuriation described in chapter 5 may be the straight road which runs more or less due east from High House in the west past Hill House, Reddings and White Horse Farm in the east, which I shall call the Reddings road. This road has three roads branching off at right angles to the south — to Asheldham in the west, Dengie in the centre, and Midlands in the east. These side roads are on average forty actus apart. The road to which they lead, which runs parallel with the Reddings road from Asheldham in the west past New Hall and Dengie Manor to a point south of Midlands in the east, which I shall call the New Hall road, is also on average forty actus distant from the Reddings road. In addition the Reddings road is twenty actus long between that point north of Moynes Farm where it ends in the west, and that point where the Asheldham road leaves it. This, added to the distance from the Asheldham road corner to the Dengie road corner, and that from the Dengie road corner to the Midlands road corner, gives the Reddings road a total length of one hundred actus. The north-south footpath east of Glebe Farm is also twenty actus east of the Dengie road and twenty actus west of the Midlands road to the east. These facts suggest that the forty actus squares may have been divided into four twenty-actus squares — which was the basic unit for centuriation in Italy.

In describing this area of centuriation at Asheldham I must make three qualifications. First, since the three north-south roads are not so arrow-straight as the Reddings road, it is necessary to measure between points which seem to represent their central line, which is why I refer to an average. Secondly, in the case of the New Hall road some diversion to the south has obviously taken place, so measurements from the Reddings road have been taken first to that point where the New Hall road turns east through a right angle just east of the earthwork at Asheldham, and second to that point where the road is joined by the north-south road through Dengie. The first point is a particularly reliable one, because travellers who in later years went round the earthwork picked up the Roman road or track again at the point I have chosen and, by turning through a right angle, proved that the road existed. Both the points I have chosen are forty actus from the Reddings road.

The third qualification is that I have extended the most easterly of the three north-south roads, which at Midlands turns east out of alignment, to an imaginary point on the New Hall road south of Midlands. It is a reasonable assumption that the original road so continued.

The result of these measurements is to find two squares each of forty actus formed by the Reddings road to the north, the New Hall road to the south and, from west to east, the Asheldham, Dengie and Midlands roads.

I have little to add to my suggestion that the northern boundary of the Orsett land settlement area was somewhere near Eastern Avenue, except that there are a number of ten actus fields immediately to the west of West Horndon station, and that the Brentwood to Tilbury road immediately south of Eastern Avenue runs parallel with, and ten actus to the east of, an artificial waterway which forms one of the many headwaters of the Mardyke. Of the artificiality of this waterway there can be no question — its straightness proves it to be man made. It follows that this ditch is Roman — the only one known to me which marks a field boundary in a Roman land settlement area. It also follows that the road which forms the eastern boundary of this ten actus strip, the Brentwood to Tilbury road, is in this section Roman also.

One possible western boundary of the Orsett land settlement area is Blackshotts Lane, the most westerly of the three parallel roads which run north and south here thirty-five actus apart. Perhaps more likely is the former parish boundary which ran parallel with Blackshotts Lane two or three hundred yards farther west. This was the boundary of the hundreds of Chafford and Barstable at the time of Domesday, and is therefore at least nine centuries old. North of Green Lane the extension of Blackshotts Lane has no obvious course, whereas the boundary has a clear extension by lane and ditch to the Mardyke and then (perhaps) by way of Old Barn, Home Farm, Old England and Hall Lane to the northern boundary.

Within the overall area whose boundaries I have described ten actus fields predominate, although there is also a small number of five actus fields, particularly near Orsett itself. The three fields south of the path which runs east from Baker Street in the general direction of the recreation ground — they are shown as orchards on my six-inch map of Orsett — have boundaries parallel with Baker Street which are five actus apart in each case. It is likely that the whole square here — that enclosed by this path to the north, by the road passing Mobbs Farm to the east, by the Stanford road to the south, and by Baker Street to the west — is one twenty-actus unit corresponding to those at Asheldham.

I referred earlier to the fact that Blackshotts Lane, Baker Street, and Rectory Road are thirty-five actus apart. I must now add that thirty-five actus east of the most easterly of these roads is a north-south boundary which runs to the east of Home Farm. Such clear thirty-five actus distances, with the existence here and elsewhere of a number of ten actus fields, suggest that the basic unit of measurement at Orsett was five actus. The suggestion is strengthened by the fact that the three five-actus fields in the line east of Baker Street form part of one thirty-five actus stretch.

The evidence of the map is so clear that confirmation of centuriation in the Orsett area is unnecessary. But reference to the six-inch map will show that one of the boundaries inside Orsett Park, that running northwards from near Orsett Hall to Fox Holes, is ten actus west of the field boundary running south from Home Farm. Many parks were enclosed in the Middle Ages and have never been under the plough since. If Orsett Park is of their number, and this boundary is a Roman land settlement boundary, then it is possible that it has not been touched since the settlement went out of use, and might repay detailed examination.

APPENDIX II

Palin's pilgrim roads

Palin refers to two pilgrim roads passing through Stifford.

The first is the main one which crossed the Mardyke by the western ford, or the bridge which later replaced it, and was continued by the Stifford pilgrim road (which he said was still remaining in his time on the brow of Millwood Hill) and so to West Thurrock church. I take this to be the road to South Stifford which passes Millwood House and formerly marked, for most of its course, the parish boundary between West Thurrock and Stifford.

The second pilgrim road, also still existing in Palin's time, took a course from the Stifford end of Long Lane indicated by a line of "very ancient oak pollards", then branched south-west and ran by the north side of the site of what was then Belmont Castle into Mill Lane, striking the main pilgrim road on the brow of Millwood Hill.

Long Lane used to continue, in the west, to a point some 700 yards west of Chalk Pit Farm, where it ended on the road which runs parallel with, and to the east of, the road from Causeway Bridge, Stifford, to South Stifford. From this point, now a crossroads on the by-pass, it would be possible to continue towards West Thurrock church, either along the road running south towards Belmont Castle, or along the footpath leading south-west to the western end of Warren Lane. Neither, except in the vaguest way, could be said to run "by the north side of the site of what is now Belmont Castle", but they do at least start from what was, in Palin's time, the Stifford end of Long Lane.

Although Palin says the western ford was that used by Canterbury pilgrims, the path in Stifford known as Pilgrims' Lane leads to a point some 200 yards east of the eastern ford. It leaves the north side of the main road in Stifford at a point north-west of the church, and runs down towards the Mardyke in a north-easterly direction. At the time I went down this lane it was a narrow gravelly track between high overgrown hedges, rank with the smell of elder. At the bottom was an iron gate with a side gate for pedestrians, both closed with strands of barbed wire. The gate had above it the sign *This place of peace is presented to Stifford in memory of Sir Fiel ing Clarke*. The "d" of Fielding was missing. It was a pleasant, haunted sort of place.

Pilgrims Lane does not lead to a footbridge today, and there is no record known to me of a ford having existed there. Nor is there any sign of a path, track or road on the opposite bank — only a mark, as it might be a grubbed up hedge, crossing a field.

Things are very different on both sides of the footbridge some 200 yards to the west. On the south side of the Mardyke the path here — it is a path rather than a lane — leads directly to the footbridge. On the north side of the Mardyke there is a track leading away from the stream, first gravelled with a ditch each side, then with concrete blocks set as steps. I imagine these have replaced stone slabs.

Palin also had something to say about another "ancient road" in the area, that which he takes from Southend to London through Stifford; and since he took it across the Mardyke by the ford now replaced by the footbridge we shall consider it here. I quote him in full. "Of the ancient high road, London-Southend, Long Lane, two miles long, and only wide enough for a time when everybody travelled on horseback, remains. It was continued on the London side, by the head of Stifford chalk quarries, and then struck across the Clapper, south-west of Stifford Hall, to the east end of the churchyard, separating it from the bowling-green (as the pasture is still called) of Stifford Hall. Thence by the lane, still remaining, opposite the rectory, to the ford on the site of the present footbridge passing the end of the Chace leading to Ford Place (facing, at that time, the old road, though now, by a modern west front, adapting itself amiably to the new) it crossed the present South Ockendon road by the elm tree near Mrs Holland's house, thence to the ancient house now occupied by Mr Joseph Manning, farmer, whence it is traced, skirting Belhus Park, Whitehall and Cockhides to the south-western corner of Upminster."

Palin's reference to the road striking across the Clapper "south-west of Stifford Hall to the east of the churchyard" shows clearly that he thought the London to Southend road parted company with Long Lane at Chalk Pit Farm, and did not follow it farther west. Stifford Hall appears neither on Chapman and André's map of 1777 nor on the first edition of the one-inch Ordnance Survey map, although Morant said it stood a little way east of the church. But the course of the road is clear enough: it followed the path marked on the 2½-inch map south-east of the church, then followed the course of today's main road to the footpath which leads to the Mardyke footbridge. Strictly speaking Pilgrims Lane, and not the footbridge path, is "opposite the rectory", but it must be the latter which Palin means.

Palin takes his old road past the end of the chace, and not down it; and thereafter as he describes. I take it that where the road skirts Belhus Park it is now represented by Blind Lane, which runs along the north-eastern boundary of the park, and must have been there when the park was laid out. Since it was followed by the boundary of the parishes of Aveley and South Ockendon it may be a good deal older than the park.

I have walked along Blind Lane from the point where it crosses the Common Sewer north of the lake in Belhus Park. Some two or three hundred yards north-west of this point the lane is some sixteen paces from ditch to ditch, and each ditch some six feet across. The wheeled track took up only one fifth or one sixth of the full width of the lane. The ditches each side of the lane were deep, and the lane gravelled.

It will be seen that Palin takes his old road to the south-western corner of Upminster — which is no way of getting to London from Stifford. Nor does he suggest by which route the road gets to Southend in the east. These confusions, which when unexplained amount almost to inaccuracy, make Palin an uncertain guide.

APPENDIX III

Miller Christy's Roman roads

Christy claims to have traced "more or less precisely" eighteen fairly distinct Roman roads in Essex. He divides them into roads which lead to and from London, and roads which lead to the river. We will deal first with the three roads he takes to the river.

Writing in the Transactions of the Essex Archaeological Society in and after 1918, Christy says there are three Roman roads which leave the London to Colchester road and finish on the Thames: one from Brentwood to Tilbury, one from Chelmsford to Canvey Island, and one from Rivenhall to Prittlewell. They are, says Christy, practically parallel, all take a south-easterly direction for the northern third of their courses, and a southerly direction for the southern two-thirds; and their changes of direction take place at or near the point where each crosses the line of a road (of which more later) which he claims ran from London to Bradwell.

Christy takes his Brentwood to Tilbury road from the northern end of Brentwood High Street, where it is crossed by the parish boundary between South Weald and Shenfield, and then along the north-east side of Shenfield Common, where it is followed by a parish boundary for part of the way, to Ingrave Green. He then takes it along, or near, the north-east boundary of Thorndon Park to Herongate (but within the boundary of the park, and not along the line of the road which skirts the park today). From Herongate (according to Christy) it ran along the line of today's road past Cockridden, but just before reaching East Horndon church, "it disappears".

I will now quote Christy directly, with minor changes and deletions which do not affect the sense of his writing. "Continuing, however, on the old line, past the church and hall (near each of which short lengths of the Roman road remain, and with existing footpaths mark its former course) one reaches Garlesters in Bulphan. Here at a sharp angle the modern road returns to the line, which has now descended to low ground. From Garlesters the road runs on quite straight and on the old line for 2½ miles through Bulphan and Orsett, over Sticking Hill, along the boundary between Orsett and Horndon on the Hill, and past the eastern side of the park of Orsett Hall. After passing the hall the road becomes irregular; but continuing, it passes through a small projecting part of Orsett [he means the parish, not the village]; then straightening, it follows the boundary between Orsett and Mucking for about a mile, till just south of Seaborough Hall it ends suddenly. After half a mile one encounters it again at an angle of the boundary between Chadwell and West Tilbury. From here the boundary continues quite straight and exactly on the line for 1¼ miles (a footpath marking the line for half a mile), passing along the western side of Shrove Hill Wood and ultimately reaching Broom Hill on the edge of the high ground overlooking the broad riverside expanse of the Chadwell and Tilbury marshes. Descending the steep slope and continuing along the line across the marshes (where there is now no sign of the road and the parish boundary seems to have been diverted a few hundred yards to the west) one finally reaches the bank of the Thames at a spot where there was in Roman times an important landing place of some kind, almost exactly opposite the present town of Gravesend."

Christy adds in a note that the point at which the road struck the Thames is now covered at high tide, and adds, "The Morant Club had it under investigation for ten years or more, but never reported on it, owing to the failure of the experts concerned to send in their promised reports on the large quantity of Roman pottery dug up". (He adds that views and particulars of the site are given in the south-east Essex volume of the Royal Commission on Historical Monuments. Unfortunately the reference he gives, clearly in error, is to illustrations of two Romano-British ovens and details of hut sites on the foreshore at East Tilbury some three miles downstream. There is no other entry to which he could have intended to refer.)

The most interesting part of Christy's account is his reference to short lengths of Roman road remaining near East Horndon church and hall, as if he were referring to a track not coincident with a modern road, and clearly recognisable as a Roman road. I have been unable to trace his road at this point.

I must now describe my own largely unsuccessful attempts to trace the course — the actual physical course — of this road, or indeed of any Roman road which connected Brentwood and Tilbury. Before doing so, however, I must make clear why I am convinced that such a road existed. My conviction is based on the fact that the Ordnance Survey map of Roman Britain marks a road leaving Stane Street immediately south-east of Braughing which travels south-east as far as a point south of Bishops Stortford. This road cannot have stopped there. I believe it passed through Ongar and then ran in a straight line to Brentwood, with two changes of alignment, one just south of Kelvedon Hatch about four miles north-west of Brentwood, where it turned slightly south-west, and one at Millfield, where it turned south-east again before driving straight to the centre of Brentwood. I have little doubt that it crossed over the Colchester road at Brentwood and continued as far as the Thames, probably reaching it at or near Tilbury. The strongest evidence for the existence of a Roman road leading south from Brentwood is therefore the fact that a Roman road so clearly leads to it from the north.

I believe that the first section of the Roman road from Brentwood to Tilbury is to be found in the Ingrave road in Brentwood itself, which continues the line of the road from Braughing through Ongar and Kelvedon Hatch. The first difficulty comes when one tries to follow its line south of the point where it goes out of alignment at the north-west corner of Shenfield Common.

It is possible that it may have followed the track which with double ditches sixteen paces apart now runs south-east across the common until it is covered by the railway cutting spoil tip. But I have not been able to trace this section of track, or drive, on the south side of the railway. It is possible that the determined might pick up some sign of it crossing Thorndon Park, but I have been unable to do so.

I have also tried without success to pick up signs of a Roman road connecting Brentwood and Tilbury south of Thorndon Park and along the former parish boundary between Chadwell and West Tilbury south of the Muckingford road. But here also, on the line Christy suggests for his Brentwood to Tilbury road, and on the northern extension of the boundary which I followed for three-quarters of a mile, I saw nothing.

If there is one place where the Roman road from Brentwood should show it is in its final section at Tilbury, and at the point where it strikes the river. There is a line which runs almost due south from Old House Wood on today's Brentwood to Tilbury road, passes east of Chadwell, down Hob Hill, through Tilbury, across the open land just east of the Riverside station, and so to the river bank opposite Gravesend High Street (which street I regard as Roman). I think this line marks the final section of the Roman road from Brentwood to Tilbury. The course of the line is followed across the open land east of the station by a track running along the top of a bank: it may be that this track also follows the course of the Roman road. But of the road where it would strike the river there is now no sign.

The second of Christy's three roads from the Colchester road to the Thames ran from Chelmsford to Canvey. He describes the course of this road from south to north, but I have reversed his account in order to make it consistent with that of the Brentwood to Tilbury road, and to make it more convenient to add at the end a note about roads on Canvey Island.

Christy takes his road from Chelmsford to a point south of Grove House at Great Baddow (presumably The Grove, south-east of the village on the main road to Southend). South of Grove House he takes the road across fields to rejoin the same main road at Little Claydons. Thereafter its course follows today's road until a point three-quarters of a mile south of Rettendon, where the Southend road turns south-east. From this point, according to Christy, the Roman road continues in alignment along the boundary of Runwell and Rettendon as far as the Crouch, which it strikes just east of the point where the river is crossed by the Wickford to Southminster railway line. It is on this last section between Rettendon and the Crouch, according to Christy, that Roman origins become particularly obvious.

The course of the road is then picked up between Shotgate and Shotgate Farm on the Wickford to Rayleigh road, passes "the rectory near Great Fanton Hall", and then North Benfleet church. From this point Christy takes it to the Bowers Gifford parish boundary, first with Thundersley, then with South Benfleet, and so to the north bank of the creek which separates Canvey Island from the mainland at that point where East Haven Creek meets Benfleet Creek. This is just opposite the most northerly point of the island and, according to Christy, "rather more than a mile east [he means west] of South Benfleet church".

Concerning Roman roads on Canvey Island, a map dated 1966 in the Dutch House museum there shows a "possible" Roman road running north and south just to the west of the bow in the road north of the station at South Benfleet. I do not think this could have been the last section of Christy's road. The same map also shows a Roman causeway running north and south just west of Thorny Creek. It would be too speculative to try and suggest a connection between this road and those earlier described.

The third and most easterly of the three roads which Christy takes from the Colchester road to the Thames is that which he says starts from Rivenhall, between Witham and Kelvedon. Here, as in many other cases, he refers to the parish of Rivenhall through which the main road passes, and not the village itself. Christy describes the course of this road in some detail. It is enough for our purposes to know that south of Maldon he takes it on much the same line as the present road to North Fambridge, although it leaves today's road west of Dyegoods Farm at Cold Norton to follow the eastern boundary of the parishes of Cold Norton and North Fambridge before arriving at the north bank of the Crouch. Christy picks up the course of the road on the opposite bank, takes it past South Fambridge Hall and by Ashingdon and Hawkwell to Rochford, and then by Earls Hall and Milton Hall to the river about a mile east of the Crow Stone. As we saw earlier, it is possible that this was the *straete* referred to in Leofwine's will of 998.

It is now necessary to consider the course of the road which Christy takes from London to Bradwell, which is crossed by these three roads in turn. First, however, I must make some general comments on the idea of a through road being planned and built by the Romans as a unit to connect London and Bradwell.

There can be no doubt that the fort at Bradwell was served by a Roman road. Its final stretch is marked on the Ordnance Survey map of Roman Britain. This section must also have been connected with the rest of the Roman road system in Essex. But one reason for viewing the overall course of Christy's road with reserve is that since the road to the fort was presumably contemporary with the fort, and therefore of late construction, it would not be taken all the way from there to London, but to the nearest point on an already existing system. A second reason for doubting whether there was a through road is that Christy first suggested that it went through Ilford, Becontree Heath, Rush Green, Havering Well, Hornchurch and Upminster, and then changed this course for one which went to Upminster through East Ham and Dagenham.

The fact that Christy could make such a drastic change in the line of a fifty-mile stretch of road planned and built as one (as he supposed) almost puts his suggested course outside serious consideration. Nonetheless certain sections of his suggested London to Bradwell road are probably Roman, although these connect nearer destinations, and might possibly form part of other through roads. Thus if a

Roman road did pass through East Ham and Dagenham it would be more likely to lead to the Southend area than Bradwell, and a road from Ilford through Becontree, Hornchurch and Upminster would be more likely to head for Rayleigh. But let us follow his road, dividing it up into three sections for the sake of convenience — although these sections are not in fact suggested by Christy.

The first, "from Aldgate through East Ham and Dagenham to Upminster", is too vague for consideration. For the second section, which passes through Cranham, Great Warley Street, Little Warley, Childerditch, West Horndon, East Horndon, Dunton Wayletts and Laindon Barn, Christy produces no evidence. Further, if Christy meant to take his road through the settlements rather than the parishes, it would have described a greater detour to the north than any Roman road would have taken. If he intended to take it through the parishes so named — and this seems to have been his general practice — then his course (and that suggested earlier by Salmon) is so vague as to be almost meaningless.

Christy takes his third section of road from Laindon Barn along Oak Lane, Blind Lane, and Borwick Lane, and then through Ramsden Crays, by Woolshots Farm in Ramsden Bellhouse, and Friern Farm in Downham. It crosses the Crouch a little to the north of Wickford, passes Runwell church and New Runwell Hall, and then goes by Rettendon and Woodham Ferrers. Christy then takes it by Hamberts Farm, south of Wellinditch Farm, and through, or by, Stow Maries, Cold Norton, Beacon Hill, Latchingdon parish church, Steeple church, St Lawrence church, and so to Bradwell.

It is clear from this list that Christy sometimes uses the name of a village to indicate the whole area of the parish, and not the village itself. Another difficulty is that between Upminster and Bradwell he records eight "jogs", as he calls them, in roads or tracks which he thinks follow the course of his Roman road. These jogs are momentary deviations from, and returns to, alignment. They do not necessarily deny Roman origins to the road, although they may deny the suggestion that the road was built as one.

These jogs resulted from medieval travellers finding the road ahead of them in such a poor state that they turned to right or left and went out of their way for a short time before turning left or right again and continuing their journey across more favourable terrain. This can only mean that when these jogs took place the north-south roads were in

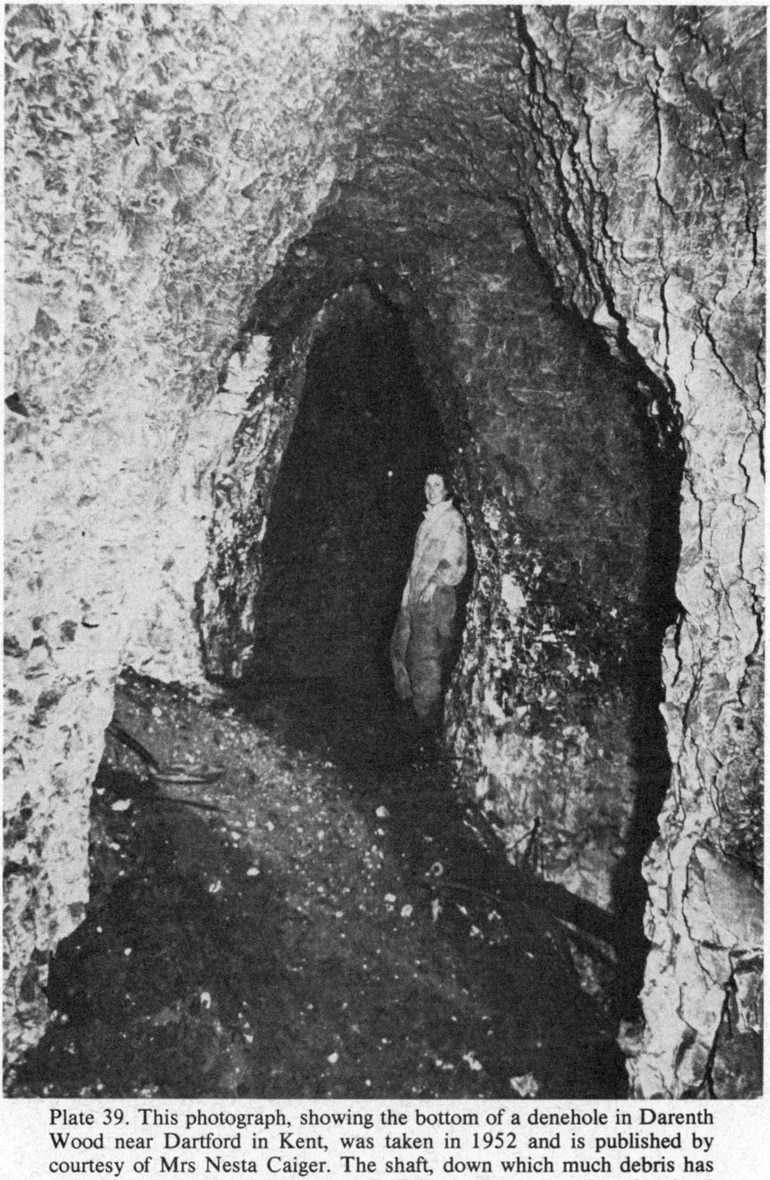

Plate 39. This photograph, showing the bottom of a denehole in Darenth Wood near Dartford in Kent, was taken in 1952 and is published by courtesy of Mrs Nesta Caiger. The shaft, down which much debris has fallen, is through the opening to the left. The chambers are behind, ahead and to the right of the photographer.

Plate 40. Grays and the container port a

Tilbury on the Essex bank of the Thames.

John Topham

Plate 41. A backward look in time and space; the Pool in days of steam.

better condition at these points than the "Bradwell" road; and this can only mean that the evidence for the north-south roads being Roman — or, while being Roman, less used — is stronger than that for the east-west, Bradwell, road being Roman. But perhaps this argument should be put the other way round: if stretches of this road which contain jogs are Roman, then it is even more likely that the cross roads are Roman too.

There is, however, another possible explanation for these right angle movements in roads thought to be originally Roman. It is set out by Laver in the Transactions of the Essex Archaeological Society for 1895; and while he is referring only to the obviously rectangular road pattern in Dengie Hundred between the Blackwater and Crouch, it may be that his explanation applies more widely.

Laver says the roads in Dengie were not made up in the modern sense until after 1783, when parishes were required to have this work done. At that time roads were little better than cart tracks and frequently passed along the edge of a field and down its side. There were usually gates on opposed sides of the field, and when a field was bearing a crop, those using the road would go through one gate, along the top of the field, and down the other side until another gate was reached. The new field was then passed in the same way. When the field was fallow travellers would go straight across the field from gate to gate.

Laver says that when the parish made up a road they would "place stones" (presumably metalling) where the road ran at that particular time; and that this accounts for the fact that many roads go through pairs of double right angles in maintaining general direction. I should, however, point out that a road which seems to have been subject to the variations Laver describes is not thereby proved non-Roman, provided that overall alignment, in addition to general direction, is maintained.

While I do not think the Romans built a through road from London to Bradwell on the line suggested by Christy, I believe stretches of his road are Roman, particularly between Hamberts Farm south-east of Woodham Ferrers and Stow Maries, where he takes it in alignment over the shoulder of Bushy Hill, while today's road goes round the hill. This refusal to be diverted by gradient is typical of a Roman road.

Christy believed that the wedge shaped piece of land between the Blackwater and Crouch rivers was crossed by six Roman roads which with one exception started from his Bradwell road and spread out like a fan to cover the whole peninsula. He traces the most southerly of these roads from Woodham Ferrers to Althorne, with roads on progressively more northerly courses from Purleigh to Southminster, Latchingdon to Dengie, Mayland to Bridgemans south-east of Tillingham, Steeple to Tillingham, and St Lawrence to Packards north-east of Tillingham village. I will deal with these in turn.

The Woodham Ferrers to Althorne road is taken from a point on today's road just east of Hamberts Farm a mile south-east of Woodham Ferrers. According to Christy the Roman road follows the line of today's road, here travelling due east, and continues in the same direction to a point just north of Great Hayes a mile south of Stow Maries, where a continuation of the same modern road turns due east after travelling north. He then takes the Roman road through the parishes — not necessarily the villages — of Cold Norton, Purleigh and Snoreham to Althorne.

Christy points out that the Woodham Ferrers to Althorne road does not make detours to the south to avoid crossing shoulders of high ground at Snoreham church and Althorne, and adds that none but a Roman road would do this. (I think his reference to Snoreham church must be, not to the church in Snoreham, which is in any case better known as Latchingdon, but to the isolated church on the Althorne road just west of Tyle Hall. This is the church which Laver refers to as Latchingdon old church.) Whether or not a Roman road did follow this course — and I think it did — one thing is clear: this Woodham Ferrers to Althorne road has no connection with the *straete* at Purleigh mentioned in Leofwine's will.

Christy takes his second road from the parish of Purleigh, some three miles south-east of the village, to Southminster. He takes it from near Dyegoods Farm, half way between Cold Norton and Latchingdon, to the road running east and west down Buttons Hill north of Althorne, along a course which he says is now completely lost. He then takes it along the modern road which runs east to Southminster Hall. (Laver, thinking of movement west rather than east, seems to accept that a Roman road runs at the back of the houses on the north side of Southminster Street, merges into the "old line" of the road at the bottom of Pantile Hill west of Southminster, and then proceeds westwards "past Caidge". This follows the line suggested by Christy.)

Christy's third road, from Latchingdon to Dengie, is the one exception which does not start from the Bradwell road. It begins at the south end of the village of Latchingdon, and can be traced on the map easily enough to Asheldham and beyond, ending within a mile of the sea shore south of the Grange. Today's road makes a detour round the ancient camp at Asheldham, although Christy says it originally ran straight through it, and for this reason he regards it as a Roman camp. It is in fact a slighted British camp. If I am correct in thinking that the road through Weald Camp is Roman, then the Asheldham road is the second Roman road in Essex which drives straight through a pre-Roman camp.

Christy takes his fourth road from a point on the Latchingdon to Steeple road about three-quarters of a mile east of Lawling Hall eastwards to a point just north of Moynes Farm, Asheldham. There is, however, little evidence of its course on the map save at the far eastern end, where Hodges Lane is in alignment. From this point the road continues east in alignment to a point north-west of Bridgemans, not far from the edge of Tillingham Marsh. I have already pointed out that this and the previous road form part of a Roman land settlement area.

Christy's fifth road, Steeple to Tillingham, runs parallel with the previous road about three-quarters of a mile to the north. It is taken from the Bradwell road where it crosses the parish boundary of Steeple and St Lawrence at The Poplars east of Steeple, and thereafter follows a footpath for most of the way. It is said to end at the north end of the village street in Tillingham.

The sixth and last of his more or less parallel, more or less east-west roads is that from St Lawrence to Packards north-east of Tillingham. This is the most northerly, the shortest, and as Christy himself realises, the least clearly defined of the branches he describes.

Christy thinks all six roads are Roman. I would say the east-west road through Althorne, which forms part of his first road; most of the road from the south end of Latchingdon to the Grange east of Dengie village, his third road; and the road from Moynes Farm to Bridgemans, part of the fourth, are Roman. They are straight, followed to a degree which Christy describes by parish boundaries, and the last two at least form part of a Roman land settlement area. But fieldwork has yet to discover physical evidence in the field of their Roman origins; and to trace, with more evidence than Christy has been able to provide, the sections which connect them with a main road to the west.

I would say that the final eastern section of the road to Bradwell, whose western section has yet to be identified with certainty, was built late in the Occupation to give access to the Roman fort when Saxon raids made shore defences necessary, and was therefore imposed on an existing road pattern.

Christy also takes a road from Chelmsford to Bradwell through Great Baddow, Maldon and Latchingdon, but produces no evidence based on fieldwork. The other roads whose courses he claims to have identified are north-west of the Roman Colchester road, and outside our area.

APPENDIX IV

Canute's Trench

It is accepted that 27,000 able bodied men were capable of digging a canal to take their shallow-draught ships from east to west of London Bridge. It is possible, however, that what the Danes did was to restore a watercourse dug by the Romans to divert some of the flow of the Thames while they built the first London Bridge. The suggestion is given mild support by two series of facts: the first, that the Romans dug such a cut-off channel to divert water from the building site of the Medway bridge at Rochester, and indeed dug transport canals on a wide scale in the Fens and other alluvial areas. The enigmatic Cnut's Dyke in the southern Fens (the spelling Cnut here being hallowed by the Ordnance Survey) whether or not Canute restored it, which is likely, was originally dug by the Romans; and Canute's Trench itself was again used as a cut-off channel when London Bridge was rebuilt in 1173. The second series of facts is that on one occasion the Danes moved their ships on rollers across the Kiel watershed between the Baltic and North Sea; and that on another they, or more likely the Norsemen, portaged their boats from Vistula to Dnieper. There is a possibility that in the absence of an already dug channel, even in disuse, the Danes might have done the same south of London Bridge.

There is a tradition that the Trench passed through Bermondsey and Southwark. It could, indeed, hardly go anywhere else. The remains of part of its central section could be seen in Southwark in recent time, but its precise course, and certainly its outlets to east and west, are uncertain. Besant, one shaky authority here, seems to suggest in his *London South of the Thames* that the canal was dug from what is now the entrance to Greenland Dock east of London to some unspecified point on Chelsea Reach to the west — a length, as the crow flies, of over five miles. After saying that it passed across what is now Tabard Street he adds, "In Warner Street all the houses are marked with the arms of St Bartholomew's Hospital . . . and close to the south ran the old trench of King Canute which on its way from Rotherhithe to Chelsea Reach crossed the Deptford Road a little to the south-east of the hospital at the lower end of Kent Street [Tabard Street, which formerly came as far as the corner of Bermondsey New Road] and proceeding to Newington Butts, intersected the road a little south of the Turnpike [at the Elephant and Castle]."

At another point Besant says that Canute's Trench is supposed to have been followed by the channel "through which the Thames was diverted at the building of London Bridge in 1173" which began "about Redrife [Rotherhithe] and ran west to Battersey". He suggests that the eastern end of the trench may have been at Greenland Dock, where piles and trundles of willows were unearthed when the dock was dug. It was thought at the time that these had been used in 1173 to retain the wall of the cut-off channel. Unfortunately at another point in his book Besant quotes without explanation a different date for the construction of London Bridge, and says that Stow's claim that the Thames was diverted from its course through Canute's Trench, or a canal based on Canute's Trench, to facilitate the building of the bridge was "manifestly impossible and absurd". Such a diversion through a trench already dug, and perhaps re-dug, would of course be possible; but it is clear that Besant has not related all of his at times conflicting information on the subject. Even so, he puts forward the Greenland Dock to Chelsea Reach course of Canute's Trench with more confidence than that from St Saviour's Dock to what is now Old Barge House Wharf, which is the second course he suggests.

The second course covers a distance as the crow flies of some one and a half miles, and for this reason alone would seem a likelier course than the other. St Saviour's Dock, the eastern end of the course, is clearly an artificial inlet, and one of some age. At one time it belonged to Bermondsey Abbey, founded in 1082. Old Barge House Wharf, at the western end, is opposite Temple Gardens and at the north end of Broad Wall, which crosses Stamford Street and runs roughly north and south half way between Waterloo Bridge and Blackfriars Bridge. But Besant, in referring to this course, uses the phrase that Broad Wall is "even mentioned as being the line of Canute's Trench", which hardly suggests that he accepts the suggestion. He also says that Broad Wall was "a bank thrown up probably as an embankment with open sewer [that is a ditch] on each side", which does not make his meaning any clearer. On the other hand, Broad Wall is the boundary of Southwark and Lambeth, which suggests that it, or the embankment, or the canal, was a feature of some age. The line of the trench in Bermondsey and Southwark as quoted by Besant also seems more in keeping with outlets at St Saviour's Dock and Old Barge House Wharf than Rotherhithe and Chelsea Reach.

Old and New London describes a course for Canute's Trench which is the same as the longer of the two courses given by Besant, that is from Greenland Dock on the east to Chelsea Reach on the west. It does not specify the points it passes through, apart from saying that the Trench "ran through St George's Fields" (between St George's Road, Lambeth Road and the Kennington Road). It also credits Maitland with the statement that Canute's Trench ran from the lower end of Chelsea Reach along the line of Spring Garden, Vauxhall, by the Black Prince, Kennington, south of Newington Butts, and across Deptford Road to "the great wet dock below Rotherhithe". This course is similar to that decribed by Besant, but with the points listed from west to east, not east to west.

Old and New London also mentions the old channel which was dug "from Redriff to Lambeth" to divert the Thames while London Bridge was being built in 1173. The reference appears in a letter to Pepys from a Dr Wallis, who reports having seen "divers remains of the old channel made from Redriff to Lambeth for diverting the Thames while London Bridge was being built". According to Wallis the channel was "all in a straight line or near it, but with great intervals which had long since been filled up".

APPENDIX V

Danish earthworks

In Essex an earthwork at Pandal Wood east of Southminster village and north-west of Southminster Hall is said to be Danish. Laver, writing in volume 19 of the Transactions of the Essex Archaeological Society, said that the earthwork, which in his time was not shown on the Ordnance Survey map, was an unequal sided pentagon. Its southern bank was 293 feet long, its western 233, its northern 379 and its eastern 320. One side seems to have got lost somewhere. Laver said it had a forty-feet-wide opening at its north-east corner, and that the camp was at the head of a stream in Danish times. I have not seen it.

The Victoria County History of Kent suggests with varying degress of confidence that there may have been Danish works at Greenwich, Appledore, Tong, Kenardington and Newenden.

The *Anglo-Saxon Chronicle* has a number of references to the Danish ships being "at Greenwich". The County History says that no trace of the Danish work at Appledore remains; suggests that Tong Castle was built on the site of Saxon or Danish defences; and that Castle Toll at Newenden is possibly Danish.

The Ebbsfleet, the stream which flowed from the Roman town at Springhead through Northfleet to the Thames, is said by Hasted to have been a Danish retreat, but I have not examined it for docks.

In the 1885 volume of the *Archaeological Journal*, Spurrell says that the earthworks in Stone Marshes, Kent, north-east of Littlebrook Farm, are "like Hasten's" — presumably Hasten's camps at Benfleet and Shoeburyness — and therefore Danish. In the 1889 volume of *Archaeologia Cantiana*, however, he suggests that the earthworks, which he refers to as "banks", are Saxon, and probably to haul boats into. The Saxons must have had docks for their ships, but I would have expected them to be in areas of concentrated Saxon settlement where the settlement itself would be a defence, and not in an isolated area like Stone Marshes, which is one to appeal more to the Danes. Nor is it easy to tell, from the map which accompanies Spurrell's earlier paper, where the boats would have been laid up, and how they would have got there from the Thames.

According to the *Anglo-Saxon Chronicle* the Danes had semipermanent headquarters in Sheppey; earthworks half a mile east of Queenborough have been suggested as the site.

There are some curious depressions by the site of Lesnes Abbey at Abbey Wood in Kent. Those to the west of the site, at the bottom of a steep combe in the northern edge of the bluff on which the abbey stood, are in the form of two rectangular basins, one leading into the other. Before the embankment which now takes the Woolwich to Erith road was made, these basins were connected with the Thames by a dyke. They may have been monastic fishponds; but they may also have been used by the Danes to shelter their boats in too.

Addenda and corrigenda

I have not tried to standardise the spelling of the Saxon word for a Roman road, which appears variously as *straet*, *strate*, or *straete* and to some extent in keeping with the varied spelling in Saxon land charters.

The archaic form of the letter 's', where it appears, (for example on page 61) has had to be represented by the modern letter 'f'.

The name of the Thurrock Historical Society Journal was changed to the Thurrock Local History Society Journal with volume 7 in 1962, so that references on pages 46, 54 and 181 should be to the Thurrock Historical Society Journal.

Higham Upshire, the larger settlement on the hill south of the original hamlet of Higham in Kent, is increasingly known only as Higham. I have, however, retained the name Higham for the few cottages and church on the edge of the marshes to the north, and referred to the larger settlement as Higham Upshire save on page 108, where references to Higham are in fact to Higham Upshire.

References to individual pages follow.

11. The Continental Shelf also includes Britain and Ireland and the seas between them.

32. The evidence from St Mary's Island came from excavation, not boring, and the post glacial land surface on which the figures are based is dated 4000 B.C. because it is thought that the layer of peat immediately above it formed at that time. The figures for peat and clay layers in the first paragraph are taken from a table in Evans' paper. In relating them in the third paragraph to land sinking since 4000 B.C. I have followed a graph published in the paper which has the two layers of peat, one one foot and one two feet thick, suggesting a land rising of some five feet in each case. As a result there will be inconsistency if the figures for land rising in the third paragraph, which are based on the graph, are compared with those in the first paragraph, which are based on the table. The conclusion that the land surface in Roman times — that is at the second peak of elevation — was fifteen feet above its present level, is however consistent.

33. The absence of Roman remains on the line of the Roman Banks is a further argument against their being Roman.

34. For F.J.C. Spurrell read F.C.J. Spurrell.

37. Although later writers have transcribed Covnvs as Covennos and Convennos, the correct form is almost certainly Counus, on the lines Avgvsta . . . Augusta. In kindly confirming this fact for me Mr C.W. Phillips, formerly the Archaeology Officer to the Ordnance Survey, gave it as his opinion that Toliatis was probably Thanet, and Counus possibly the lost land of Lomea, now the Goodwin Sands.

63. Stansted Mountfitchet (the correct spelling) is better known simply as Stansted.

75. St Peter's Church is actually on the site of the wall of the fort, not nearby.

81. There were "gaps" in the line of the south coast forts between Lympne and Pevensey and between Pevensey and Portchester.

84. Payne, unidentified here, was George Payne, a former secretary of the Kent Antiquarian Society.

98. I refer to the Broomway "going down into the sea at Wakering Stairs" because it is most easily seen at that point. The stretch of road here is, however, the first feeder to the main road, which leaves the coast slightly to the south.

171. Two Grain Marshes are marked on the first edition of the Ordnance Survey one-inch map. The reference here is to the more northerly one.

207. The Danes who invaded Northumbria came from elsewhere in the Danelaw. The word "vultur" in the quotation is as in the original.

208. The spelling Eadwig is accepted, although the commoner form is Edwy.

211. The village of Penselwood itself is in Somerset half a mile from the meeting place of Somerset, Dorset and Wiltshire.

213. The unexplained delay in executing Edric Streona suggests that not all the facts in this sordid business have come down to us.

223. The modern spelling is Stansgate.

224. I fancy Defoe lived at Chadwell Place.

224, 225. I have described Ethelwald as the son of King Oswald of Deira on Bede's authority, although works of reference refer to his kingdom as Northumbria.

226. Saunders also points out in his article that in 1254 East Tilbury was called Great Tilbury, and West Tilbury, Little Tilbury. If the former, being larger, was also earlier, then this would further strengthen the probability that Bede's Tilaburg was East Tilbury.

238. The title of Lambarde's work is *A Perambulation of Kent.*

249. Joyden's Wood is at Bexley in Kent and, like Hangmans Wood, noted for its concentration of deneholes.

259. A reference to the fact that I was leaving the well-tilled subject of Dickens and the lower Thames to others was deleted in reducing the length of the book.

272. It may help if the reader is reminded that the western ford referred to in the second paragraph was replaced by a road bridge, Causeway Bridge, and that the eastern ford was replaced by the footbridge referred to on the following page.

280. Miller Christy's Oak Lane is now Oak Road and his Borwick Lane appears on the map as Barrick Lane.

283. The Grange is simply *Grange* on the map.

INDEX

Entries in brackets, such as (3B) for Grays, refer to the square in which place names, or neighbouring place names, appear in the folding map. Roads and railways are indexed in groups, all else individually. Essex and Kent are not indexed, except (in the case of Essex) for the Saxon period under *East Saxons*. Kent during the same period is dealt with in chapter 12. More detailed maps of the Orsett and Asheldham areas of Essex appear on pages 67 and 68. In some cases where there is a double entry, for example Friern Farm, Downham, the position on the folding map is given in a separate entry for the second name. Refer also, in general, to the list of plates.

Those interested in Roman roads are asked to refer to all section headings under *Roads, Roman.* In that and some other subjects a general entry is also given precedence.